Radio

Essays in Bad Reception

John Mowitt

UNIVERSITY OF CALIFORNIA PRESS

Berkeley • Los Angeles • London

University of California Press, one of the most distinguished university presses in the United States, enriches lives around the world by advancing scholarship in the humanities, social sciences, and natural sciences. Its activities are supported by the UC Press Foundation and by philanthropic contributions from individuals and institutions. For more information, visit www.ucpress.edu.

University of California Press
Berkeley and Los Angeles, California

University of California Press, Ltd.
London, England

© 2011 by The Regents of the University of California

Library of Congress Cataloging-in-Publication Data

Mowitt, John, 1952–.
    Radio : essays in bad reception / John Mowitt.
        p.   cm.
    Includes bibliographical references and index.
    ISBN 978–0–520-27049-7 (cloth : alk. paper)
    ISBN 978–0–520-27050-3 (pbk. : alk. paper)
    1. Radio broadcasting—Philosophy.   I. Title.
    PN1991.5.M69   2011
    384.54—dc23
                                            2011026053

Manufactured in the United States of America

20 19 18 17 16 15 14 13 12 11
10 9 8 7 6 5 4 3 2 1

In keeping with a commitment to support environmentally responsible and sustainable printing practices, UC Press has printed this book on 50-pound Enterprise, a 30% post-consumer-waste, recycled, deinked fiber that is processed chlorine-free. It is acid-free and meets all ANSI/NISO (Z 39.48) requirements.

THE FLETCHER JONES FOUNDATION
HUMANITIES IMPRINT

The Fletcher Jones Foundation has endowed this imprint to foster
innovative and enduring scholarship in the humanities.

Radio

We still do not have the kind of analysis of the brief moment
of radio that people have so passionately undertaken for
the cinema on the one hand, and television on the other;
but Brecht's modernism—and the very modernism of his
moment of history in general—is bound up with radio, and
demands the acknowledgment of radio's formal uniqueness
as a medium, of its fundamental properties as a specific art
in its own right, a form in which the antithesis of words and
music no longer holds, but a new symbiosis of these two
formerly separate dimensions is effectuated and rehearsed.

—Fredric Jameson, *Brecht and Method*

Radio confuses the philosophers. What is it that I am not
present for the speaker at the microphone while he is present
for me? Does presence itself split itself up? This is a very
serious psychological problem.

—René Sudre, *Le huitième art: Mission de la radio*

Contents

Acknowledgments

Near the core of Carl Sagan's *Contact* stands an episode, perhaps even an event, pertinent to the genre of which this is an example: acknowledgments. As those familiar with either the novel or the film will remember, the eponymous "contact" is discovered when the protagonist detects an electromagnetic signal repeating in what might otherwise pass as the noise of interstellar space. In time this signal is recognized as a broadcast, in fact, the televised broadcast of Leni Riefenstahl's *Triumph of the Will*. This leads not only to the onto-theological crisis of contact itself but—and Sagan's shrewdness shines through here—to panicked speculations regarding intentions, speculations that quickly include the conspiratorial question of hoaxes and the like. In the end, the novel itself succumbs to this hermeneutical panic, but not before reminding us that the question of where any text comes from is of fundamental, because elusive, import.

If I emphasize this instance of scientist fiction, it is because it has long been my impression that this text—*Radio: Essays in Bad Reception*—has been approaching for some time. If you will, it came to me ("the seeds were planted in my brain") while I was teaching a graduate seminar in the nineties at the University of Minnesota, "Radio and the Politics of Mass Culture," where, among other things, I was interested in crossing the analytical "pessimism" so frequently ascribed to the Frankfurt School with radio as opposed to literature, film, and television—the more typical roster of "bad objects." Or so it seems now. At the time, the students present queried me early and often about "my objectives," and it seems fitting here to thank them for underscoring the flawed character of the reception that I was struggling to improve in the seminar.

In a sense, this situation has repeated itself throughout the duration of this project, but in configurations as distinctive as they are worthy of grateful acknowledgment. For the sake of exposition I will distinguish among hosts, curators, and enablers, that is, colleagues and friends who have—both at length and in passing—helped me figure out what this text is trying to tell me.

Chief among the hosts who deserve acknowledgment are Joan Scott and her colleagues (the late) Clifford Geertz, Eric Maskin, and Michael Walser, who invited me to join the School of Social Science at the Institute for Advanced Study in Princeton for the academic year 2004–5. Joan in particular allowed me to recognize that the object of radio was transmitting to me from deep within the recesses of my earlier thinking on antidisciplinarity. She also brought me into association with an extraordinary group of scholars from whom this project has benefited in incalculable ways. I want to thank especially Caroline Arni, Mark Beissinger, Matteo Casini, Patricia Clough, Paulla Ebron, Duana Fullwiley, Bruce Grant, Sarah Igo, John Meyer, Kenda Mutongi, Helen Tilley, and Marek Wieczorek. Patricia, in particular, emerged as a consistently provocative interlocutor, and Caroline's paleographic talents proved indispensable.

In the course of researching and writing *Radio*, I was invited to present it as a work in progress in various venues. I am especially grateful to the following (in the order of invitation from earliest to most recent): Negar Mottahedeh for inviting me to give one of the humanities lectures at the John Hope Franklin Center at Duke University; Tina Mai Chen for including me on her Canadian Council of Areas Studies and Learned Society panel, "Culture and Globalization"; Lars Iyer and Richard Middleton at Newcastle-on-Tyne University for inviting me to participate in "Versions of the Popular;" Barbara Engh, Eric Prenowitz, and Ashley Thompson at the University of Leeds for inviting me to address the "Voice" seminar; Ika Willis at Bristol University for inviting me to inaugurate the "Beyond the Text" lecture series; Joshua Lund for including me on the Latin American Studies Association panel "After the Washington Consensus"; Meredith McGill at Rutgers for inviting me to speak at "Sound Effects"; Donna Haraway for inviting me to present my work to her colleagues (faculty and students) at the University of California, Santa Cruz; and Martin Harries for including me on the "Radio" panel at the American Comparative Literature Association's annual meeting. As is customary, in several of these venues particular people took it upon themselves to respond or otherwise formally comment on my work, and I want to acknowledge and thank for their effort and insight Nicole Archer, Roman de la Campa, Patrick Madden, and Barry Parsons.

When I arrived at the Institute in September of 2004, I appeared before Joan and her colleagues with a broken left wrist from a car accident (pace Virilio). Being unable to type, that is, write (at least for me), I was hurled into the world of the archive, where I met the first in a long list of librarians, curators, and archivists without whose help this transmission would have remained unsent. I want especially to thank Momota Ganguli and Marcia Tucker, both Institute librarians; Dan Linke and Susan White, both librarians and reference specialists at the Mudd Library at Princeton University; Tara Craig, a rare books and manuscripts archivist in the Butler Library at Columbia University; Angela Carreno, a manuscript archivist at the New York Public Library; Susan Irving, a reference specialist for the John Marshall papers at the Rockefeller Foundation; Marie Walsh, a reference specialist in the Department of Sociology at the University of Birmingham; Ike Egbetola and Rod Hamilton, both archivists in the British Library for the BBC Sound Archive; Paul Spencer-Thompson, an editorial assistant at *Tribune;* Alena Bártová, a curator at the Prague Museum of Decorative Arts (my cover is indebted to her); and last, but certainly not least, Elissa Guralnick, who kindly shared with me her transcript of the radio program "Radio: Imaginary Visions." With the likely exception of Elissa, I am virtually certain that none of these people will remember me, but if I have remembered them it is because they helped me tune in something faint but in the end crucial to the nebulous text I described when first contacting them. This said, now is the appropriate time to thank the late Phyllis Franklin, who, several years ago, spent a good hour with me on the phone discussing *What's the Word?* That she cannot remember me is all the more reason to remember her generous spirit and commitment to the humanities "in dark times."

Which leaves the enablers. The list is long, but it ought properly to begin with Michelle Koerner, who, over the years, has given me extensive feedback and wise counsel but who has also, when necessary, reminded me what thinking is for. Among other students (former and current), I want especially to acknowledge Ebony Adams, Nick de Villiers, Lindsey Green-Simms, Doug Julien, Andrew Knighton, Jovan Knutson, Niki Korth, Erin Labbie, Amy Levine, Roni Shapira-Ben Yoseph, Julietta Singh, Michelle Stewart (my DJ), Paige Sweet, Mousa Traoré, and Rachel "Raysh" Weiss—all of whom, in ways big and small, helped turn my receiver in the right direction. Among faculty both here and elsewhere, special, and in several cases very special, thanks are due to Franco "Bifo" Berardi, Hisham Bizri, Paul Bowman, Polly Carl, Cesare Casarino, Paula Chakravartty, Chris Chiappari, Lisa Disch, Frieda Ekotto, Barbara Engh, Jarrod Fowler, Andreas Gailus, Daniel Gifillan, Michael Hardt, Jennifer Horne, Rembert Hueser, Bob Hulot-Kentor, Qadri Ismail, Dave Jenemann, Jonathan Kahana, Doug Kahn, Michal Kobialka, Kiarina Kordela, Liz Kotz, Premesh Lalu, Richard Leppert, Silvia López, Alice Lovejoy, Julia McEvoy, Ed Miller, Andy Parker, Thomas Pepper, Victoria Pitts-Taylor, Jochen Schulte-Sasse, Adam Sitze, Ajay Skaria, Laura Smith, Richard Stamp, Jonathan Sterne, and Charlie Sugnet.

Three other more formal, but no less essential, acknowledgments are due: to Anthony Alessandrini, whose anthology, *Frantz Fanon: Critical Perspecitives,* provided me with an early occasion for publishing on *What's the Word?;* to the University of Minnesota and specifically its College of Liberal Arts for providing research support—in various forms—for key aspects of the project; and to Mary Francis, my editor at University of California Press, who convinced me early on that she knew what this text was about and where it needed to go.

Last, I want to thank—and it always feels like such a meager gesture—my daughter Rosalind, who, when she hung stubbornly onto the weird little transistor radio that we received from our car dealer, got me thinking, and my wife, Jeanine, who in the midst of her struggle with cancer still found the energy to draw vital signs to my attention, confer about much-needed support, and be profoundly "there" in the nothing that connects everything.

The Object of Radio Studies

The object in question has two aspects, and it will help if I begin by distinguishing them. At one level, "the object" designates the cultural technology of radio itself. At issue is not exactly the thing called a radio, for a radio can be reduced to the status of a thing only if regarded as an appliance, a component of a home entertainment system, however modest. As has been argued by others, radio is composed of certain techniques of listening, a diffused network of social interaction, an industrialized medium of entertainment, a corporate or state system of public communication, in short an unwieldy array of cultural institutions and practices. In this it bears striking resemblance to what film scholars sought to capture in the term *apparatus* when applied, not to film as such, but to the institution of the cinema. Thus an important aspect of what I am doing bears on radio as a cultural technology, an apparatus, with a social and political history. In this I am channeling an intellectual tradition that reaches back to Bertolt Brecht, Hadley Cantril, Gordon Allport, Walter Benjamin, and Theodor Adorno, all of whom in the 1930s and 1940s attempted to theorize the distinctive sociopolitical history of radio.

At another level, "the object" also designates the aim or purpose of a field of scholarly inquiry called radio studies by its partisans. At stake here is not the question of why one might study radio but rather the question of what this new disciplinary project hopes to gain by studying radio in the way that it does. Thus an equally important aspect of what

I am doing bears on the matter of constructing the intellectual history, or, as Michel Foucault preferred, the genealogy, of this field, paying special attention to how its partisans characterize both the importance and the necessity of the aim of their research. In this I am channeling a tradition that reaches back at least as far as Max Weber, Georg Simmel, and Karl Mannheim in the discipline of sociology.

An appropriate question might well be: What, if anything, do these two objects have to do with one another? To answer, I am obliged to say a bit more about the concept of the object this study leans upon.

In *Text: The Genealogy of an Antidisciplinary Object,* I analyze something I call a disciplinary object, largely concentrating on the shift described by Roland Barthes from the literary object of "the work" to the postliterary or antidisciplinary object of "the text." Doing this matters because it shows, among other things, how a group of subjects, in this case masters and disciples (professors and students), forms the distinctively social character of its bond through the sharing (however unequally) of an object. This object serves as the referent for the questions and answers deemed pertinent within a given discipline. If the literary work once served such a function, it was because the institutional practices conducted in its presence—reading, writing, examining, and so on—produced the literary work as the occasion for the constitution and reproduction of the discipline of literary studies. So, to put the matter succinctly, on this construal the literary work is an object and not a thing. In fact, it is an object precisely because it invests some *thing* with an intellectual aim and through this investment generates a social relation. That aim, henceforth confused in perpetuity with the thing itself, is the good (ultimately knowledge) that is to come from its study if conducted in accord with certain methodological protocols.

All of which is to say that the two objects I have described belong together more than orthographically. They belong together because disciplinary objects are the volatile zone of indistinction between the world—whether physical or psychical—and the institutionally organized production of knowledge—whether hard or soft—about that world. In short, *object,* as I am putting the term to work here, is a name for the place where knowledge and world can be neither differentiated nor confused. Moreover, this way of approaching the object situates my study squarely within the frame of media studies (whether one thinks here of Harold Innes or Jean Baudrillard), although my concerns aim more narrowly at the articulation of media and theory than one typically finds in the study of mass culture.

To ward off the usual misunderstanding, I am not saying that there are no things in the world; I am simply saying that from the standpoint of the discourse of the university—which is, for better *and* for worse, our standpoint (I harbor few illusions about who might be reading these lines, certainly *not* "the poorest woman in the South," to use a familiar example)—things are mediated by the social formation through which our encounters with them, as we say, come to matter. Writ large, of course, this means that "things in the world" is a meaningful and pressing concern because more than the grammar organizing the English phrase is at work within it. This "more" is at once the numerous and multiform disciplinary projects charged with knowing "things in the world" and the world that solicits and acknowledges the attention of disciplinary reason.[1] To study, as I am proposing to study, the object of radio studies thus involves cocking one's ear toward the socially organized zone of indistinction in which radio and its study encounter each other. Obviously, I am—as one who studies radio, indeed as one who studies radio studies—present in and at this encounter. Consider this ineluctable metacritical state of affairs as something like the faint but persistent *Hörstreif* (hear stripe) to be heard in the margins of this entire study, a study, then, less about radio (and there are many excellent ones) than about the scholarly interest in it.

To discern some of the signals being emitted from this zone, I urge that we consider two developments: first, the dramatic arc of radio history, the oft-repeated fact that after coming into national prominence in the so-called Golden Age of the 1920s and 1930s (at least in the United States) radio precipitously faded, only later to return at the end of the century with what can properly be called a vengeance; and second, the emergence of what called itself radio studies, the novel, defiantly interdisciplinary initiative seeking to wrest radio from (to exaggerate for melodramatic effect) the "clutches" of journalism and mass communications, that is, a more administrative or professional study of the mass media. These developments interact, of course, but more than that, they interact in a geopolitical context that both conditions and outdistances them. Not to put too fine a point on it, radio did not fade in quite the same way in Europe, nor, for that matter, has it ever faded in the Third World. Likewise, radio studies so-called is a largely Northern (visible in the United States, Canada, and the United Kingdom) phenomenon. Grasping its emergence must therefore come to terms with this fact without thereby granting such things as facts undue intellectual authority.[2]

For the sake of a consistency whose principle has not yet been established, I will take up the second of these developments first. This involves taking advantage of the serendipitous fact that, in a certain sense, our moment is a moment of gestation and maturation. Just as, I suppose, the pulses of astrophysicists race upon witnessing the "birth" of some astrophysical phenomenon, so too do those interested in the genealogy of disciplines begin to vibrate when a discipline emerges in our midst, as radio studies did in the last decade of the twentieth century. The thrill here is largely one of opportunity. Though there has been much discussion within both the humanities and the "qualitative" social sciences about the reconfiguration of the disciplines, about what Immanuel Kant once called "the conflict of the faculties," it has been difficult actually to trace how a discipline negotiates a space, at once intellectual and institutional, for itself, especially since so much of the recent reconfiguration of disciplines has been stimulated, not by scholars, but by administrators seeking ways to get more for less. Interdisciplinarity, touted now by scholars of all stripes, aside from always already having taken place, alas harbors no intrinsic animus toward neoliberal corporatism, where, after all, it has long gone by the more anodyne term *synergy*. With radio studies and, lest it go unsaid, with its fraught yet enabling precursor, cultural studies, we have, if not a golden era, then certainly a golden opportunity to trace a discipline in the event of its emergence. To what end? Not, I assure you, simply to herald its "birth," but to sift its descriptions for something rather more like an explanation of what earlier I called the aim of radio studies and to tease from this the terms that, in cycling back and forth between radio and its study, signal something like the very conditions of emergency themselves. In other words, studying radio studies must be pitched so as to tune in studying as much as broadcasting.

If I have repeated the word *emergence* in the preceding, I have done so deliberately. For I wish to put this term to work in a way that is in direct dialogue with the British (although he might prefer "Welsh") scholar Raymond Williams, who sought, in any number of works but perhaps most systematically in *Marxism and Literature,* to produce the concept of emergence. What matters to me about this is not primarily the question of intellectual debt (in fact, I will reveal myself to be a somewhat fickle debtor, perhaps even a "frenemy") but rather the fact that in producing the concept of the emergent Williams also produced a concept profoundly relevant to the apparatus of radio and its history, namely, the concept of the residual. This helps one think about the broadly asserted notion that radio's day has passed, that its comeback in the digital AM era is from some sort of prior moment. Moreover, no doubt as an overdetermined confirmation of my earlier point about disciplinary objects, Williams is also responsible for making radio and cultural studies matter deeply to one another, as a later chapter will attest.

In *Marxism and Literature,* Williams defined the emergent by contrasting it with both the residual and the dominant. His purpose was to find a way, within the broad contours of a Marxism committed to distinguishing the economic base of society from its cultural and political superstructure, to designate something like the spatio-temporal structure of the superstructure. No fan of the sort of mechanistic determinism that would render Marx's own thought unthinkable, Williams deployed his three terms to capture how, across class society, interests could form that might lag behind or even race out ahead of those that might otherwise be said to form the prevailing consensus. To designate this last (for example, what we in the United States might call neoliberal economic policy), he used the term *dominant.* To designate those traditions and interests that the prevailing consensus appeared to have superseded (to adduce his own example, monarchism), he used the term *residual.* And last but hardly least, to designate practices that managed to get out in front of the prevailing consensus (to again adduce his example, a socialism "beyond actually existing socialism"), he used the term *emergent.*

To clarify how precisely I want to bring this to bear on radio studies, we need to consider one further distinction drawn by Williams. Within the emergent, Williams differentiated between two tendencies, one "alternative" and the other "oppositional." His point was to concede that certain ways of getting out ahead of the prevailing consensus were, in fact, *mere* alternatives to it and not deep critiques and/or rejections of either its logic or its founding institutions. Although capable of ambivalence on the matter, Williams saw aspects of the "counterculture" of the 1960s and 1970s in the West as largely an alternative mode of emergence rather than a truly oppositional one. Less ambivalently, his considerable and vividly drawn misgivings about Soviet Marxism and the Labour Party in Britain notwithstanding, socialism was the only coherent vision of the oppositional mode of the emergent that Williams would live to provide.

What interests me here is the logic of these distinctions, not their referents, or at least not primarily their referents. Applied to radio studies, what this logic rather obviously invites is a consideration of whether its "emergence" exhibits one tendency or another, either alternative or oppositional. Complicating this, however, is precisely the object of radio studies, the fact that in articulating its aims radio studies has presented the device of radio in consistently residual terms. Complicating the matter yet further is the fact that Williams did not draw a correlative distinction within either the residual or the dominant to match the one drawn in the emergent such that one might be able to trace carefully the interchange and interaction between his categories either in general or in the context of a given analytical project.[3] Rather than give up in frustration, I propose that we float such a distinction with regard to the category of the residual and see how far it takes us. As the terms of such a distinction are not indigenous to or otherwise forthcoming in Williams's work, it will be necessary to appeal to the work of others, specifically to two moments in Adorno's correspondence with Benjamin. I propose that we differentiate the residual in terms of the vestigial and the archaic.

For the sake of brevity I will urge that we regard the vestigial as distinctly developmental. In other words, despite the reference to comparative anatomy and paleozoology, the vestigial underscores that aspect of what Williams calls the residual that is simply surpassed in the normative unfolding of a process, whether physical or psychical. So one might say that polymorphous perversity is vestigial vis-à-vis genital, that is Oedipal, sexuality in Freudian psychoanalysis, although, I hasten to add, in having derived the normative from its failure, Freud complicates this example in a decisive way—so decisive, in fact, that he largely fails to acknowledge it.

By contrast, the archaic is defined not by development but by metalepsis and resistance. Two epistolary formulations of Adorno capture this with concision. In one, Adorno conjoins the archaic and the modern by saying, "The archaic itself is a function of the new; it is thus first produced historically" ("To Walter Benjamin" 38) in and by the modern. It is the temporal inversion of the old and the new that I associate with metalepsis, and it implies that the residual registers what the dominant has produced as something like its enabling past. In other words, if the monarchy still matters in Britain this may have more to do with the contemporary political value of crafting a nationally inflected form of Tradition, or for that matter the dramatic chops of Dame Helen Mirren, than with an abiding popular investment in the divine right of kings.

The resistant aspect of the residual manifests itself when, in further specifying the archaic, Adorno writes that it is "the site of everything whose voice has fallen silent because of history" ("To Walter Benjamin" 38), a phrase as important for what it says about the archaic as for its appeal to the voice, indeed voices, that have been turned down, silenced, in order to say it. If I link this to resistance, it is because it specifies that metalepsis is interested. In other words, Adorno suggests that the modern produces the archaic in order to resist those demands voiced against it both in the present and in the present's past. Presumably, then, President Jimmy Carter, however dimly, had something like this in mind when, in the wake of the seizure of the U.S. embassy in Tehran, he characterized Iranian grievances against the United States for installing and supporting the shah as "ancient history." In effect, to give voice to its presumed radical novelty, the modern produces the archaic as silent, a gesture whose consequences for the concept of resistance are taken up repeatedly in the chapters that follow. For now, I urge only that we hold onto the notion that the archaic might be said to represent what Williams understood by the oppositional, but articulated around the category of the residual. The point is not that the archaic is a rewording of a "socialism to come" but that it clarifies theoretically what it means to differentiate that version of the future from some other—for example, our own.

To justify this theoretical digression, I return to radio studies. Why not start with the basics? For example, what evidence is there that something called radio studies has emerged as a field of academic endeavor? And further, how precisely does the residual, whether vestigial or archaic, figure in or otherwise illuminate this emergence?[4]

In scholarship on the infrastructures of intellectual power those attentive to it have been repeatedly invited to pay less attention to the debates and controversies triggering paradigm shifts, than to such apparent banalities as conferences, research grant proposals, publications, reviews, dissertation projects, seminar offerings, job placement, in effect all the institutional micropractices of academic social reproduction. With this in mind, I invite consideration of two issues of the *Chronicle of Higher Education*.

The first of these appeared in February of 1999 and contains an article written by Peter Monaghan, a staff writer assigned to the "faculty research" beat at the *Chronicle*. Apparently sparked by "Radio Voices and the Construction of Social Identities," a panel devoted to radio at the 1998 annual convention of the American Studies Association, Monaghan set out to register for the large, multidisciplinary, national audience of the *Chronicle* the advent of something new.[5] As if to contradict one of her own claims about the field (that radio studies knows nothing of auteurism), Monaghan adduces the work of Michelle Hilmes as a sign of this breakthrough. He writes:

> Ms. Hilmes is now prominent among a fast-growing number of researchers who are rectifying that deficiency [that radio had disappeared from the scholarly radar screen] by asking what radio programs and audiences reveal about American culture and society. Her *Radio Voices: American Broadcasting, 1922–1952* (University of Minnesota Press, 1997) is the most-cited publication in a recent spate of cultural studies of radio. . . . The new scholarship focuses on the tension between two disparate poles. One: radio's complicity in advancing some now-well-documented features of American culture—its intense consumerism and its questionable notions about such factors as race, gender and ethnicity. The other: the ability of the invisible medium to transgress accepted cultural norms and to feed new ideas into American homes. (A17)

Doubtless Monaghan, like anyone else, says more than he means, but let me first attend to what he has said. First, note that he actually avoids the expression "radio studies," preferring instead the telling circumlocution "cultural studies of radio" (about which, more later). This notwithstanding, he makes it clear that the pursuit of the cultural study of radio remedies a deficiency, it supplements a lack. Well and good, but a lack in what? Presumably, a lack of focus, not on radio per se, but on the disparate poles that according to radio studies partisans should organize the aim of one's approach to the study of radio, at least in the United States. To give a certain urgency to the discussion and to provide the whole story with a certain *frisson,* Monaghan resorts to "intensifiers" like *fast-growing, most-cited, spate,* and the ever-reliable if utterly exhausted *new,* all words that struggle to perform the sudden, irreversible advent of a breakthrough. Thus, to summarize: readers of the *Chronicle* are presented with a perceived lack in scholarly approach being quickly supplemented by a fast-growing group organized around a shared new belief in disparate poles. In effect, the key coordinates of an emerging disciplinary body are here in evidence.

So now what did Monaghan say without meaning? He said, "Her *Radio Voices: American Broadcasting, 1922–1952* (University of Minnesota Press, 1997) is the most-cited publication in a recent spate of cultural studies of radio." In citing this citation (an event he could certainly not have intended), I felicitously enter the hall of mirrors of Monaghan's sentence, whereby an utterance that is itself a scholarly citation (note its bibliographic form) adds its own gesture of citation to the counter clicking away under Hilmes's most-cited text and, in doing so, solicits, as it were, my own hit. Monaghan obviously means to tell us something about the way Hilmes's work exemplifies the new scholarship, but in saying so he does more, he also co-produces something like the factual density of this scholarship and its centrality. Moreover, he does so conspicuously, if not exactly wittingly.

To what effect and with what significance? Especially important here is the general theme of citation and what the late Jacques Derrida has called the logic of iterability. By stressing the said but unmeant performative character of Monaghan's text, I am trying to draw attention to how the discourse, in this case that of academic journalism, collaborates in the production of the significance of what it reports upon. This, in a nutshell (a term Derrida himself once risked), is what the logic of iterability tries to capture: the way authority actually derives from citation and may, in a certain sense, be nothing without it.

To further justify this invocation of the logic of iterability, I turn briefly to the second *Chronicle* story on radio studies. Written five years later by a well-regarded scholar, Thomas Doherty (from Brandeis), it contains the resonant subtitle "Radio Studies Rise Again," drawing attention, I should think, less to the absurdly precipitous rise, fall, and return of radio studies (what happened to the fast-growing, to the spate, to the new?) than to the *Chronicle*'s own prior story about the rise of radio studies. As if acknowledging its iterative responsibilities, the article opens with a citation of a citation (the narrator in Woody Allen's *Radio Days*) and proceeds, I suppose inexorably, to the site of the most-cited, *Radio Voices,* characterized by Doherty, not as part of a mere spate, but as the start of a veritable "wave," thereby intensifying an intensifier but also more deftly wiring the rhetorical register of his own discussion so as to solder its form and content. Although Doherty's characterization of the aims of radio studies (this time called by name) is important—he says that its identifying "call signals" are close Analysis of programs, due consideration of listener Response, and reliance on "postmodern Theory" (or WART?)—more important by far is the reiteration, or repetition, of coverage itself. The whole exercise has something of the feel of the bandleader's exasperated call, "Once more, with feeling." And were it simply that, it would deserve no further attention from us, but what remains crucial is the evidence it provides for the role that the discourse of professional reviewing, and its iterative logic, plays in the "emergence" of new academic fields.

Lest I be misunderstood, the logic of iterability is not, in any sense, unique to the discourse of professional reviewing and reporting. It is not, therefore, a sign of something like degradation, and I am not interested in casting suspicion on the *Chronicle*'s motives or in denigrating the talent of its contributors. In fact, iterability can be shown to belong to the very object of radio studies once we recognize that device and aim cite one another through the coverage that takes them as *its* object. This difficult though important point can be further clarified by a brief look at some of the scholarship heralding the birth of radio studies.

Between the two stories in the *Chronicle* appeared no doubt the decisive avatar of any and all new fields, a reader. Perhaps predictably, *Radio Reader: Essays in the Cultural History of Radio* was edited by none other than Michelle Hilmes and, it turns out, a Minnesota alum, Jason Loviglio. The oblique filial connection is trivial (Loviglio has gone on to have his own distinguished career) compared to the role played by Hilmes in this project, and for this reason it is worth thinking carefully, if only in passing, about what she says in the introduction to the volume.

Readers are largely pedagogical devices. With the prosecutions of copying centers for copyright infringement, the heightened emphasis put on publication in matters of academic promotion, and the ubiquity of interdisciplinary initiatives in virtually all fields of academic endeavor, the task of providing postsecondary teachers with a bound selection of "key essays" in any given field has assumed new urgency. This is as true of emergent fields as it is of established ones, where the emphasis falls on something like "canonical statements," such as, in cinema studies, Laura Mulvey's oft-reprinted "Visual Pleasure and Narrative Cinema." Invariably, readers sport introductions in which their editors make, as it were, a first pass over the anthologized material. For Hilmes, the first pass is complicated by her need to introduce both the volume *and* the field, a task that has the advantage of allowing her to go on at length. Strategically, she proceeds by pointing to the very developmental arc emphasized by Doherty. After a somewhat scrappy beginning, radio came to national prominence during the 1920s and 1930s. Then, just as radio was beginning to attract serious scholarly attention (one thinks here of the Princeton Radio Research Project, about which more later), it was eclipsed by the advent of television and the virtually immediate scholarly interest in the medium, especially on the part of those concerned about its role in inciting violence and inducing rampant imbecility. Then radio, Phoenix-like, returned both as a cultural technology (especially, of course, with the advent of talk, or, as some prefer, hate radio) and as an object of scholarly scrutiny—witness the advent of radio studies itself.[6] For the readers of the reader, two points are thus emphatically underscored. First, radio matters because its importance was prematurely usurped by another medium, television—an implicit appeal to something like the fairness *of* broadcasting. And second, radio matters because we now know better than to ignore it: an only slightly less implicit appeal to a notion of intellectual or, even more particularly, theoretical progress. If I emphasize this, it is with an ear toward amplifying how, in effect, Doherty repeats a repetition in Hilmes, as if to associate with radio itself its reiterative, or, if one prefers, wavy character. In other, albeit somewhat cryptic words, radio must always have mattered twice in order to matter once.

Turning from what amounts to first contact with the hardwired residualism of radio and its study, I now set my dial on the rhetoric of her introduction and cite the most-cited author in radio studies when she subtitles the penultimate section of her introduction "The Return of the Radio Repressed" (8). This blatant citation of Freud clarifies several things, even if unwittingly. First, as Doherty suggested, radio studies partisans do indeed care about the currents of critical theory that have convulsed the humanities and social sciences over the last forty-five years (notably psychoanalysis); second, the iterative logic at work within the object of radio studies is one thought to be illuminated by free association with Freud's account of the psychic economy of repression; and third, when read in the mode of a bold headline, the return of radio is *itself* repressed ("the return of the radio repressed"). While apparently the most counterintuitive, this last simply bespeaks the fact that iterability is so deeply inscribed in both radio and its study that even its return will have to take place twice in order to happen at all.

This aside, and I realize it is an important, even controversial claim, what is perhaps most telling about Hilmes's rhetoric is the way it invites us to recognize the residual in her invocation of Freud. My point here is not that radio studies is actually residual rather than emergent but that fundamental to its emergence is the way its partisans deploy the concept of the residual, applying it at once to radio and, through the history of the device, to its study. More particularly, let me propose that when invoking the "return of the repressed," Hilmes appears to emphasize more the "archaic" and less the "vestigial" aspect of radio's residual character. How so? Contrary to received opinion, Jean-Paul Sartre was not right when he accused Freud of incoherence in insisting that a mental content could both be repressed and unconscious. The repressed returns not because it finally overpowers the bouncer assigned to it by the ego but because the mute affective charge of a previously lived event takes place for the first time as a mental content when, through the work of analysis, it is made to mean. If radio can return as the repressed, according to Hilmes, it is because the event of its advent and perhaps even more of its decline has acquired meaning, for the *first* time, with its return, its reiteration, *in* radio studies.

At the risk of revealing that I, like anyone working in words, have stacked the proverbial deck, I will observe that Hilmes comes by her recourse to psychoanalysis honestly. For reasons that call for elucidation, the study of radio has long directed its interdisciplinary beacon toward these depths and perhaps nowhere more plainly than in the enigmatic line from Adorno and Horkheimer's *Dialectic of Enlightenment* that invites us to conceive "the radio as a sublimated printing press" (2). Written in 1944 and republished (reiterated?) in 1947, presumably on the eve of radio's eclipse by television, the authors invoke Freud's account of sublimation to think the technical and historical relation between the medium of print and the medium of wireless communication. But in what sense do they mean what this odd formulation says?

Although two other invocations of "sublimation" occur in the chapter from which this sentence derives, it isn't until the third chapter—their well-known cancellation of the "culture industry"—that the printing press and the radio are again paired in a way that allows one to attune to the role of sublimation in their argument. Elaborating on the proposition that radio has become the nation's "mouthpiece," they write: "In fascism radio becomes the universal mouthpiece of the *Führer;* in the loudspeakers on the street his voice merges with the howl of sirens proclaiming panic, from which modern propaganda is hard to distinguish in any case. The National Socialists knew that broadcasting gave their cause stature as the printing press did to the Reformation. The *Führer*'s metaphysical charisma, invented by the sociology of religion, turned out finally to be merely the omnipresence of his radio addresses, which demonically parodies the divine spirit" (*Dialectic* 129). True, the word *sublimation* does not reappear here. However, if it makes sense to say that radio is a sublimated printing press, then this passage tells us that this is because the Reformation returns, as it were, in National Socialism, specifically, might we not add, in the form of the radial network whereby isolated individuals converge in their identification with the word, not as they come to it (say in Mass), but as it comes to them (say in the printed vernacular Bible). But then shouldn't it be the other way around? Isn't the printing press/Reformation a sublimated radio/National Socialism? Only if we insist upon misunderstanding sublimation as what recasts an asocial act or belief in a socially acceptable form. Key here is not just that the radio comes *after* the printing press but that for Freud—as Adorno and Horkheimer well knew—sublimation was organized by the same psycho-logic of repression and, as such, exhibited the same structure as the return of the repressed, whereby unspecified and undelimited psychic energy assumed meaning (as the "asocial") for the first time, as it were, in print. Not to put too fine a point on it: these exilic Jews were keen to suggest that Luther's passion had returned in the meaning of National Socialism. Radio, as a secular apparatus, became the socially acceptable form of an evangelism whose more vicious sectarian inflections might otherwise have been, as Marshall McLuhan would later insist, too "hot" to handle (although—I hasten to add—not for nothing do right-wing demagogues—Father Coughlin, George Allison Phelps, and Martin Luther Thomas—figure prominently in several of the early studies of radio).

Two relevant points follow. First, as has been implied, the appeal to psychoanalysis within radio studies is neither new nor original. It is worth mentioning here that the first sustained scholarly study of radio, by Cantril and Allport, was titled *The Psychology of Radio* (1935), and that, even more tellingly, when Paul Lazarsfeld initiated the Princeton Radio Research Project two years later, he assembled a team of psychoanalysts, including Erich Fromm, Karen Horney, and Harry Stack Sullivan, to advise him on the preparation of his audience response questionnaires. Additionally, there appears to be a decisive reiteration, mediated through the concept of sublimation, of the sociohistorical character of the radiophonic apparatus *in* the very rhetorical preoccupations ("obsession," "repression" "sublimation") of radio studies. This suggests, does it not, that emergence takes place in the feedback loop in which disciplines scan the networks of communication from which and to which they contribute material, while projecting into the world networked by communication just those signals their analytical tools are designed to pick up. To put the matter simply, if reductively, *that* radio has returned is perhaps no less true of radio than it is of radio studies. Reduction notwithstanding, putting the matter this way helps us tune in the object, now strictly in the sense of "the aim," of radio studies. What does it want to know, how does it want to know it, and why must a return structure its way of knowing?

As we have seen, the necessity of radio studies' emergence has consistently been premised on two claims: one, that radio was eclipsed by television, and two, that scholarship that was just starting to pay serious attention to radio initially shifted its focus to television and then zoomed in on film. Put differently, in the era of television and film, radio became residual in Williams's sense of the term. However, in light of the complex interplay of radio and its study to be discerned in radio studies, it is surprising indeed that the persistent and often fraught attention paid to radio within many, if not all, of the major currents of philosophy and critical theory in the twentieth century has not been picked up by radio studies partisans. This is an omission worth countering, both for what it helps us to understand about the aims of radio studies and for what it can tell us about the sociocultural history of critical theory in the West.

In proceeding along this line, my thinking has been sparked by two rather different projects. In "Observations on Public Reception," the German critical theorist and cultural historian Friedrich Kittler argues that media reception participates in what for some time now he has been calling discourse networks *(Aufschreibesysteme)*. More particularly, through a close, though brief, consideration of Martin Heidegger's early work Kittler shows that the former's reception of German radio played a formative role in the articulation of his philosophical project, manifesting itself initially in a preoccupation with the tendency of *Dasein* to encounter Being in the experience of nearness, and later in Heidegger's recasting of nearness, especially accelerating nearness, as giganticism. In effect, radio was the name for a mode of revealing that in sparking across the gap between beings and Being gave Heidegger a fix on the worldliness of *Dasein*. While dissatisfied with Kittler's angle (he often seems a bit too taken with the machine in the ghost), I find both the seriousness of attention paid to theoretical discourse and his refusal to separate even its most arcane preoccupations from the social process to be at once provocative and enormously useful.

A second spark has been the work of the French political theorist Jacques Rancière, especially his text *The Philosopher and His Poor*. In ways that resemble Sarah Kofman's and Michelle Le Doeuf's studies of the figures employed by philosophers, Ranciere's study traces how the figure of poverty, and specifically the figure of those condemned to their one and only task in life, animates the indispensable register of examples in philosophical texts, arguing that philosophy has an essential and therefore ethically compromising dependence on the fact of poverty and its figural representative. While my own project is less concerned for the status of philosophical discourse as such, I do feel that if the radiophonic apparatus is co-produced by radio studies then it will be vital to consider how radio is figured in the theoretical traditions whose messages have not been picked up by radio studies.

Seen from high ground, the figure of radio assumes the contours of a problem, not simply the familiar problem designated by Adorno and others under the rubric of infantilization (the "dumbing down" of listeners), but a problem given critical detail by what Pierre Schaeffer (92) has called the "acousmatic" character of radio sound. Schaeffer derives this term from the Greek philosopher, mathematician, and cult leader Pythagoras, who deployed it in two related ways: first, as a name for that group of his followers, the *akousmatikoi,* who sat outside the inner circle composed of the *mathematikoi* and who, as a result, listened to Pythagoras lecture from behind a curtain; and second, as the name for the enigmatic sayings, the *akousmata,* shared with the *akousmatikoi,* sayings offered up as mnemonic devices that supplemented the necessarily garbled messages transmitted from behind the curtain. Key here are three things: one, the notion of a voice transmitted and received in such a way that its source is absent from the visual field; two, the reciprocal invisibility of the voice's audience to the voice's source; and three, the notion of its message being propagated despite, or even on the condition of, its lack of full intelligibility—all aspects of what is here referred to as bad reception, a formulation to which repeated attention will be directed in the chapters that follow. One senses that many issues having to do with power, communication, technology, collectivity, and so on are knotted up in Schaeffer's concept of the acousmatic, and for this reason it strikes me as a productive way to turn attention on twentieth-century philosophical and theoretical figurations of the radiophonic apparatus, which, after all, sends from and is received across a space of invisibility. The tendency to treat the acousmatic as a condition of the voice, namely, its state of disembodiment (as found, for example, in Ed Miller's work), is one I will counter by stressing instead the often expressly disciplinary tension between vision and sound (who or what "fields" the relation between these faculties) that structures Schaeffer's concept. For me the issue is not disembodiment but delocalization, where the accent falls on the way acousmatic sound allows for an uprooting that exposes those affected to what Welles called an "invasion," not the influx of the other but the voiding of the boundary against or across which flux or flow can be oriented. As this might suggest, radio is not simply a problem *in* philosophy, a topic of reflection, but, more important, a problem *for* philosophy insofar as radio's acousmatic character forces philosophy into a certain encounter with its disciplinary limits, an encounter brilliantly distilled in the title of J.L. Austin's radio lecture "Performative Utterances," where the question of what is thereby titled haunts every word of the broadcast. Is he lecturing *about* such utterances, or is a radio lecture meant to give such utterances illocutionary and perlocutionary force an instance of such utterances? Who knows? What knows? It is perhaps suggestive that René Sudre, who provided one of the epigraphs for this study, was also hugely invested in parapsychology.

My chapters 1 through 5 are essays or thought experiments in which I attempt to trace how the problem that is radio arises within and between various philosophical and theoretical projects. In all cases the objective is to tease out how recognition of the conceptual difficulties posed by thinking the question "What is radio?" produces effects that scramble not only intellectual alliances but also the sociohistorically given contours of intellectual life, say, in the case of Heidegger, what truly constitutes the "beyond" of Western philosophy. Thus in chapter 1, "Facing the Radio," this articulation of the problem posed by radio is shown to produce a surprising array of contacts—agreements and disagreements—between and among Heidegger, Adorno, and John Cage. Although the interest in radio held by many members of the Frankfurt School is well known—perhaps only Leo Lowenthal's extended involvement with the Voice of America routinely flies beneath the radar—less well known are the surprising engagements with phenomenology, physiognomy, and psychoanalysis that appear in Adorno's exclusively English-language writings about radio from the late 1930s and 1940s.

Chapter 2, "On the Air," extends this rethinking of the Frankfurt School encounter with radio by tracing how the problem posed by it arises in the philosophy of Marxism, especially as this last came to be thematized in the confrontation between Georg Lukács and Jean-Paul Sartre and the collaboration between Bertolt Brecht and Walter Benjamin. As the chapter title suggests, the interplay between using radio as a means of philosophical and/or political communication and using radio as a provocation to philosophical and/or political thought—what I seek to render in the prepositional instability of the "on"—serves as a tracking device.

Further elaborating the political questions stirred by the radiophonic encounter between Marxism and phenomenology, chapter 3, "Stations of Exception," turns to Frantz Fanon, whose brilliant and far-reaching essay "Here Is the Voice of Algeria," from *A Dying Colonialism,* obliges us to revisit many of the keywords—*resistance, voice, people, nation*—put in play by the movement of decolonization in Africa and elsewhere. Once on the proverbial table, the role of radio in revolutionary struggles prompts considerations of policy and piracy that urge one to think twice about the status of the voice in the political confrontation with contemporary neoliberalism, especially as it informs thinking about communications.

Fanon's discussion of radio in revolutionary Algeria casts only fleeting glances at psychoanalysis, despite his professional training in it and its critical role in the French articulation of phenomenology and Marxism. Continuing my effort to establish how insistently radio mattered to twentieth-century philosophical and theoretical reflection, chapter 4, "Phoning In Analysis," scans three sites of the encounter between radio and psychoanalysis: the role played by Erich Fromm in the formulation of the Princeton Radio Research Project; the two radio lectures by Jacques Lacan, "Petit discours à l'O.R.T.F." and "Radiophonie"; and the various statements—some broadcasted, others not—made by Félix Guattari regarding "free popular radios" and the Bologna-based station Radio Alice in particular. Here the encounter between politics (whether Marxist or not) and philosophy (whether phenomenology or not) occasions a twisted set of queries about the conditions, the channels, of psychoanalysis and psychoanalytic teaching.

Chapter 5, "Birmingham Calling," is yet another pass over the encounter between Marxism and philosophy, but one that considers at length the notion that the study of radio, and especially the question of local versus commercial radio, played a founding role in the Birmingham project of cultural studies. Three figures are central to the chapter: Richard Hoggart, the founding director of the Centre for Contemporary Cultural Studies (CCCS) at Birmingham; Raymond Williams; and Rachel Powell, whose pamphlet *Possibilities for Local Radio* was not only the first of the now legendary "Occasional Papers" produced by the CCCS but the explicit intellectual and political inspiration for Williams's confrontation with Labour over its radio policy. Here, because of the persistent theme of radio's pedagogical power, Brecht returns to restate, from the beginning of the century, the question: What *is* radio? Can reflection upon it transform the institutional organization of humanistic knowledge? Is cultural studies the institutional name of that transformation?

The final chapter, "We Are the Word"?, is a sustained consideration of the Modern Language Association's recent foray into radio broadcasting, "What's the Word?" The ambition here is, through an extended reading of the broadcast "Radio: Imaginary Visions" (the sole early engagement with the actual medium of the broadcast), to reflect upon the strategic merits of the association's turn to radio, a turn prompted—and the fact is well publicized—by the attack on the humanities in general and the MLA in particular carried out by conservative partisans in the culture wars. Here, the issue of radio's relation to education is read in light of the political and philosophical problems tracked through the preceding five chapters.

Perhaps inevitably, a conflict of opinion over the situation of the contemporary humanities surfaces. It is the reiteration of another. To specify, I return briefly to Peter Monaghan's double take as a way to address, if not answer, questions bearing upon the object of radio studies and the status of the residual within it.

Recall that Monaghan described the event he was heralding by describing it as a "recent spate of cultural studies of radio." When, five years later, Doherty reheralds the event, he refers to it by name, as the advent or breakthrough of radio studies. In the interim, an evocation has become a displacement. Specifically, Monaghan's evocation of "cultural studies" (but in the innocuous, predisciplinary form of "studies of radio that are cultural as opposed to something else") has been displaced by "radio studies," where "radio" spells the nominalization of the adjective "cultural." My point here is that in addition to everything else that is being said without being meant, there is the matter, earlier intimated, of two emergences, that of cultural studies itself and that of radio studies. As such, it is clear that radio studies wants to have its culture and eat it too: it wants to lean on cultural studies without thereby being simply derivative. But might we not also say that cultural studies is in some sense residual within radio studies?

Insofar as radio studies comes after and develops out of cultural studies, the latter would appear to have a distinctly vestigial relation to the former. Cultural studies is residual in the sense of belonging to the gestation or maturation of radio studies. But precisely because radio studies risks overlooking the founding role of radio study in the institutional emergence of cultural studies (see "Birmingham Calling"), it is hard to settle for this construal of residualism in the relation between cultural studies and radio studies. It is better, I think, to reflect more specifically about the trace of cultural studies, a trace that manifests itself most clearly in Monaghan and Doherty (not to mention Hilmes herself) when they describe the principles or theoretical convictions deemed characteristic of radio studies. Monaghan got at this by invoking the two poles, the tension between radio as medium of social control and radio as medium of social contestation. For his part, Doherty framed the matter in terms of "call signals" (WART), that is, the commitment on the part of radio studies partisans to close analysis, audience response, and critical theory. In both of these cases, distinctive methodological and even political preoccupations of cultural studies are very much in the foreground—with a telling exception.

In consulting virtually any portion of the mushrooming literature on cultural studies, one notes persistent concern with the vexed status of theory. In some cases, one finds cultural studies explicitly identified with the institutional initiative that became possible in the wake of theory, dated in the humanities with the so-called de Man scandal. The vexed status of theory has prompted certain writers, such as the late Bill Readings and more recently Gayatri Spivak, to distance themselves emphatically from cultural studies, Readings arguing that it is political only to the extent that it has no impact on politics, and Spivak arguing that it is monolingual, presentist, and identitarian. Thus, given that radio studies is apparently committed to theory (the T in WART), it would appear that it is reiterating the self-reflection of cultural studies, but with a difference, and, as we have seen, with a difference that legitimates, indeed justifies, if not necessitates, the very emergence of the field. Presumably, this difference is that radio studies has a less vexed, more affirmative relation to theory, even as one might properly insist that it is monolingual if not precisely presentist. Miller's *Emergency Broadcasting and 1930s American Radio* is an excellent case in point.

This more archaic inflection of the residualism of cultural studies, where it is posited as deficient in what must then be supplemented by radio studies, might be compelling were it not for the fact that, as this study will seek to show, precisely the absence of attention to how radio figured in the philosophical and theoretical projects—phenomenology, existentialism, Hegelian Marxism, anticolonialism, psychoanalysis, and cultural studies itself—that span and largely define the preceding century allows Hilmes and others to argue, now from a different angle, that of scholarly neglect, for the *necessity* of radio studies. It would appear either that the notion that radio studies is theory friendly is at best overstated or, and this is much more interesting, that theory means something rather particular to the partisans of radio studies. One is prompted in this direction by the "call signals" delineated by Doherty, who clearly distinguishes theory from the close reading of specific broadcasts, as though theory were something that guided reading instead of belonging to the very difficulties that arise in the practice of reading, as though poststructuralism did not contain—in the vexing figure of Paul de Man—this very insight. The undisclosed location from which the guidance system of theory emanates would appear to resemble strongly the sort of transcendental position, the zone of methodological abstraction, that deprives theory of just the sort of history that seems to have fallen out of range of radio studies. Is this necessary?

It may, then, be worth suggesting that one of the aims of radio studies is a paradoxical, but therefore telling, repudiation of the very theory its partisans otherwise regard as having been wrongly abandoned by cultural studies. As such, the emergence of radio studies, despite its abiding and undeniably novel commitment to a form of critical interdisciplinarity not typically found in the institutional practices of mass communications studies, partakes more in what Williams urged us to call an alternative as opposed to an oppositional state of emergency. In setting aside the politics of its own relation to theory, radio studies risks its progressive political ambitions. I'd like to think that this is not necessary, but one cannot help but be struck by the canonical status, in virtually all treatments of radio—from Adorno and Cantril to Ed Miller and Wolfgang Hagen—of the Mercury Theater broadcast of Welles's *War of the Worlds,* a story that allegorizes the arrival of the radically and menacingly new as being overturned by the epidemiological comeback of the vestigial, that is, the germ.

But then this is not really the point. The point is not to nail down certain philosophical or political keywords but rather to recognize in the nuances they invite us to make—how *does* the earlier remain active in the later?—a problem for reading as much as for theorizing, a problem whose perplexing involvement with the apparatus of radio is trying to tell us something. But what?

In keeping with my emphasis on the conceptual problems stirred by nuance, I have essayed here to engage them at the level of expository gesture, what might also be called "midlife" (as opposed to "late") style. The reader will have noted recourse to the rhetoric of radio, to tuning dials and the like. But there is an enunciative dimension in play that might otherwise escape notice. It includes the expository shifts, the switches of rhetorical register, fields of discourse, presumed audience, and the like. This is deliberate, if not precisely calculated, and for some it will read as interference. My aim is to submit my writing practice to the demands of what I began by calling the object of radio study. At one level, this gives frank and rather direct expression to the difficulty of tuning in, of giving sharp focus to the vexed encounter between radio and its study. In effect, my own reception of what is going on in this zone of indistinction is, if not bad, certainly compromised. By the same token, it seems both attractive and imperative to write from within this vexed encounter, neither to pretend to approach it from outside nor to abandon oneself entirely to its inside, an approach that carries its own risks of distraction, but to convey the feedback, the whistle that results when a signal loops and amplifies too quickly—put differently, to practice a mode of immanent critique that takes the form of content seriously. The chapters that follow exhibit this commitment through the logic of what might be called "indirection." They get under way in odd places, they loop, they fade, but in all cases they stress that studying the study of radio repeats something with a difference. They urge that all the remarkable things we have come to learn about stations, broadcasts, markets, personalities, and patents are not enough. Radio calls out for more. This text, then, is a response trimmed to the shape of the letter(s) of that call.

CHAPTER I

Facing the Radio

A distinction useful for my purposes is drawn in scene 11 of Wilder and Brackett's *Sunset Blvd*. In it Norma Desmond, played by Gloria Swanson, and Joe Gillis, played by William Holden, are discussing her script, *Salomé*. The dialogue is as follows:

> *Norma:* I've written it myself. It's taken me years. It's going to be a very important picture.
>
> *Joe:* It looks like enough for six important pictures.
>
> *Norma:* It's the story of Salomé. I think I'll have de Mille direct it.
>
> *Joe:* De Mille!? Uh-huh.
>
> *Norma:* We made a lot of pictures together.
>
> *Joe:* And you'll play Salomé?
>
> *Norma:* Who else?
>
> *Joe:* I'm only asking. I didn't know you were planning a comeback.
>
> *Norma:* I hate that word! It's return! A return to all those who have never forgiven me for deserting the screen.
>
> *Joe:* Fair enough.

Comeback versus return. On the face of it, what's the difference? For Norma the difference is clear: a return is a response, in effect, an acknowledgment of a debt owed to those who have otherwise not forgiven her for the withdrawal of her presence, her desertion of the field of the visual. A comeback, by contrast, involves no such acknowledgment. It appears to be utterly narcissistic, utterly scripted. Whether tenable in the long run or not, what strikes me as useful about this distinction is that it cues us to a subtlety that calls out for attention when we are thinking about the contemporary theoretical status of the voice. How, in other words, should we think about the resurgence of scholarly interest in the topic? Or, put differently, what do those involved in this resurgence think they are doing? Is this the voice's comeback or its return? Or is it something else altogether? Moreover, is the difference here yet another way to approach the problem of residualism?

This may seem like an odd place to begin, especially to begin what is conceived as an examination of the relation between philosophy and radio, so allow me to explain. Certainly one way to think about what I have called the "resurgence" of interest in the voice is to grasp it as part of a response to the waning of poststructuralism, or, more precisely, to the attenuation of the critique of "phonocentrism." Although many have jumped onto the bandwagon of this critique, it was put in play with exemplary rigor by the late Jacques Derrida. In its emergent formulations this critique sought to draw out the consequences of the collaboration between Saussurean linguistics and Husserlean phenomenology. Specifically, Derrida found in Husserl's fuzzy and ultimately untenable distinction between expression and indication the same ambivalence to be found in Saussure's risky reduction of the signifier to an acoustic image (literally, *image acoustique*), that is, an entity devoid of all physicality yet capable of yoking together something seen and something heard. Recognizing this allowed Derrida, through the distinctly French pun on the heteronymic word *entendre* (that is, "to hear" and "to understand"), to tease out the centuries-old open secret of the essential link between the voice and meaning. The fact that this insight derives from a heteronym, a word whose written or spoken signifier produces two apparently different signifieds, is interesting but does not merit further elaboration here.

In the opening section of *Of Grammatology* Derrida fastened phonocentrism not only to logocentrism but also to ethnocentrism, arguing that logocentrism is "nothing but the most original and powerful ethnocentrism" (3). Once in place and taken up by those interpellated by the grammatological project, the voice became untouchable. To engage the voice, perhaps even to pronounce it, was understood to consign one to an ethnocentrism that, in the sixties, was under siege in every corner of the decolonizing globe, most conspicuously, perhaps, in Vietnam.[1] Indeed, an entire, carefully cultivated rhetoric of the voice as the very embodiment of revolutionary agency was suddenly and fundamentally challenged. It was as though Derrida had discovered, a decade before Foucault, the "repressive hypothesis," not in the vow, but in the voice itself.

I am not, of course, saying anything terribly fresh, so let me get to the point. What remained, as Don Ihde and others sensed, foreclosed in the critique of phonocentrism was precisely the matter of sound. For it is one thing to show how hearing and understanding collude or collide but quite another to say that the voice is *nothing but* the sounds heard in the event of understanding. Saussure himself struggled with the matter when, in the chapter on "linguistic value" of the *Course in General Linguistics,* he pondered over how the sound units of the phoneme, that is, the acoustic molecules of the signifier, were initially separated from the chaotic flux of sound without, at any point, presupposing the arbitrary conventions made possible through this very separation. Even if we grant him the principled disciplinary procedure of simply setting certain things outside the purview of linguistics, one cannot fail to recognize the sonic dross left in the wake of this procedure and his lack of theoretical interest in it. What is the relation between this remainder and phonocentrism? Can sound gain access to meaning only through the mediation of the voice, not primarily as the faculty of human speech, but as the philosopheme of the understanding that is at bottom a hearing? Is a meaningless listening possible?

These questions are but samples. One could certainly proliferate others (indeed, the whole notion of "secondary orality" might immediately come to mind). However, if such questions herald what I have called a resurgence of interest in the voice, then what this clarifies is that this resurgence takes place, not just anywhere, but specifically in the wake of the critique of phonocentrism. That is, instead of being an anxious denial of this critique, the resurgence is an immanent requestioning of the voice, by which I mean that it retrieves and reanimates questions that the critique of phonocentrism could not, on its own terms, answer. Obviously, one of those questions is the question of sound itself, precisely the sound escaping the call and response that Saussure located at the heart of the sign.

I turn now to the distinction between *comeback* and *return* teased out of Wilder and Brackett's *Sunset Blvd.* My aim is to flesh out this distinction in two ways: first, I will deploy it as a rationale for pondering the implications of two figures in what I have called the resurgence of scholarly attention to the voice, Mladen Dolar and Giorgio Agamben;

and second, I will import this distinction into the concept of resurgence in order to evaluate it both theoretically and politically. Is it, as I have suggested, an avatar of one residualism or another? And the residualism of what? The voice? The radio? Their theoretical superimposition?

Doubtless the most sustained recent reflection on the voice, in English, is to be found in Dolar's *A Voice and Nothing More* (2006). This is a very rich, very compact book that seeks to change the way we think about everyone from Derrida and Lacan to Kafka—and change in a rather specific way. As Slavoj Žižek puts it in his introduction to the series in which the book appeared: "After reading a book in this series ["Short Circuits"], the reader should not simply have learned something new: the point is, rather, to make him or her aware of another—disturbing—side of something he or she knew all the time" (viii). Because Žižek also blurbs Dolar's book, insisting that, all evidence to the contrary notwithstanding, its author is "not an idiot," one can safely assume that this book is one through which we will encounter something disturbing about ourselves that we knew all along. The obvious question is: What?

For my purposes the most immediately relevant aspect of the text is its discussion of Saussure, Derrida, and Lacan. Here Dolar seeks to tease out the radicality of the voice by clarifying its status as an object, invoking the series of *objets a* enumerated by Lacan in Seminar 11 from 1964: the gaze, the voice, the breast, and the turd. Structurally, these are all objects that tear a hole in our wholeness, meaning that they mark a limit of and in our identities. We cannot, as it were, leave home without them. Dolar's discussion is as rich as it is intricate. Although it resists easy summary, this is how it concludes.

> So, if for Derrida, the essence of the voice lies in its auto-affection and self-transparency, as opposed to the trace, the rest, the alterity, and so on, for Lacan this is where the problem starts. The deconstructive turn tends to deprive the voice of its ineradicable ambiguity by reducing it to the ground of (self-) presence, while the Lacanian account tries to disentangle from its core the object as an interior obstacle to (self-) presence. This object embodies the very impossibility of attaining auto-affection; it introduces a scission, a rupture in the middle of full presence, and refers it back to a void—but a void that is not simply a lack, and empty space; it is a void in which the voice comes to resonate. (*Voice* 42)

Stated semantically, the choice is clear: the voice as object or the voice as ground. If I may risk repeating Dolar's own strategy of attributing to his interlocutor values the latter is known to have repudiated, less clear is the "real" difference between these voices. One senses the difficulty instantly when Dolar pulls his punch, saying, "The deconstructive turn *tends to* deprive the voice of its ineradicable ambiguity," as if conceding in advance that the more blunt and theoretically decisive formulation, "The deconstructive turn deprives" (that is, as a matter of principle, that is, as a matter of credo) "the voice of its ineradicable ambiguity," is both unfair and untrue. Despite my having raised the issue of the truth about deconstruction, the issue here is not quite as petty as all that. Instead, what calls for attention is not only that in Dolar's hands the voice as object, all protestations to the contrary notwithstanding, is unambiguously set opposite the voice as ground, but also that its ineradicable ambiguity cannot easily be disambiguated from precisely what Derrida means by the trace. To say, as Dolar does, that the object is an "interior obstacle to (self-) presence" is not thereby repeating the structure of the trace, except for the careless invocation of an "interior" that neither he nor Derrida believes in. In effect, Dolar gives us a voice, even *the* voice, that *is* the trace, simply now rebaptized as "voice." Armed with this voice, he then goes about separating himself from a position he is obliged to caricature, as if conceding that the whole exercise is, at bottom, a performative articulation of the structure of the *objet a.* In effect, the voice as ground tears a hole in the voice as object so that the latter can get on with the pressing business of demonstrating that the voice resonates in the void left by this tear.

One is reminded here of chapter 25 in *Tristes Tropiques,* "A Writing Lesson," except that what is at stake here is not finally about the right word and how to spell it properly. The intellectual historical question of precedence is not without interest—who came up with the logic of post-dialectical difference, if it makes any sense to say this, "first"—but a responsible, that is, thorough, treatment of the prolonged confrontation between philosophy and psychoanalysis will take us out of signal range.

I will settle for a few observations. First, regardless of whether one agrees with Dolar's reading of Derrida, what is beyond serious doubt is that the former's approach to the voice, his reinvestment in it, is marked profoundly by the perceived impact of the critique of phonocentrism. In this sense my characterization of the resurgence of interest in the voice is at least partly justified—about which more in a moment. Second, and this is closer to the gist of the matter, Dolar's discussion, while it certainly succeeds in disambiguating the voice and presence as the phenomenological condition of meaning, avoids wrestling with precisely the acoustic character of the void within which the voice as object is said to resonate. How are we to think the resonance of the void? Is it to be ceded to the concerns of psycho-acoustics? In short, sound again drops out. Perhaps the clearest symptom of this is in Dolar's effortless gliding from voice to music, a gliding rendered in an arresting formulation late in the text: "What Freud and Kafka have in common . . . is their claim that they are both completely unmusical—which made them particularly susceptible to the dimension of the voice" (*Voice* 208). While on the face of it this would appear to oppose music to voice, my point is that Dolar appears here to assume that the relation between music and voice is so intimate as to be organized by the law of inverse proportion. The less you think you know about music, the more you clearly don't know you know about the voice, and vice versa.

Needless to say, the work of one thinker—however much he is not, as Žižek insists, "an idiot"—does not a resurgence make. Consider, then, in addition to the ample bibliography that appears at the end of *A Voice,* Giorgio Agamben's trilogy, *Homo Sacer, The Open,* and *The State of Exception,* all of which appeared between 1995 and 2005.[2] Rewarding though it might be, I have no intention of working carefully through each of these delicately argued texts. Instead, I want to scan immediately to the discussion of Aristotle that sets the stage for *Homo Sacer* and, by extension, for the trilogy as a whole.

Precisely because Agamben is concerned in *Homo Sacer,* as he says in chapter 3, to articulate a theory of politics "freed from the aporias of sovereignty," he establishes and crosses the threshold of his text by putting in play the distinction that will ground the theory of politics that must be overcome. This is the distinction between the Greek terms *zoe* (life in general, singular) and *bios* (particular, or distinctive forms of life in the plural). Almost immediately Agamben will move to clarify that *zoe* encompasses the form of living that he, following Benjamin, calls *vita nuda,* the form of living that must be excluded from lives ordered by activity that is properly political. If this distinction is read too quickly, one fails to see that it not only triggers a subsequent one between voice and language but in so doing triggers the second volume of the trilogy. How so? What is crucial to the distinction is what is gathered on either side of it. Under *zoe* in its undifferentiated singularity are gathered "(animals, men and gods)" (*Homo* 1). Under *bios* are gathered the myriad *different* life forms. In other words, what might be said to require the political exclusion of *zoe* is the fact that under its auspices the animal and the human are not yet differentiated. Differentiating them will require the very distinction triggered by the first.

This is how Agamben presents the matter. He derives it from *The Politics,* where Aristotle writes:

> Among living beings, only man has language. The voice is the sign of pain and pleasure, and this is why it belongs to other living beings (since their nature has developed to the point of having sensations of pain and pleasure and signifying the two). But language is for manifesting the fitting and the unfitting and the just and the unjust. To have the sensation of the good and the bad and of the just and the unjust is what is proper to men as opposed to other living beings, and the community of these things makes dwelling and the city. (1253a, 10–18)

In setting up this citation, Agamben makes it clear that he sees and appreciates the important link forged in Aristotle between the voice and *zoe.* Indeed, Dolar himself is drawn to this very discussion, confirming—if only obliquely—the common ground of their respective projects. The link at issue is that between *zoe* and the animal, or, to put the matter more carefully, the exclusion from the properly political—that is, the politics sustaining the aporias of sovereignty—the exclusion of the being who has a voice but not language, that is, the animal.

Voice, animal, bare life, politics: these terms, virtually in this syntagmatic order, reappear in *The Open,* Agamben's unsettling meditation on the human-animal relation. He does not here return to Aristotle but instead restages the discussion of voice by appealing to Ernst Haeckle's *Anthropogenie,* a text in which the origin of the human is grounded in an evolutionary transformation of a *sprachloser Urmensch,* a primordial man without speech. As in *Homo Sacer,* what Agamben wants to foreground is the relation between a politics founded on the aporias of sovereignty and the becoming human of the prehuman. And while this might lead one to assume that he aligns the animal, and therefore the voice, with naked life, he does not. Instead, what he aligns with naked life is the form of existence that serves as the background out of which emerged the human/animal distinction, that is, "a life that is separated and excluded from itself" (*Open* 38). Significantly, this life excluded from itself recalls Agamben's earlier alignment of *zoe* and voice by stressing the fact that *zoe* refers to the undifferentiated background out of which the animal/human distinction will emerge. Nowhere in the trilogy does Agamben call for an evolutionary reversal, but it is clear that voice must be brought back, if for no other reason than to remind us of how deeply into the human sensorium the political cuts, and what precisely a politics freed of the aporias of sovereignty must seek to give expression to.

On the face of this, it is hard to recognize here the motif of phonocentrism. And while Agamben nowhere appeals to the Lacanian concept of the voice as the *objet a,* his treatment of voice as a concept through which to approach the means by which life excludes itself from itself certainly implies a somewhat less occulted affiliation with the psychoanalytical discussion—or so might one conclude before considering carefully how Agamben's discussion of the animal takes up the work of Heidegger.

As Agamben acknowledges, his title derives from Heidegger's lectures from 1929 to 1930 collected as *The Fundamental Concepts of Metaphysics: World, Finitude, Solitude.* There, Heidegger following Rilke's invocation of "the open," sets up an organizing tension between the animal, who is "poor in world," and man, who is "world forming." In the course of Agamben's intricate and thought-provoking discussion, this tension is recast in ontological terms as one between concealedness and unconcealedness, a distinction that in the final paragraph of chapter 15 is made to reconnect with politics. To wit, the unconcealedness that sets the tone of *Dasein* is understood by Heidegger to find its proper locus in the polis, that is, a social order in which the animal's mode of openness, that of captivation and extreme boredom, is left radically outside, as it were, both day and night. On Plato's city map of Athens, and this would not have escaped Rilke, the poet and the animal are found in the same place: outside howling at the moon.

What brings this presentation into connection with the theme of phonocentrism does not, in fact, appear on its face. Instead, phonocentrism functions like what Michael Rifaterre used to call a "hypogram," a borrowed, often unconsciously borrowed, grit of text matter that allows the pearl of a subsequent discussion to form. In this case, Agamben's hypogram is the entirety of chapter 6 in Derrida's *Of Spirit* (1987). Although Derrida is there concerned with the status of *Geist,* indeed, the difference between *geistig* and *geistlich,* and Heidegger's avoidance of it, he too comes upon the animal that hides in the thickets of *The Fundamental Concepts of Metaphysics.* Precisely because Heidegger defines the world as spiritual, *geistlich,* the animal, that is, the being poor in world, is essentially without spirit. What Derrida adds, and this will come as no surprise, is the problem of language. Specifically, starting from Heidegger's acknowledgment that "the leap from the animal that lives to the man that speaks is as great . . . as that from the lifeless stone to the living being" (*Of Spirit* 53), Derrida lingers over Heidegger's use of the "strike through," the "crossing out" that is put to work in these pages. In discussing the poverty of the animal, Heidegger emphasizes that this bears on the matter that while a lizard may be stretched out on a rock, strictly speaking, the word *rock* should be crossed out (much as Heidegger will later cross out Being itself) because the lizard cannot relate to "the rock" *as such.* That is, the animal is poor in phonocentrism. It cannot be present to the signified of the signifier *rock,* a situation figured in the crossing out of the written word. Note that Heidegger insists that the lizard is certainly present to the referent, the rock upon which it lies, but not to the signified of the phonemic bundle *rock.* Linking this to the philosophical *as such* clarifies that we are indeed on the terrain of phonocentrism, that is, that the meaning of the rock in general is tied to the acoustic image that the lizard cannot fail to miss. Perhaps, if Thomas Sebeok is right, the lizard is simply poor in zoosemiotics. To be sure, we may never know.

My point: although manifest in a completely different way, to summarize crudely—through the crossed-out or suppressed Derridean hypogram—Agamben's discussion of the voice is every bit as engaged with the legacy of its phonocentric critique as is Dolar's. Whether one thinks about the voice as an object or as the avatar of a life that can be killed without sacrifice—and I am by no means saying that these are the same thing—what matters is that in both cases the voice is redeployed theoretically to get at something, to produce an insight, thought to be inaccessible without it. Because thought, whether philosophical or not, cannot thrive in the absence of such maneuvering, one must concede that what I have called the resurgence of the voice finds its most principled motivation here. But the question remains: Does this get us where we want to go? And where, precisely, is that?

This is where the exchange between Norma and Joe finds its pertinence. *Comeback* versus *return.* It seems to me that what Norma protests in Joe's word is precisely its predictability, the fact that he is already narrating his encounter with her as part of a Hollywood script. The comeback is thus an effort to get started again, but one whose logic and motivation have already been determined by what no one—not even Norma herself—had recognized as her "last" performance. Now, it is certainly true that "return" is every bit as scripted, especially to whatever extent it responds to the call of forgiveness, but what is important here is the very thematization of the temporal join. Norma insists, nay, demands, that we think twice about how one step follows upon another. Brought to bear on the matter of the voice—which, as some will recall, is the topic of discussion in the immediately preceding exchange between Norma and Joe (they quarrel about the sound-image relation in the cinema)—the issue is not so much whether the resurgence of interest in it is either a comeback or a return as whether, as I have said, it gets us where we want to go. If this is to a concept of sound that is radically postphonocentric, it will come as no surprise when I aver that I have my doubts. To clarify why getting here is worth the effort, let me turn yet again to *Sunset Blvd*.

As Norma and Joe enter her study just prior to the exchange regarding her *Salomé* script cited earlier, the cut to their passage over the threshold finds it sonic articulation in the beginning of a persistent but distinctly haunted wheezing of the organ on the opposite wall. Norma gestures in its direction, noting that it should be either removed or repaired (we later find Max, her butler, playing it). Joe then quips that she might also consider teaching it "a better tune." Because the scene is structured sonically around the toggling back and forth between Joe's voice-over narration and the dialogue of the characters, both the wind playing, poorly, on the organ and the voice-over come from an acousmatic if not quite nondiegetic space. A structural relation is thus forged between the voice and music. Here is my point: of interest in the scene is not so much the rather typical way in which the sound of the organ is buried beneath the dialogue (the very noose of words Norma has only just decried) as the way sound, and here its distinctly acousmatic character, is boxed in between music and voice, as if it can be grasped, or picked up, only on this disciplinary frontier, that is, somewhere between philosophy and musicology.

Thinking outside this particular box is not easy, a fact demonstrated with instructive clarity by Adorno's voluminous writings on the box he calls radio.[3] Several of these are well known. Less well known are the writings recently compiled and edited by Robert Hullot-Kentor in his contribution to Adorno's ever-completing works titled *Current of Music,* a volume that gathers virtually all of the work written by Adorno—and, I might add, written in English—while he was affiliated with the short-lived Princeton Radio Research Project. The only significant omission, one addressed in Hullot-Kentor's detailed introductory remarks, is the *still* unpublished "Memorandum: Music in Radio," a text one must consult in the Rare Books Room in Butler Library at Columbia University. In this indispensable collection two texts call out for attention: "Radio Physiognomics" and especially "The Radio Voice." Elaborations of "Memorandum," both engage in rich and compelling ways the problem of the box, as furniture and as philosophy. They lead us directly to the vexing interplay between radio and philosophy.

Adorno's correspondence establishes that he and Gretel arrived in New York from Great Britain in late February of 1938. Adorno writes Benjamin on letterhead from Princeton University, the Office of Radio Research (located in, of all places, Eno Hall), on March 7, 1938, saying that they have taken an apartment on 45 Christopher Street, once the heart of queer Manhattan. He goes on to solicit from Benjamin a short paper on "listening models" that he hopes to integrate into his work at Princeton ("To Walter Benjamin" 240–41). Almost a year later to the day, Adorno presents to the faculty of the Psychology Department at Princeton the paper "Radio Physiognomics," in which he lays out what he takes to be the most serious limitations of the "experimental methods" of psychology. Hadley Cantril and Gordon Allport—the authors of the 1935 study *The Psychology of Radio*—were, whether in attendance or not, his intended audience. Those familiar with the Frankfurt School critique of "instrumental reason" and the "re-enchantment of positivism" will find nothing particularly interesting in these remarks. Truly interesting, however, is the methodological alternative that emerged in their wake.

This alternative is formulated through an appeal to Johann Kaspar Lavater's concept of physiognomy, a figure that although translated into English at the dawn of the nineteenth century required the curiosity of Allport and others to make him matter to psychology. As Adorno reminds us, *physiognomics* referred to the analytical practice of discovering the truth of personality beneath or behind facial expressions. Although in his discussion Adorno has recourse to the English vocabulary of Peirceian semiotics, notably the notion of the index and the sign, he does not underscore the extent to which physiognomy is clearly a rearticulation of the very derivation of semiotics from the Greek practice and technique of symptomatology, that is, the reading of an inner, invisible condition through the decipherment of outward, visible signs. Nevertheless, he is insistent upon the structural value of the channel, the communication, between an inner and an outer, a hidden and a manifest—something of an inverted acousmatics. Brought to bear on the phenomenon of radio, physiognomy leads Adorno almost directly to the concept of the radio voice. Aware that this invites immediate comparison with Lavater's concept of personality, Adorno embarks on a somewhat tortuous but telling justification for both physiognomy and the radio voice that it allows one to pick up.

On the face of it, Adorno's material would appear to surrender to phonocentrism in advance by seeking the social meaning of the radio in its voice, and to some extent this is true. Moreover, insofar as he addresses himself to sound he does so by turning immediately to music, again as if the meaning of sound must be made to resonate within and across the frontier bordering philosophy and musicology. Although true, these are not the only conclusions that can be drawn from his discussion. Indeed, it is precisely the way Adorno's analysis sidles up to phonocentrism without succumbing to its charm that is at once interesting and important.

After provisionally setting aside the matter of the obsolescence of physiognomy, Adorno turns to the problem of the face. What is the equivalent of the human face in the domain of the radiophonic? Does physiognomy have more than a merely metaphorical value? It does if we recognize that, like the face, the radio presents us with a unity, something that synthesizes psychological, sociological, and technological elements. It does so by exhibiting voice. In other words, just as we might say that Don LaFontaine had a voice that exuded aggressive masculinity (his was the ubiquitous promotional voice of summer blockbusters in the United States), we might want to say that the radio has a voice that can be delimited and read as the sign of something, if not someone, behind it. Voice then becomes the very means by which Adorno wants to salvage physiognomy in the face of its obsolescence. It thus has, as it were, two faces: one turned toward the radio and the other turned toward the disciplinary field in which radio appears as an object of inquiry.

But what precisely can be said about the radio voice? Adorno is quick to point out that it has nothing to do with the voices or other sounds that are broadcast over the radio. That would be too empirical.[4] The issue, instead, has to do entirely with what he insists upon calling the "how" of the radio. In other words, the radio voice is different from both voices and music, presumably because it emanates from somewhere that neither the voice nor music can name.

Because Adorno's discussion of the impact of radio on symphonic music (in "The Radio Symphony") numbers among his better-known writings on radio, I will only point briefly to the aspect of this discussion that bears on physiognomy. In essence, radio is at odds with symphonic music because it deprives this music of its sonic power. It does so in two ways: first, it generates an acoustic image of the music that miniaturizes it, making it impossible for the listener to be surrounded, absorbed by the forces of the symphonic orchestra. Second, this act of miniaturization blocks what Adorno elsewhere calls "structural listening," forcing the listener to engage in atomized listening, a form of listening that in failing to feel the whole of a musical composition seeks to recognize and isolate fragments of melody or thematic passages and motifs. It contributes to what he regards as the patently offensive practices of humming and whistling—both, it should be pointed out, sounds that fall somewhere between voice and music. This is a point that ought to have attracted more of Adorno's attention and less of his impatience.

Famously, or perhaps infamously, this discussion does not settle for a technical dressing down of the radio as a device, as a piece of furniture. It goes after the theoretical jugular instead: the claim that radio so transforms our relation to the listening required by symphonic music that it destroys this music from within. Trivializing this analytical proposition through the psychologism of "pessimism," a polemical weapon drawn these days almost as quickly as Göbbel's famed Browning, is really more of a bluff, a feint. It is certainly no argument against the theoretical ambition of Adorno's insight—or so I am contending here. With this caveat in mind, we return now to the physiognomic problem of the voice.

Consider then the following extraordinary passages from "The Radio Voice":

> What actually "speaks" through radio is man: by his voice or by musical instruments. Thus the term "speaking" appears to be a purely metaphorical one. One attributes to the instrument what is due to man merely because of his invisibility and remoteness. Still, when the phenomenon is analyzed, man's remoteness from the loudspeaker and his invisibility are part of the phenomenon. Whenever one switches on his radio, the sounds pouring out bear an expression all their own, an expression which is related to the men behind it, only by reflection and not by the primordial awareness of the phenomenon. Radio speaks to the listener even if he is not listening to a speaker. (533)

And on the following page, segueing from a summary of his critique of the radio symphony:

> Radio has its own voice inasmuch as it functions as a filter for every sound. Due to the comprehensiveness of its operation as a filter, it gains a certain autonomy in the ears of the listener: even the adult experiences the radio rudimentarily, like the child who personifies radio as an aunt or uncle of his. It is the physiognomics of this radio voice wich [sic] provides the key for an understanding of how the expression of the radio tends to become a model for its social significance. (534)

More worthy of close attention follows thereon, but for now let me underscore a few especially salient issues. First, there is the complex interplay between metaphor and attribution. Obviously, Adorno remains haunted throughout by the epistemological status of physiognomy. Here he supplements metaphor with belief, that is, while hanging on to the physiognomic idea that something is signified behind the radio voice, he not only points to the invisible man but also emphasizes the role played by listeners in attributing an identity to the source of what is heard. Moreover, as if defending his appeal to appearances, Adorno builds into the radio itself the remoteness and invisibility of the human subject. In other words, what the radio *is* includes the irreducibly acousmatic character of what lies behind it, the missing subject whose absence is compensated for in the listener's attribution of voice to the radio. Because this very dimension of radio arises only in reflection, it is otherwise essentially unconscious; indeed, it is through this unconsciousness that the human and the radio belong to each other.

In the second passage, the motif of the unconscious manifests itself in the figure of the filter. This is not just a filter for what "man" says or the music he plays, it is a filter for every sound, a specification that finds in the compensatory structure of the radio voice a deflective processing of all sound transmitted by the radio. Here, one might reasonably suggest, sound breaks away from voice and music in serving as the index of a filter that explicitly extends beyond the two. Importantly, as with the discussion of radio's impact on the radio symphony, the filter becomes a prosthetic earpiece. It at once enhances and preempts our listening. In Eisenberg's formulation, it listens for us. As Adorno says, the filter gains a certain autonomy in the ear of the listener, but instead of miniaturizing the power of the symphony it consigns the human subject to an infantilized personification of radio in which, regardless of what is being broadcast, "he" is spoken to by the invisible and remote brother or sister of one of his parents. Is sound filtered here, in and as radio, through what we could properly call Oedipalization? It is worth recalling here that one of the preoccupations of the psychoanalysts assembled by Lazarsfeld to consult with the Princeton Radio Research Project was that of the radio's interference with parenting. In effect, Fromm, Sullivan, and others worried that radio functioned as an alternative authority in the family. Does such a function have a sound? What would such a sound sound like?

Before attempting to respond, consider the closing formulation of the second passage. This is the sentence in which physiognomics is mentioned by name and advocated as an approach to radio because through it one understands how its expression becomes a model for its social significance. It is not hard to grasp how expression and signifi- cance fall in line with the physiognomic distinction between the hidden and the manifest, but what does pose difficulties is the notion of an expression that becomes a voice by virtue of an absence for which it compensates. Moreover, what, if anything, does this have to do with the filter?

Recall here that it is because the radio filters that it has a voice. It is as though Adorno were here anticipating what Barthes would later call "the grain of the voice," the material quality of speaking—the pace, timbre, volume, in short, the sound qualities of a voice. Indeed, turn- ing back briefly to the discussion of the radio symphony in the same essay, Adorno goes on at some length about what he calls the "hear stripe": the surface noise of a phonograph or the static hum of a public broadcasting system, noise that adds a relentless pedal tone to the score of every piece of music broadcast by radio. This grain, this irreduc- ible materiality of transmission, would certainly qualify as the audible presence of a filter. Indeed, one might think of the haunted wheezing organ in *Sunset Blvd.* as an incarnation of the hear stripe, or at least its screen. But what bears repeating here is the fact that voice is what lies, in the terms of Adorno's exposition, behind or beneath a face. Given that the radio is faceless, a voice must be invented for it and then at- tributed to it—in which case radio would thus appear to call to or for the physiognomist.

The voice as the "face-like unity" is precisely what cues the physi- ognomical analysis of radio. As such, the filter—the audible sign of the radio voice's functioning—is as much about radio as it is about theory. Adorno, by locating the filter in the ear of the listener and declaring both it and the absent speaker to be parts of the radio apparatus, would appear to be including in radio its physiognomic study. Because the social significance of radio would presumably derive—at least in part— from such a study, one can then say, as Adorno does, that the radio's expression "models" its social significance. In short, because the face- voice relation repeats in advance the expression-significance relation, theory as a critical mediation of the whole is apparently already active in the radio itself. It is as if the radio voice were calling from behind its purely metaphorical face, not to a listener per se, but to a theory capable of picking up its signals. What does this call sound like? How does the filter that is the voice deflect or channel it? To begin to amplify this sound, or at least the problems that it poses, I want to approach it by thinking about closeness, invisibility, and spooks.

To the reader familiar with Adorno's cranky rejoinder to Benjamin's essay "The Work of Art in the Era of Its Technical Reproducibility," his advocacy of the critique of aura in "The Radio Voice" comes as a bit of a surprise. In an early pass over this material, Adorno, invoking the work of Robert Havighurst, puzzles over the matter of the "live-ness" of radio music. Preparing us for the physiognomic turn, Adorno quotes approvingly Havighurst's assertion that radio listeners feel that they know the personalities of those speaking on radio because of the "illusion of closeness," which makes the listener "feel that he is actu-ally present at the place where the broadcast originates—or purports to originate" (Radio Voice" 501–2). Because the motif of "knowing personality through voice" is, as we have seen, properly physiognomi-cal, it is clear that this discussion is asking us to bring together the "face-like-unity" of the radio with the illusion of closeness, the notion that we are present to/at the origin of the broadcast. In further charac-terizing this closeness, Adorno first reminds us to consider that we listen to the radio in the privacy of the home, as he says—tellingly—"in face of [our] wireless set" (502), and that the "amplified noises" emitted by it approach the listener as an "owner victim," or, as he later specifies, they "approach one bodily." Thus closeness is clearly more than prox-imity: it is about a feeling that sound, amplified noise, is penetrating, breaking into something or someone who can face a wireless. In this sense, Kafka's "The Burrow" surely provides the template for Adorno's encounter with radio.

Adorno, of course, is here more interested in the puzzle of the live ver-sus the reproduced, but it is important to note how quickly in the piece the physiognomic motifs enter and how intimately they become associ-ated with the acoustic or sonic problem of what pours into or through the body. Perhaps not surprisingly, later, when Adorno's anxiety about the metaphoricity of the physiognomic method is at its height, he trots out not only a catachrestic justification for it—we refer, he notes, to the sound source as a "loudspeaker," the "diaphragm" of the microphone is modeled on the ear, in short, "the radio mechanism is patterned after human sense organs" ("Radio Voice" 535)—but a psychoanalytical one. Indeed, in the long footnote on 534–35 he rehearses the dispute between Ferenczi and Bernfeld regarding the physiognomic symptom-atization of the human organs whereby they can function as expressive centers of personality disorders. His comment on this debate, where he characterizes the radio "as an organ of society" ("Radio Voice" 535), leaves no doubt that if such exaggerations, in the end, nevertheless help one understand something fundamental about radio, then they are ana- lytical risks worth taking. And what, apparently, is fundamental about radio is the "illusion of closeness" generated in and by its voice.

But does this not contradict the earlier emphasis on the remoteness of the invisible man whose voice breaks into one's home? It does, until one recognizes that this invocation of the acousmatic character of radio sound is treated by Adorno as an avatar of the uncanny, that is, the sense of its sound being "here" but in such a way that one cannot be, as he says, 'face to face" with it ("Radio Voice" 503). To flesh out this uncanny "hereness" of radio, Adorno appeals to Günther Stern's (later Anders's) 1930 study "Spuk und Radio." Although Stern's concern is to illuminate the odd spatiality of broadcast music—the fact that it has a precise "when" while lacking a precise "where"—Adorno draws on Stern's discussion of ubiquity to extend his insight into hereness, and by extension the illusion of closeness. In effect, what ubiquity pro- vides is a way to talk about how the remote comes near precisely in being everywhere. The invisible man, in falling outside a certain con- strual of the domain of the visible, is someone or something that can, in principle, be anywhere. If listeners feel themselves addressed as owner victims by the invisible voice, and especially if the nearness of this ad- dress spirits them off to the site from which the broadcast purports to originate, then it is not hard to understand what appeals to Adorno about Stern's figure of the spook. Moreover, given Adorno's unusually receptive relation to psychoanalysis in this essay, it is hard to believe that he was not aware of Freud's use of Goethe's *spuk* from *Faust II*— "Now the air is so filled with spooks, that no one knows best how to get out"—a line that stands as the epigraph to *The Psychopathology of Everyday Life* but that in this context suggests that ubiquity and the psychopathological character of the everyday are mixed together in the sound of closeness. Perhaps this sheds light on the curious fact that this essay of Adorno's, like several others of those done under the auspices of the Princeton Radio Research Project, finds an occasion to reference the *War of the Worlds* broadcast that took place in the fall, on Halloween Night, to be precise, of his first year in the United States. Recall that in exculpating the Mercury Theater and NBC Radio, Welles described the broadcast as a Halloween prank, our "own radio ver- sion of dressing up in a sheet jumping out of a bush and saying Boo!" (Cantril, *Invasion* 42).

Boo. What kind of sound is that? Semantically, of course, it registers both disapproval and menace. But it is also one of those so-called imitative or onomatopoetic words that, in apparently defying the principle of the arbitrariness of the linguistic sign, gave Saussure fits. But rather than puzzling over precisely the sort of sound that *boo* is, and remembering that the larger aim here is to get at the sound that escapes the radio voice, consider that *boo,* as an imitative and thus analogical word, challenges the discipline of linguistics as Saussure is seeking to found it. To exaggerate if only for effect, *boo* is the sound of something whistling, maybe even humming, through or around the limits of a discipline. This means, of course, that I am rather obviously pressuring the notion of what sound is, where it takes place, indeed whether it can or should be heard/understood at all.

To move beyond these unsettling abstractions, it is crucial that we follow the lead of Adorno in adducing the relevance of Heidegger to his discussion of the radio voice. Adorno invokes Heidegger to help clarify in what way Stern's analysis succumbs to the ahistorical tendencies of "existential philosophy," and although Adorno makes no immediate reference to those pages in *Being and Time* where Heidegger discusses the radio, the pointed ambiguity of his remarks essentially prompts one to do so. In effect, the reader has, as it were, been transferred—not to the source, even purported, of the broadcast, but perhaps to the source of reckoning with it in certain terms.

Virtually all media historians of the Weimar period—Pohle, Currid, Jelavich, Bergmeier, and Lotz—insist that radio underwent a profound transformation and reorganization in Germany after World War I. This was due to the emerging consensus among educators and politicians that Germany had decisively lost the propaganda war; indeed, this very concept appears to have come into its own during this conflict. As an expression of this device envy, Germany embarked upon an aggressive centralization of radio broadcasting, a process that might be said to have culminated in Göbbels's appointment as *Reichspropagandaleiter* of the Nazi Party in 1929. Immediately following the war in the winter of 1918–19, many still-equipped veteran wireless operators lent their talents to an ugly confrontation with the uprighting and rightward-tending German state, a confrontation that came to be referred to subsequently as the *Funkerspuk* or radio scare. Doubtless, this and the fact that it was taken as the pretext for an aggressive state centralization of radio under the Postal Ministry cannot be far from the minds of Stern and Adorno, both, as we have seen, eager to articulate the radio-spook link. Finding its ideal echo at the level of reception, as early as 1933, almost immediately after Hitler's seizure of state power, his government developed and began aggressively distributing the *Volksemfänger,* or people's set, a low-cost radio receiver designed to interact with the broadcast signals transmitted from the Berlin *Funkhaus.* Brian Currid is surely not exaggerating when, in his study, he refers to this situation as exhibiting what he calls a "national acoustic," that is, an experience of a sound envelope, the "unisonality" described by Benedict Anderson as key to a meaningfully bounded national imaginary.

Of course, Stern and Adorno were not the only Germans picking up the process reputedly triggered by World War I and the *Funkerspuk.* Friedrich Kittler, as stressed in the Introduction, has draw attention to the fact that Heidegger was also following these events, and doing so in the course of writing *Being and Time,* his still-resonant essay in fundamental ontology. The key passage reads as follows: "*In Dasein there lies an essential tendency towards closeness.* All the ways in which we speed things up, as we are more or less compelled to today, push us on towards the conquest of remoteness. With the 'radio' for example, Dasein has so expanded its everyday environment that it has accomplished a de-severance *[Ent-fernung]* of the 'world'—a de-severance which, in its meaning for Dasein, cannot yet be visualized" (*Being* 140, italics in the translation).

As if miming its own insight, this passage is crowded with dense and important ideas. It appears in Section Three of Division One, titled "The Worldhood of the World," and specifically in those passages dedicated to the problem of the spatiality (note the convergence with Stern) of Being-in-the-World. In these passages Heidegger is keen to distinguish between a form of being in the world that is to a certain degree empirical, that is, a form of being-in that is subject to measurement, and a more ontological form. To adduce one of his own examples: the garment is in the closet, the closet is in a room, the room is in a house, the house is in a city, and so on. Precisely where the garment is in this configuration is determinable by and through calculation. Against this stands the spatiality of ontology, that is, the experience *Dasein* has in being *with* things in what then deserves to be called a "world." Recall that this is the very world Heidegger thought animals, that is, those without language, were decidedly poor in.

In the midst of this discussion, Heidegger turns to the radio. In the context created by my remarks, his immediate attention to "closeness" captures our own. Oddly enough, it would appear, on the face of it, that Adorno, who otherwise has very little time for Heidegger, is essentially recycling this discussion. But this seems decidedly less possible when one sorts out precisely how Heidegger understands "closeness." The important first step lies in confronting the difficult concept of what is here translated as "de-severance." Macquarrie and Robinson tell us important things in explaining how, in the footnote on pages 138–39 of their translation, they confected the term. Heidegger's word *Entfernung* has *fern*, or, "far," at its root. The privative prefix *ent-* takes farness away from itself, a semantic effect that is intensified when, as in the case of the passage cited, the prefix is set off by a hyphen. In other words, *Ent-fernung* is not simply a remoteness that is less remote, but a coming near of the remote, of the far. Given the topic of spatiality, one might reasonably conclude that we are dealing here with an insight into the essential spacing of the being of *Dasein,* an insight that Heidegger virtually picks up from the radio, one that points directly at the difference between disembodiment and delocalization. Although no reference is made to *Dasein,* it seems obvious that Adorno has modeled the "illusion of nearness" on Heidegger's treatment of *Ent-fernung.* In fact, when, in 1964, Adorno turns the full intensity of his critical glare on Heidegger—I am thinking here of *The Jargon of Authenticity*—it is striking that in challenging the latter's approach to the immediate he rehearses in condensed form the arguments from "The Radio Voice," down to reiterating the motifs of the "voice of the announcer" that "resounds" in the home, the nearness of the whole, and the atomized individual (*Jargon* 76).

Before, however, we get distracted by the question of influence and its *Angst,* I want to dwell briefly on the closing sentence in the passage cited from *Being and Time:* "With the 'radio,' for example, Dasein has so expanded its everyday environment that it has accomplished a de-severance of the 'world'—a de-severance which, in its meaning for Dasein, cannot yet be visualized." What draws attention here is the distinct way in which Heidegger evokes the acousmatic character of the radio. He does not frame this in terms of the invisibility of the sound source. Instead, he deftly traces the dilemma that arises as an ontological structure, that of *Dasein* itself, undergoes an expansion whose effect—the de-severance of the "world," that is, the no-place where *Dasein* is with itself and with others—cannot yet be visualized (the German, *übersehbare,* might be better rendered as "fore-seen," even "looked over," scrutinized). Such a formulation might appear to be inconsequential, except that a page later Heidegger writes: "Seeing and hearing are distance senses *[Fernsinne]* not because they are far reaching, but because it is in them that Dasein as deseverant mainly dwells" (*Being* 141). In other words, when one insists upon the limits, even if provisional, of vision, one is pointing to an asymmetry in the ontological structure of *Dasein* itself. Radio is thus obliging hearing to speed out ahead of seeing, producing a de-severance out of step with itself, recalling, I should think, the importance of thinking about the sound of this racing hearing. Indeed, when Heidegger returns to these questions ten years later, in "The Anaximander Fragment," he envisions the press "limping after" radio, whose speed has overtaken even historiography itself, establishing the world dominion of historicism (*Early Greek Thinking* 17).

It is tempting, especially since the interventions of Françoise Fedier and Victor Farias, to approach this racing sound as the voice of Hitler that resounds in the speaker of the *Volksempfänger,* mixing, as Horkheimer and Adorno insisted, with the sirens in the street. Or, put differently, it is certainly possible to read this asymmetrical de-severance at the heart of *Dasein,* especially as indexed to the nationalizing of German radio in the twenties, as the vulnerability of *Dasein* to the Nazi temptation—in effect, to invoke Berel Lang's anguished study, as Heidegger's rehearsal for his silence on the Jewish Question. Doing so, however, suppresses too hastily the unsettling proximity between Adorno and Heidegger on the radio, that is, the fact that *Dasein*'s vulnerability refers with equal immediacy to an ontological structure and to the fundamental ontology—the philosophical project—putting this structure, as it were, on the playlist. In other words, if the full implications of de-severing the world are not yet fore-seeable, this may well cast the shadow of the acousmatic upon philosophy itself, to the extent that the source of its sounds, its rumblings, falls outside *its* construal of the visual field. In short, the sound that haunts phonocentrism could be said to fall out of the range of our hearing, but hearing understood as a faculty or capacity of a subject that belongs to the knowledge, at once rational and affective, that we have of what passes for the acoustical. Here we face squarely the sound of both knowing and not knowing, a philosophical dilemma of shared interest to both Adorno and Heidegger.

But surely there is a political circle to square here? While not wishing to suggest that they are the same, much less identical—although each finds his own way to the retreat from politics (Heidegger in the name of "thinking," Adorno in the name of "negating")—it is instructive to witness how effortlessly Denis de Rougement aligns Heidegger not only with antifascism but with a Frankfurt School–style repudiation of mass culture. Written while de Rougemont was in exile in the United States, *The Devil's Share* is a probing, even desperate study of the status of the diabolical in modern society. In a pugnacious chapter, de Rougement advances a thesis pitched to scold Americans about both their political, moral, and ultimately military failure to recognize the diabolic character of Hitler and, almost paradoxically, their too automatic reduction of Hitler to a largely Judeo-Christian symbol whose cardinal virtue lies in its ability to persuade us that the devil does not exist. Seeking the conditions for this everyday, ordinary damnation, de Rougement turns, in chapter 47, to the theme of "depersonalization" and, surprisingly, radio.

Noting that the devil, in the twentieth century, has lost interest in conscripting individuals and has thus turned its attention to the masses, de Rougement points to the work of Kierkegaard as the first systematic diagnosis of this development. Supplementing Kierkegaard, he points to not only the dialectical fact that "the radio, the press and mass meetings" (*Devil's Share* 144) address themselves to masses, leading people to lead lives they do not have, but for him the essential corollary that "masses would not be possible, in the precise sense of a concentration of men, without the radio, loudspeakers, the press and rapid transportation" (145), insisting upon the perverse, onto-technological dimension of depersonalization. Radio produces the reception that scans for it, a reception just as bad as the designs of the device. It is when de Rougement teases out the distinctly diabolical character of the contemporary situation that the Heideggerian themes, doubtless cued by the references to Kierkegaard, enter the mix. In quick succession, under the titular heading of "The Tower of Babel" (an allusion later taken over by Erik Barnouw for his volume on early radio), de Rougement appeals to formulations such as the "frames have grown too big," we "clamor for bigness," things are "too large for our capacities," we have "moved too fast," and perhaps most tellingly of all, "society has become too gigantic to be taken in at a single glance." Given these characterizations of mass-mediated depersonalization coupled with the syntagmatic fact that this list segues to a discussion of boredom (one of the recurrent preoccupations of both *Being and Time* and *The Fundamental Concepts of Metaphysics*), one is hard-pressed to deny that Heidegger, and specifically Heidegger's discussion of radio, haunts this analysis. De Rougement is virtually repeating, but now in the context of mobilizing the confrontation with fascism, Heidegger's anxious discussion of de-severance. While today (and to some extent already in the thirties) we recognize that the so-called romantic anticapitalist critique of fascism was compromised, the all too readily at hand—because tendentious—opposition of Adorno and Heidegger's politics around the implications of mass culture is hard to sustain. Moreover, the obsession with alignment is the surest means by which to subject politics to what Agamben called "the aporias of sovereignty" (*Homo Sacer* 48). This said, the fraught and contentious proximity between Adorno and Heidegger is perhaps not as interesting as the fact that radio brings it out. Indeed, radio as something like a metonymy of mass culture appears precisely as the locus for a certain form of philosophical crisis, as though the political meaning of philosophy's position were directly transmitted by or otherwise channeled through it.[5]

By way of bringing the discussion to a provisional rest, I will dwell for a bit longer on Lang's underdeveloped, yet politically charged concept, that of silence. In solidarity with Margaret Attwood's laconic assertion that "context is all," indulge me as I repeat an oft-repeated anecdote, firm in the belief that the context generated by these remarks will realize the formalist goal of estranging the familiar. As John Cage himself tells it in a 1955 essay, the story goes like this:

> There is no such thing as an empty space or an empty time. There is always something to hear. In fact, try to make a silence, we cannot. For certain engineering purposes it is desirable to have as silent a situation as possible. Such a room is called an anechoic chamber, its six walls made of a special material, a room without echoes. I entered one at Harvard University several years ago and heard two sounds, one high, one low. When I described them to the engineer in charge, he informed me that the high one was my nervous system in operation, the low one my blood in circulation. Until I die there will be sounds. ("Experimental Music" 8)

The immediate aim of this anecdote is, on the one hand, to defeat the neo-Romantic notion that music emerges from, and thus gives transcendental order to, the Pascalian universe of silent, infinite space and, on the other hand, to assure readers that music, once retheorized, has a future. For me, however, what is striking is the way Cage re-poses the question of listening and the range of hearing. In effect, the two sounds he identifies, radiating as they do from the living body, from what Agamben would have to call the sheer animal capacity for voice, point to the haunted wheezing, the hear-stripe, that conditions all hearing we are prepared to recognize as such. The point here is not to resurrect the bio-anatomical body but to recognize that hearing is, to use a Lacanianism, mediated by listening, that is, by the signifier, or, as I prefer, by disciplinary reason. In this sense, Cage can be read as proposing that we produce silence as the form of the not-hearing that our listening rests upon in order to identify its objects of acoustic attention. Or, to translate the point back into the terms of this discussion, Cage finds in the absence of silence a sound calling for attention, not in and of itself as some ethereal avatar of the *musica universalis,* but as an index of what the contemporary, disciplinary organization of listening receives badly, if at all.

Formulating the point in these terms directs us immediately back to *Being and Time,* not to its meditation on de-severance, but to its analysis of the call, *der Ruf.*[6] This material appears in Heidegger's effort to grasp "conscience," specifically "the voice of conscience," not as a psychological experience but as an ontological structure. The formulation inviting the comparison between Cage and Heidegger reads as follows: "The call does not report events; it calls without uttering anything. The call discourses in the uncanny mode of *keeping silent.* And it does this only because, in calling the one to whom the appeal is made, it does not call him into the public idle talk of the 'they' *[des Man],* but *calls* him *back* from this *into the reticence [Verschweigenheit] of his existent* potentiality-for-Being. When the caller reaches him to whom the appeal is made, it does so with a cold assurance which is uncanny, but by no means obvious" (*Being* 322). To be blunt, I do not find the matter of conscience, per se, what is most interesting about this material. More interesting is the way Heidegger anticipates Cage's complication of silence by discovering in the call a sound that does not utter anything. Sensing that enunciating such a call complicates the entire motif of the "voice of conscience," Heidegger insists not only that the caller of the call is the neutral "it" (*"Es" ruft*) but that, to the extent that it speaks at all, it does so with an *"alien voice" (eine fremde Stimme).* Obviously, one finds here—in the no one who is the speaker, in the uncanny, in the odd fascination with *des Man*—elements that vividly recall Adorno's discussion of the "Radio Voice," but before these are elaborated, note that just as the voice of conscience is a sound but not a voice, so too is the reception of the sound a listening that is not a hearing. Indeed, Heidegger is careful both here and in "Logos" (his reading of Heraclitus from 1954) to insist upon the need for philosophy to think the ontology of hearing differently, specifically with an ear pricked toward the philosophical limits of the thinking of hearing.

The point is simply this: in both Cage and Heidegger the silence that is not one produces both a practical possibility and a theoretical provocation. Specifically, what is called for—and I use the expression advisedly—is an approach to sound that situates it in the "neutral zone," the zone of indistinction, between a musicology straining to capture noise as something other than sheer alterity and a philosophy struggling to apprehend meaning, as it were, outside the vox. The acousmatic, that is, the sound whose source falls outside the visual field, finds here its evil twin, its double, that is, the sound whose source falls outside the audible field. Isn't this precisely what Cage is getting at in the closing paragraph of his 1958 statement on film: "Therefore, the most important thing to do in film now is to find a way for it to include invisibility, just as music already enjoys inaudibility (silence)" (116)? Sound when thus pitched against the limits of the image becomes about the "listening models," as Benjamin called them, although he was not, alas, thinking in the disciplinary terms I prefer.

To anticipate the concerns that may have arisen with regard to whether Heidegger's discussion of the call has anything to do with radio, it should be emphasized that between the earlier discussion of de-severing the world and the later discussion of the alien voice stands the problem of the near. It is in fact not difficult to discern here a relation, perhaps even a necessary relation, between the closeness that speeds toward us through the radio and the urgency with which Heidegger contrasts "the call" to the idle chatter of the "they," the medium through which world events are reported. Crucial is not that the call is remote while the report is ever nearer, but that the call is uncanny: it is, as he puts it early in the discussion of conscience, "from afar unto afar." Or, put differently, precisely to the extent that the radio hastens our perdition among the "they," it isolates, frames, that which the call meaningfully but silently calls to. Radio in this sense belongs not only to the ontological structure of conscience but to the very theoretical practice of fundamental ontology, that is, to Heidegger's phenomenology. Because this, as I have argued, forms a land line between Adorno's and Heidegger's approach to radio that is, as it were, off the radar (officially Adorno held Heidegger, his jargon if not his person, in contempt), perhaps the alien voice that is coming ever nearer and distancing us ever further from our world is not a voice at all but the sound of philosophy, or, for that matter, musicology, seeking to catch up with or otherwise attune to the it, *das Es,* that whistles between them. This may, in the end, be the most important feature of the "illusion of closeness," of nearness, or, as Heidegger puts it in "Age of the World Picture," of "Americanism," in that it calls upon us to hear differently the hum, the rumble, the flutter that foils the suppression of all echoes, a sound that in falling below the voice cannot be either picked up by our models of listening or taught a better tune.

Can we not say, then, that radio spooks philosophy, that radio, not film, not television, is historically the medium that obliges the field to confront the question of where both its questions and its answers come from? Recall, if you will, that each of us is a radio receiver, that our bodies are fully shot through with radio waves, and that, as Neil Strauss reminded us now almost twenty years ago, all we have to do is clench a simple device in our teeth to begin broadcasting (192).

This is a sound that has, in the end, neither come back nor returned. To treat it as such, in the manner of Dolar and Agamben, is to attempt to avoid or at best contain radio—in effect, to redeem the field of philosophy from the sound that haunts its voice. Instead, radio might better be thought to operate as the residual, as Williams taught us to say, the residual in the mode of the archaic that progress produces to have a temporal atmosphere in and against which to fire its retro-rockets. Perhaps this is why, when the alien voice does show up, as it was thought to have done on Halloween in 1938, it is always already defeated by a lingering "before" that progress cannot leave behind. Welles, as has been argued, wanted to grasp this in vestigial, that is, Darwinian terms, and if we are not all to succumb to the wave of evolutionary biology now sweeping and reorienting the field of interdisciplinary studies, we will have to come up with terms of our own—even if, or perhaps especially if, they are difficult to hear. One such term, word, name, may well be *radio* itself.

CHAPTER 2

On the Air

Simon Winchester, in his witty, informative, and hopelessly balanced history of the *Oxford English Dictionary,* archly draws attention to a detail so obvious that it might otherwise escape notice. It appears in a footnote to chapter 4, where, in commenting on the Herculean labors of Frederick Furnivall (an early editor), he points out that at a certain moment one can detect, and detect with certainty, a change in the daily paper read by Furnivall. How? All of a sudden his quotations establishing current usage of word entries shift from the *Daily News* to the *Daily Chronicle.* This anecdote, coupled with the many pages Winchester devotes to documenting the precarious history of the quotation slips gathered by the *OED*'s volunteer readers, casts an immediate shadow on the reliability of the dating that appears in every entry of the dictionary. Is this truly the first recorded use of a certain word, or is it the one to have survived, the one to have ended up in the right pigeonhole, as the boxes in the dictionary's filing mechanism were called? Or is a dictionary, maybe even "the" dictionary (in the Anglophone world), structured like a language, defined, as Roman Jakobson might have put it, by the twin axes of selection and combination, where both activities, at best, cut through an unwieldy, even impossible dispersion? With such precautions taken, note that the first appearance of *air* used as it is used in the title of this chapter, as part of the phrase "on the air," occurs in 1927, the year when, among other things, Heidegger's *Being and Time* first appeared. According to the anonymous volunteer reader, the phrase is to be found in the British newspaper the *Observer*. The quotation reads: "The only New York church that is 'on the air.'" The sense that this quotation bears witness to is one in which *air* is, in effect (the point, yes, of the scare quotes?), a synonym for *radio*, drawing attention to how in 1927 a certain metonymic perplexity characterized thought about the radiophonic medium. Was the medium of transmission part of the device, or was the device part of the medium of transmission? Put differently, where is/was the radio, and where is one when one is "on" it? Moreover, given the essayistic use of *on* (for example, "On Friendship"), do not these perplexities redouble when we ask where or what an essay is when it is "on" the radio, especially when—and this will be one of the core concerns in this chapter—essays, or other philosophical texts, are delivered over the radio? Is one here not faced with the anxious prepositional spiral of the on on the on? Indeed, but with what consequence?

To pursue this I concentrate here on two engagements with radio: those of Jean-Paul Sartre and Walter Benjamin. As Benjamin's radio work was deeply entangled with his friendship with Bertolt Brecht, the latter's writings will also be taken up. My concern will be to track how each figure thinks the relation between radio and philosophy (or perhaps thought more generally) in terms of the politics of using radio as a means by which to disseminate ideas—in effect, as a teaching machine. Two complications are stressed. First, these figures struggle instructively with the fact that philosophy is not simply radiophonic content. Instead, in ways that invite us to think twice about radio itself, Sartre and Benjamin (and Brecht for that matter) all urge us to recognize that radio is intimately caught up in the enunciation of philosophical self-reflection. Second, and this follows from the preceding, the political use of radio does not come to the medium from the outside. It is not a matter of discovering the tendency that finds expression in a given appropriation of the medium; rather, of interest here is the way the radiophonic enunciation of philosophy raises urgent questions about the very nature of the political as articulated in the cultural sphere. Not surprisingly, given the figures in play, the question of politics bears decisively on the status of Marxism, and in particular on the status of Marxism as the sublation of Western philosophy. I turn first, then, to Sartre's *Critique of Dialectical Reason,* for which the fiftieth-year anniversary of publication has just been celebrated.

Although not separated out in the French text (as it is in the Sheridan translation), the discussion of the radio broadcast marks an important development in the section of the *Critique* devoted to the concept of "collectivities." As such, it represents a comparatively rare engagement with what Adorno and Horkheimer had called the "culture industry" in the context of Sartre's Herculean struggle to reconcile the account of the subject to be found in existentialism with the account of the object to be found in Marxism, the "unsurpassable philosophy" (as he called it) of his present. As the first section of the text, detached in English as *Search for a Method* (in French, and the rejoinder to Descartes could not be more obvious, *Question de méthode*), makes clear, Sartre's ears are still ringing from Lukács's boisterous attack on him (and Heidegger) from 1949, "Existentialism," or, in the original German, "Zwei europaische Philosophien (Marxismus und Existentialismus)," an essay written in the wake of his return to Hungary and on the very cusp of his disillusionment with Stalinization in the emerging East Bloc. Indeed, the title of the first section of *Search* is a direct citation, "Marxism and Existentialism," with the significant exception that the homonymic pun on the French *et (est)* provocatively, even heretically, equates Marxism with existentialism. Eager to defend existentialism from the charge of solipsism and bourgeois decadence, Sartre moves to challenge both Lukács's sociology (if existentialism is determined by a particular class's experience of the "collapse" of social democracy, how do we account for Jaspers's and Heidegger's quite different reactions to National Socialism?) and his anthropology (what precisely remains of the concept of human *freedom* in historical *determinism?*). Sartre's ultimate concession that existentialism is to be metabolized by a thus reinvigorated (i.e., post-Stalinist) Marxism should not be understood to vitiate the importance he attaches to fleshing out his theory of the subject. Indeed, this is precisely what compels the attention to collectivities and groups where the question of the radio broadcast arises.

As if to underscore the importance of the question of collectivities, Sartre announces his turn to it thus: "We can now elucidate *[éclairer]* the meaning of serial structure and the possibility of applying this knowledge *[connaissance]* to the study of the dialectical intelligibility of the social" (*Critique* 269). Both serial structure and dialectical intelligibility are essential concepts of the *Critique*. That they are "now" in a position to be clarified marks an important, perhaps even decisive moment in the text.

Immediately prior to the discussion of the radio broadcast is Sartre's startlingly evocative analysis of riders waiting at a bus stop in Paris. Using a distinction between "series" and "group" (as well as between *praxis* and the practico-inert), he demonstrates how something, some agency, external to the riders organizes them as a unity in isolation from one another: the bus, its route (indeed, urban space as a whole), and even more fundamentally the ticket that, by virtue of its articulation of an arithmetical series determining the boarding sequence (clearly a bygone procedure), is interiorized by the riders as a version of what Marx in volume 1 of *Capital* called the commodity, that is, as an object producing in its circulation the occulted system of their social relations. To thus restate what Marx understood by "fetishism," Sartre invokes the concept of the series, that is, an unintelligible ordering out of which a group, through a concerted praxis of dialectical intelligibility, might emerge. Key here is the structure of seriality, the now familiar—given the enduring, if erratic, relevance of Debord and the Situationist International—motif of separation, or, more specifically, the fully interiorized sense of being alone together. This insight is crucial to Sartre's project in the *Critique* because, as he says plainly at one point, he is concerned to identify how human freedom is constrained, not by the deliberate pursuit of conflicting interests, but by the interiorized forms of exteriority that render humanity, as he says in an evocative footnote, a race haunted by robots of their own making. Aware that the gathering at the bus stop lacks sufficient explanatory scope, Sartre reaches for the radio dial, or, as he says, the communication through alterity that characterizes "all mass media" (*Critique* 271).

Here one is brought directly to the highly charged humanistic motif of presence. This most phenomenological of concepts is deployed by Sartre to restate the relation between the bus stop and the radio in terms of direct (the bus stop) and indirect (the radio) gatherings. Both, to be sure, exhibit the structure of seriality, but in a manner clarified by an inflection of the present/absent variety. What, then, does Sartre mean by presence? He writes: "Presence will be defined as the maximum distance permitting the immediate establishment of relations of reciprocity between two individuals, given the society's techniques and tools" (*Critique* 270). He offers the telephone and the two-way radio on an airplane as examples—both importantly acousmatic—as if to make sure that "distance" is not construed too narrowly. In then turning to absence—"the impossibility of individuals establishing relations of reciprocity between themselves" (270–71)—he establishes the full significance of distance. It is a way to represent the space that contains what Sartre understands, following Hegel, reciprocity. This last is more than a mere affirmation of cooperation or mutuality. It refers to the ontological work of recognition and thus undergirds what Marxism understands by "solidarity." In Sartre's hands reciprocity stands opposite alterity, that is, the form of social mediation premised on a passive interiorization of the "given," the so-called nature of things. Presence names the limit of reciprocity and thus also of alterity. It is not about the face to face but about the anthro-technological conditions of a totalizing proximity. It is about the Near that may also be far, the distance that is not distant, in effect, the essence of humanity such that that essence might express itself in common with others concerned to wrest praxis from the robotic grasp of the practico-inert, or what Marx called dead labor.

How, then, does this bear on the two radios: the ground-to-air or two-way radio and the broadcast radio? The latter, by virtue of exemplifying an indirect or absent seriality, would appear to fall squarely into the experience of alterity, that is, a distance that in compromising the conditions of reciprocity would appear to fall beyond the far into the purely remote. Does this not undercut presence as the conceptual link between Heidegger and Sartre on the radio? Actually, no, but to understand why one needs to trace attentively the political dimension of Sartre's analysis, a dimension that has direct and sustained recourse to the concept of voice *(la voix)*.

As should be obvious, Sartre's analysis anticipates important concerns of radio studies in several ways, but perhaps no more so than when he urges us to think carefully about how the form and content of the radio broadcast interact. To be sure, such thought is prompted by his attention to a rather particular (and, one might also say, overdetermined) type of broadcast, namely, the political speech. After detailing the contradiction lodged in the voice of *"le speaker"* (the not-yet-scandalous *franglais* here works to evoke the physiognomic scene), where, by its very "humanity," its relation to the space of reciprocity, the voice functions as an agent of reification, Sartre writes:

> Yet I can, if I wish, turn the knob, and switch off the set or change stations. But here the gathering at a distance emerges. For this purely individual activity changes absolutely nothing in the real work of this voice. It will continue to echo *[résonner]* through millions of rooms and to be heard by millions of listeners; I will merely have rushed into the ineffective abstract isolation *[solitude]* of private life, objectively changing nothing. I will not have negated the voice; I will have negated myself as an individual member of the gathering. And, especially in the case of ideological broadcasts, it is really as *Other* I will have wanted this voice to be silent, that is to say, in so far as it can, for example, harm Others who are listening to it. . . . In fact, I feel as though

I could challenge the arguments put forward by this voice in front of these Others, even if they do not share my views; but what I actually experience is my *absence* as my mode of connection with the Others. In this case, my impotence *[impuissance]* does not lie only in the impossibility of silencing the voice: it also lies in the impossibility of convincing, *one by one*, the listeners, all of whom it exhorts in the common isolation *[cette solitude en commun]* which it creates for all of them as their inert bond. (*Critique* 272–73)

Impotence? The concept, introduced earlier in his study, is reinserted here to underscore on a visceral and unabashedly masculinist register the analytical themes of passivity and reification. As such impotence makes clear, it is precisely in obstructing presence, in positing distance or alterity within the listener's relation to both the speaker and other listeners, that the radio belongs to presence but *reactively*, that is, through a politics of reaction inscribed both in the offending broadcast and in the apparatus of radio as such. Remember, the discussion of the radio broadcast is set opposite the discussion of the two-way radio, emphasizing that, in accordance with the principle of dialectical intelligibility, reciprocity and alterity lean on each other just as much as do presence and absence. That within the radio broadcast—that is, a particular social deployment of the apparatus—presence is contaminated by an absence that pacifies it strongly suggests that all Sartre adds to the Heideggerian discussion of the Near is a more carefully inflected political critique of the modern. Importantly, this political inflection, however much it resembles one to be found in Adorno and the Frankfurt School more generally, never quite homogenizes. Even as Sartre presciently eviscerates the entrepreneurial defense of the mass media—one cannot, as industry apologists for offensive content claim, simply "turn it off," because doing so merely obliges one to collaborate in the inertia of solitude—he stubbornly insists, throughout his discussion, on the possibility of wresting a group *from* a series. Because, on his terms, passivity is an activity that is constantly developing, it "can *to some extent* be resisted: I can write, protest, approve, congratulate, threaten, etc." (*Critique* 271). Here the permanent possibility of presence—the capacity to affect and be affected—reveals itself to be not simply the more tenacious element in the dialectic but also the broader framework within which the relation to the radio is to be conceived. As such it would appear to underscore, as bluntly as possible, the ontological solidarity between Heidegger and Sartre around the motif of what Derrida will later call the metaphorics of proximity. One cannot but be struck that the radio serves as the relay station at the core of this fraught encounter.

Mere historical accident, or an invitation to consider what radio must be to be able to serve in this capacity?

In Michael Scriven's *Sartre and the Media* there is an important chapter on Sartre's involvement with radio. What it underscores is the fact that Sartre, well before he wrote about radio in the *Critique,* used the radio as a propagating medium for his thought. Sartre, beginning already in 1944, that is, during the Occupation, was "on the air." Quite usefully, Scriven traces what he calls four "key phases" (71) of Sartre's involvement with radio: the program *Tribune des temps modernes* (nine broadcasts); the broadcast "L'avenir de la France" (1950); an interview with Sartre broadcast during the events of May 1968 (a broadcast pointedly transmitted by a Francophone station in Luxembourg); and the *Radioscopie* interview with Jacques Chancel in 1973. Scriven's analysis of Sartre's discussion with Chancel, where the former deftly uses the format of the celebrity interview as a forum to launch his new paper, the still-thriving *Libération,* is especially compelling. Considerably less compelling is Scriven's silence on two important matters: "La république du silence," the title of Sartre's first "on the air" experience in 1944, and the fact that between 1950 and 1968—phases two and three—Sartre wrote and published the *Critique* and its prescient analysis of the radio broadcast. This last seems especially important because one of the puzzles Scriven is attempting to solve is why Sartre abandoned radio for television and video. Was it just an opportunistic exploitation of modernization? My preceding discussion of Sartre's analysis suggests that it might well be otherwise.

First, "The Republic of Silence." This text recommends itself for scrutiny not simply because of its status as origin but because of the way its rhetoric and its argument set up core preoccupations of Sartre's later analysis of radio, especially through the motif of silence, preoccupations that resonate with Heidegger's thinking on the radio. Remember, their exchange (as mediated by Jean Beaufret) over humanism occurs within three years of its broadcast. The statement was originally prepared for publication in the journal *Lettres Françaises,* a literary publication clandestinely published by members of the National Front. It appeared in print shortly before Sartre read it on the air. It begins with a defiantly counterintuitive sentence, "Never have we been more free than under the German Occupation," and continues: "We have lost all of our rights and first and foremost that of speaking; we are faced with insults every day and it is necessary that we keep quiet; we are deported en masse, as workers, as Jews, as political prisoners; on all the walls, in all the magazines, on every screen, we find that unworldly and pale look [visage] that our oppressors want us to adopt for ourselves: because of all that we are free. . . . Because an all-powerful police seeks to condemn us to silence, every word becomes precious as a declaration of principle" ("La république" 11, my translation). Here silence makes its first appearance in the body of the broadcast, not appearing again until the final sentence: "We now stand on the edge of another Republic: we can only hope that it will preserve, when the big day has come, the austere virtues of the Republic of Silence and of Night" (14). What precisely authorizes the comparison to Heidegger beyond the shared terms (*das Schweigen* and *le silence*) and the evocation of Hegel's night?

Essential here is the logic of Sartre's argument. In the passage cited it is clear that he is working a patently dialectical vein, establishing how utter destitution, complete oppression, produces a subtle, ubiquitous, and fully energized freedom. Because silence is belligerently imposed, the smallest, most modest utterance becomes more than a sound; it becomes a declaration of principle, the principle of repudiating silence, in effect, the declaration of the Rights of Man. Sartre extends this logic not only to generate a new account of democracy—one grounded in the organizational structure of the Resistance, where everyone shares the same risks and responsibilities—but also to fold the Resistance into France and ultimately the *réalité d'homme,* or, in a more explicit evocation of Malraux, *la condition humaine* ("La république" 12). Politically, of course, this strategy pays homage to his literary patrons, Jean Decour and Jean Paulhan, and, more importantly, produces in its terms of address the nationalization of the Resistance. But more than simply generating a fecund principle of solidarity, this move also inevitably collapses the distance between the leaders and the led, the active and the inactive, the living and the dead. As Sartre says, under the conditions of night everyone wonders whether he or she can stand up under torture. Little did he realize that in less than a decade the French would provide Algerians with occasion for posing precisely the same tormenting question. In this sense and to this degree the Occupation functions like the gigantism, the monstrous nearness, that Heidegger and, even more emphatically, de Rougement wired to radio. As he says: "However, at the most profound depth of this solitude, there would be the others, all the others, all the comrades of the Resistance that one might protect; a single word would suffice to provoke ten, a hundred arrests" ("La république" 13). In other words, although within the Republic of Silence each and every word is a declaration of principle, the utterance of a single word under the pressure of interrogation implicates all the others who form the social order of one's solitude. One never decides for him- or herself without deciding for everyone else—according, let us not forget, to "*le* speaker," that is, the singular voice of a radio broadcast, a voice that insists, "We are all *in this* together."

Perhaps because Scriven is concerned to carry out the essential spadework of simply unearthing and cataloguing Sartre's activities, he neglects Sartre's repeated recourse to the concept of "solitude," the very concept that, as we have seen, figures so prominently in his discussion of the indirect gathering in the *Critique*. There, hidden beneath his translator's preference for "isolation," solitude functions to designate the condition to which the subject retreats in seeking to effect agency from within the realm of the practico-inert. In turning off the radio, one negates *oneself,* not the offending broadcast. Put differently, one lives his or her self-negation in the shared solitude of seriality. In "The Republic," solitude expressly enters the discussion in the wake of Sartre's repudiation of psychoanalysis—"a man's secret is not his Oedipus complex or his sense of inferiority" ("La république" 13)—where the concept is used to disclose the new and distinctive experience of the Resistance fighter. Unlike a soldier who fights among comrades on the field of glory, the Resistance fighter is tracked and arrested in solitude, and it is in "his" solitude, abandoned and naked, that the meaning of resistance is crystallized: he or she must resist torture, must not compromise others. In the text, as has been emphasized, the confrontation with torture is understood to constitute the deepest form of self-knowledge *(connaissance)* that a subject can have of him or herself. It is the locus of personal agency, and to that extent it contrasts sharply with the presentation of solitude in the *Critique*. But does it really?

Although there is no evidence that Sartre read Maurice Blanchot's 1955 essay "The Essential Solitude," it is clear from his essay on Blanchot and the mode of the fantastic that he was certainly paying attention to the man. Equally clear is the fact that as both men turned toward communism in the forties (and there are clear signs in *The Infinite Conversation* that Blanchot had read the *Critique*), the problem of how to complicate solipsism and the model of the human subject it presupposed loomed large on their shared horizon. Ultimately, Blanchot was moved to sacrifice humanism to communism, but in both their cases solitude undergoes a conceptual modification that casts its opposing term differently. Sartre, who matters more immediately in the context of this chapter, by 1960 contrasts solitude no longer with fraternity (the group psychology of the army) but with alterity. Moreover, the contrastive relation itself succumbs to the pressures of dialectical logic. In fact, in the *Critique* the contrast gives way to a fully socialized account of the individual member of a group structured by the asocial logic of the commodity, where solitude becomes an expression of a particular form of living in common. When compared to the discussion of solitude in "The Republic," what leaps out is a surprising parallel to the analysis of radio to be found in Adorno and Horkheimer's *Dialectic of Enlightenment,* a book whose first draft was exactly contemporaneous with Sartre's inaugural broadcast. In other words, in "The Republic," Sartre discovers the Nazi torturer seeking to transgress the very limit of human freedom in the depths, indeed the deepest depths, of solitude. In the *Critique,* solitude, as it is lived in common with all other members of the indirect gathering, encounters what menaces it in the form of what Sartre calls "the mass media," implying—does it not—an ontological if not political intimacy between such media and fascism, the very intimacy at the core of the chapter on the culture industry in *Dialectic of Enlightenment.* Granted, the link is belated, but striking just the same is the associative logic that appears to have forged it.

That one discovers here a perhaps surprising solidarity between French and German anti-Stalinist Marxism is not as important as what light, however indirect, this solidarity casts on Sartre's decision to abjure radio as a means of political or philosophical communication. Scriven rightly stresses the importance of Sartre's decision to broadcast his remarks concerning the student uprising in May 1968 from a "peripheral station" (though one very much on the Parisian radar, as it were), but he doesn't explore the relation between Sartre's communications strategy and the analysis of seriality to be found in a book published just eight years earlier, a book, in fact, thought by many to have had a decisive impact on the student movement in France. Scriven's inclination is to address the matter entirely in terms of Sartre's critique of the state, a focus that makes it hard to see what precisely the difference would be between radio and television, both predominantly state controlled in France to this day. A different, perhaps more compelling account would stress the way radio figures, and figures decisively, in the articulation of Marxism and existentialism, an articulation whose challenges are known to have had an enduring impact on Sartre.

We have seen the extent to which the *Critique* responds to Lukács's dressing down of Sartre's existentialism, a response that pivots around the concept of human freedom. While in *Search for a Method* Sartre is prepared to concede that *Being and Nothingness,* or, for that matter, *No Exit,* promulgates an infernal account of the intersubjective field, he insists that Lukács has sacrificed Marxism to its Soviet (i.e., Stalinist) incarnation, in effect, blithely surrendering the realm of freedom to the realm of necessity. Not content to formulate the matter polemically—he has the chutzpah to call Lukács's perspective a "lazy," "paranoiac dream" (*Search* 53)—he sets out to elaborate in considerable detail a social ontology of human agency. One of its vital features is the theory of the group, that is, the social formation within which the individual becomes possible. As the reading of the *Critique* has established, the emergence of the individual is deeply menaced by solitude, that encounter with alterity that distributes individuals along a chain of impotent associations with the Other. Radio, through the event of the indirect gathering, is where the group is re-asocialized, reconstructed, as the series. In effect, to exaggerate slightly, radio is where all—at least all that might separate solitude in 1943 from solitude in 1960—is lost. Both name the onto-political stakes of something fundamental. Radio is not unique in this regard—Sartre follows his discussion of it with a treatment of the impotent bonds forged by consumption—but it assumes an importance in the elaboration of his analysis that solicits further attention.

How might we make sense of this failing distinction? Perhaps some clarity arises if one recalls that an account of listening figured prominently in Lukács's attack on existentialism. Early in "existentialism," so as to crystallize the methodological target of his remarks, Lukács discusses the work of Wihelm Szilasi, a student of both Husserl and Heidegger and the author of *Wissenschaft als Philosophie.* Lukács quotes Szilasi as saying the following about a lecture: "This space with its variously worked boards is a lecture hall only because we understand this mass of wooden objects as such, and we do understand it so because from the outset we mean it as something presupposed in our common task—namely, lecturing and listening." From this Lukács concludes, "It is the way of being together [*Miteinandersein,* my interpolation] that determines what the thing is" (248). Predictably, given his brief, Lukács posits that the understanding that arises in the common task of lecturing and listening does not, indeed cannot, determine what the thing, the lecture, is. Although he indulges in a bit of kettle logic—this is nonsense; this is what the seriously philosophical Immanuel Kant *already* said—Lukács tenaciously stresses that the appeal to the understanding, to intuitive consciousness, avoids confronting the reality of the "worked boards" (the fact that they *physically* erect the

division between the lecturer and the listeners) precisely to avoid dealing with the more political reality that Szilasi is lecturing in Switzerland
because the Nazis have chased him out of Germany. In a flourish, and
therefore without clarifying whether Szilasi "says" his example derives
from Switzerland (how could it not?), Lukács proposes that this relay
of avoidances constitutes the decadent politics of existentialist method
qua method.

Now, Sartre's introduction to the *Critique* in which he squares off
against Lukács is *all* about method. As has been established, it is called
(in French) "Questions of Method." This suggests that Sartre is keen
to rebut precisely the charge made through the lecturing/listening example. By the same token, it also suggests why the case of the radio,
where Sartre delineates with considerable care the onto-political effects
of a serialized speaker-listener dyad, defines the core of his articulation
of Marxism and existentialism, not just in the sense of reconciling the
two perspectives, but, just as importantly in the sense of embodying his
duel with Lukács, a guardian of Marx's European legacy. In this sense
radio as a metaphor for listening stands at the midpoint in a confrontation between two lecturers each trying hard to shout the other down.
Given that Lukács succumbed to cancer before finishing a study provisionally titled *The Ontology of Social Existence* (fragments of which
have been published in English translation as *The Ontology of Social
Being,* vols. 1–3), and given that in the truncheon inscribed with the
title *The Destruction of Reason* Sartre fares comparatively well (Lukács
enthusiastically supports his critique of Camus, whose fiction he otherwise respects), one might reasonably conclude that Lukács was, in the
end, outshouted by Sartre, or, put differently, that he reconciled himself
to listening, not lecturing. Either way, what is clear about Sartre's position is that listening, and the status of the subject's socially constructed
passivity within it, functions to represent a decisive part of the hinge
between two incarnations, two moments of his thought. As such, the
account of radio listening in the *Critique* might very well have blown
back against his radio lecturing in a manner consistent with the oft-
cited subtitle of Cage's book *Diary:* "How to improve the world (you
will only make matters worse)." In other words, if the analysis of radio
in the *Critique* is correct, then even those who in a fit of freedom might
decide to turn Sartre's voice off end up just as summarily condemned to
solitude as those whose attentive lecture notes might have come to serve
as the basis for a *Course in Existential Generalities.* Not only is this a
defeat of radio as a political medium, but it implies that radio names

the impossibility of an existentialist Marxism or, as Derrida will later insist, what Sartre meant by a true humanism. The issue is not the state control of radio, or even the matter of its purported residual techno-logical status vis-à-vis television, but the crystalline clarity radio brings, via the theme of listening, to the politically charged problem of the social construction of consciousness. That Scriven fails to see this point is only part of the story, for the more important point is that behind his inattention radio operates so as to suggest strongly that its relation to the debates defining Western philosophy in the twentieth century is intimate indeed.

Sartre, of course, is not the only leftist philosopher of the last century who thought on the air, that is both over and about radio. So did Wal-ter Benjamin. Moreover, what the two men share is a complex, even delicate, negotiation with Marxism, and—to invoke a term that will fast become loaded—it is thus "instructive" to stage a confrontation between their radio writings.

If the word *instructive* deserves to be underscored, this is because Benjamin's thinking "on" (in the sense of "about") radio was deeply marked by his interest in Brecht and epic theater, where the concept of the *Lehrstück,* the learning or teaching play, figured prominently. Indeed, his perhaps most sustained and polished analysis of radio was written initially for a theater journal and bears the title "Theater and Radio." Brecht, as is generally known, both wrote "on" radio and wrote *Hörspielen,* radio plays, and it is clear that Benjamin's angle on epic theater is set in relation to this work. It is thus worth recalling what Brecht had to say on radio.

Doubtless the most substantial contribution to the "Radiotheorie, 1927 bis 1932" section of the *Gesammelte Werke* is the essay titled "The Radio as a Communications Apparatus," translated originally in *Screen* (as "Brecht on Radio") and now available in *Brecht on Film and Radio.* As if attuned to Heidegger's nearly contemporaneous distinc-tion between *Rede* (discourse) and *Gerede* (chatter), Brecht's comments are subtitled "Rede über die Funktion des Rundfunks," a discourse on, over, about the function of radio.[1] Because Brecht proceeds almost im-mediately to affiliate early radio and, as we've seen, the much-mined figure of the "Tower of Babel," this insistence on *Rede* can also be read as Brecht's struggle with the problem of the *über,* the on/over. The ap-paratus may be mired in *Gerede,* but his reflections on the apparatus are not. Really. No, really. Not for nothing does his statement open with a self-conscious paradox, the notion of an anarchy of orders.

How, then, does the motif of instruction enter Brecht's discourse? At the core of the piece stands Brecht's influential call to end radio's one-sidedness. Indeed, the notion of "two-way communication" championed half a century later by Enzensberger in "Constituents of a Theory of Media" finds its signal source in Brecht's analysis. What prompts Brecht's call is his concern about the prematurity of radio, what in another context he calls its antediluvian *(vorsintflutlich)* character ("Radio: An Antediluvian Invention?"; "Radio: Eine vorsintflutliche Erfindung?"). In "The Radio as a Communications Apparatus" this concern takes two forms. On the one hand, he stresses that radio was invented before there was a need for it. As he puts it: "The public *[Öffentlichkeit]* was not waiting for the radio, but rather the radio was waiting for the public" (41; "Der Rundfunk" 128), a formulation that was meant to contrast planning with anarchy and that, no doubt unwittingly, put in play a term Habermas was to incorporate into his later analysis of the press. On the other hand, prematurity finds expression in Brecht's maxim "Suddenly there was the possibility to say everything to everyone, but upon reflection there was nothing to be said" (41; "Der Rundfunk" 128), a formulation that repeats an insight from a 1927 essay, "Explanations [about 'The Flight of the Lindberghs']," in which Brecht had emphasized more the class-analytical dimension of the problem. There, he bemoaned the fact that the bourgeoisie was obliged to follow the invention of the radio with an invention designed to hide the fact that just as it acquired the means to "tell the whole planet what it had to say," it simultaneously "enabled the planet to see that it had nothing to say" ("Explanations" 38). In effect, radio places before the public the blatant fact that those using it to address its members have not yet learned to speak—they have not, put in the idiom of Lacanian psychoanalysis, entered language for the second time.

To pry radio free from the nothing that now streams out of its acoustic warehouse *(akustischen Warenhaus)* requires instruction. As Brecht puts it: "The technology that needs to be developed for all such undertakings . . . must work according to the principle that the audience *[Publikum]* is not only to be instructed but also must instruct *[belehren]*" ("Radio as a Communications Apparatus" 43; "Der Rundfunk" 130). Indeed, what obliges radio to abandon its one-sidedness is precisely the fact that since the radio has nothing to say it must be taught to speak by the public, a public interested in realizing its publicness, its distinctly public character, by using the invention of the radio to document and intervene within daily life. Brecht describes this by using the keyword

Umfunktionierung, refunctionalization ("Radio as a Communications Apparatus" 42; "Der Rundfunk" 129), which I would translate as "re: working."[2] As if anticipating the entire tradition of Paolo Freire and Augusto Boal, he links instruction to the work of re: working, stressing that radio cannot be rendered two-sided, that public instruction cannot be properly realized, if at all, within an anarchistic social order. Sensitive to the skittishness of his intended audience, Brecht concludes his statement by simply calling for the propagation of another order *(anderen Ordnung)* ("Radio as a Communications Apparatus" 45; "Der Rundfunk" 134). That Brecht includes in his statement an awkward apology for its blatantly utopian cast should come as no surprise. Not only is a properly instructive radio futural, it is neglected, even unwanted, by an audience happy to improve its capacity to talk *at* others.

Also caught up in the dialectic of instruction and the re: working of radio is the relation, indeed the antediluvian relation, between instruction and entertainment and along with it the relation between theater and radio, as well as, at a somewhat more practical level, the relation between Brecht's theatrical and radiophonic plays. In "The Radio as Communications Apparatus," entertainment enters the mix as Brecht puzzles over the problem of how to make "interests interesting," especially to the young, or, as he says in his 1927 introduction to a radio broadcast of *A Man Is a Man*, to the evolving "new human type" ("Radio Speech" 18). Instead of resolving the matter theoretically, he observes, drawing on the sort of antemetabole that characterizes many of his dialectical formulations, that "radio's attempt to give instruction an artistic form would support efforts on the part of modern artists to give art an instructive form" ("Radio as a Communications Apparatus" 44), a formulation that allows him to cut directly to a discussion of one of his own radio plays, *The Flight of the Lindberghs* (renamed *Ocean Flight* after Lindbergh's fascist sympathies became widely known). A significant alignment or association is thus forged between the project, at once political and aesthetic, of epic theater and the re: working of radio, as if the call to social revolution emitted by an apparatus as it is made to shift from the work of distribution to the work of communication found its immediate and therefore silent echo in the entertaining instruction realized by the learning play. In a startling metaphor, Brecht, anticipating Adorno by a decade and perhaps channeling Franz Rosenzweig's writing on records, insists that radio cannot broadcast operatic music because the idiom and the apparatus conspire to submit the performance to the destructive listening practice of "solitary tippling," in a word, addiction. Put differently, radio shamefully reprivatizes the sociality of opera. Today, of course, we refer to this as mystification, or more polysyllabically, ideological manipulation, and do so in the same breath that we characterize Brecht's critique as "optimistic."

I would argue that it is precisely the political and theoretical *intricacy* of the encounter between epic theater and the radiophonic apparatus that spurred Benjamin's interest in the medium. Indeed, an exchange in the Benjamin-Scholem correspondence suggests that Brecht's Lindbergh radio play in particular seems to have inspired Benjamin. As part of a persistent back-and-forth about radio (Benjamin waxing enthusiastic, Scholem less so), Benjamin writes on February 28, 1933 (the very day of the Reichstag Fire decree, which rescinded the right of habeus corpus for, among others, German communists): "The rest of the day was taken up with work and the dictation of a radio play, 'Lichtenberg,' which I must now send in, in accordance with a contract the better part of which has long been fulfilled and which facilitated my flight to the Baleares" (Benjamin, *Correspondence* [with Scholem] 27). *Lichtenberg* was never broadcast, although it figures as one of the three 'listening models" *(Hörmodelle)* to be found in the collected works and is presumably one of the texts requested by Adorno upon his arrival in New York. Apart from the rather blatant phonetic resonance between *Lindbergh* and *Lichtenberg,* the vital importance of Brecht's radio play is signaled in Benjamin's own 1930 radio lecture on Brecht, where, in attempting to articulate what is new in Brecht's work, he cites his favorite line from Lichtenberg's aphorisms ("It is not a person's convictions that matter, but what they make him") and then links the important "newness" of Brecht's stance to the citable gestures of *The Flight of the Lindberghs* ("Bert Brecht" 366). The concept of the citable gesture—by the way, not unlike Derrida's later concept of "iterability"—figures centrally in Benjamin's account of epic theater, thus implying not only that radio is key to Brecht's practice but also that his own relation to radio is mixed in with his relation to and friendship with Brecht.

It is important to resist the temptation to reduce the relation between the two radio pieces (the model and the play) to the serendipity of language; for that would encourage one both to overlook the importance of Lichtenberg for Benjamin and to underplay what is said on radio in the listening model bearing his name. To be sure, Lichtenberg is referred to largely in passing, but unfailingly his work is described in superlatives: *brilliant, excellent,* and so on. Be that as it may, an epistolary exchange between Lichtenberg and G. H. Amelung does figure prominently in the series of letters Benjamin published in the *Frankfurter Zeitung* under the title "German Men and Women: A Sequence of Letters," and cross-promoted on radio through the, alas, undelivered talk, "On the Trail of Old Letters." In this letter Lichtenberg is confessing to what might now be called "child endangerment" (he convinced a thirteen-year-old girl to move into his home as his "assistant") and, stated baldly if ahistorically, a pedophilic fantasy (the letter virtually "blushes" as Lichtenberg reveals that he regarded the girl as his "wife"). Its purpose is to share his anguish over the girl's sudden death, a death rendered cruelly ironic by Lichtenberg's recent decision to legitimize their relationship. Benjamin comments, in ways that resonate directly with remarks made in "Author as Producer"—yet another text in which Brecht and "the excellent Lichtenberg" are set side by side—that Lichtenberg's letter achieves a form of realism compared to which the New Objectivity must be found sadly wanting. Although one might have expected more from a vocal opponent of the state's control of pornography, it is clear that Lichtenberg figures decisively in Benjamin's cultural politics, the turn away from philosophy and theology that so irritated Scholem and, in a somewhat different way, Adorno. But who precisely is Lichtenberg?

Georg Christoph Lichtenberg is certainly more than the "feared satirist" cum aphorist described repeatedly by the editorial group responsible for the Harvard edition of Benjamin's *Selected Writings*. Creator of the Electrophorus, Lichtenberg is credited with having founded "dielectrics," the technique for mapping the branching of electrical discharge. Indeed, the maps derived from this technique are still referred to as Lichtenberg figures. A contemporary of Franklin's (and an acquaintance of Kant, Gauss, Volta, and Goethe), Lichtenberg was perhaps the foremost German researcher in the physics of electricity. He was also a well-known Anglophile, hosting and being hosted by British artists and intellectuals of the period. One might also say that he was the founder of what Lacan was later to call *poubellication* in that he tirelessly scribbled in a series of notebooks he came to call *Sudelbücher* or "wastebooks," and it is largely here that many if not all the brilliant aphorisms he is credited with are to be found. He took an aggressive polemical stand against Lavater's science of physiognomy—certainly a view that would have brought him to the attention of both Adorno and Benjamin, as would the fact that he suffered from scoliosis of the spine. In short, he was a hunchback, a profoundly overdetermined figure in Benjamin's conceptual bestiary.[3]

In his final "Curriculum Vitae" ("Curriculum Vitae, VI"), Benjamin announces his intent to complete, for a commission, a bibliography of the writings of Lichtenberg, strongly suggesting his familiarity with more than the two aphorisms he repeatedly cites. But surely the clearest account of his engagement with Lichtenberg—the one that clarifies in what sense Lichtenberg, however counterintuitively, fits in with the Brechtean cultural politics Benjamin felt committed to—appears in the *Hörmodell,* the listening model, *Lichtenberg: A Cross Section* (but also, given the German *Ein Querschnitt,* a paraplegic).

The two other "models" with which *Lichtenberg* has been editorially paired (*What the Germans Were Reading While Their Classical Authors Were Writing,* and *Much Ado about Punch*) are, in fact, labeled *Hörspielen* (radio plays, but literally listening plays). *Lichtenberg* extrudes here, urging us to take seriously—despite its obviously dramatic form (there are characters, indeed Lichtenberg is one, they deliver lines, there is a plot, etc.)—its status as a *model,* a way of theorizing the nature of listening, and one that places radio both at the core and at the periphery.[4] Anticipating Welles's *War of the Worlds* broadcast by five years, Benjamin plots his model as an interplanetary deliberation concerning the value of humanity, conducted between members of the Moon Committee for Earth Research, headed by one Labu, and configurations of people that include the eighteenth-century British thespian David Garrick, the renowned and eponymous eighteenth-century Anglophile dielectrician Lichtenberg (accompanied by his female companion, Maria Stechardt), Justice Councilor Pütter, three middle-class men from Göttingen, a pastor, a crier, and, last but not least, a speaker/announcer (indeed a crucial figure in Benjamin's conception of the "listening model"). In setting the plot in motion, the speaker—and the physiognomic intricacies underscored by Adorno are explicit (see the preceding chapter)—explains that at the industrial plant of the Society of Earth Research the moon beings have, in addition to a coffee grinder, three machines (and the German here is significant, *Apparate*) that make what is to follow in the "listening model" possible: a Spectrophone that allows the moon beings to see and hear everything everywhere on earth (surely a savvy evocation of the paranoid line taken from Welles's novel that opens the *War of the Worlds* broadcast, "We know now that in the early years of the twentieth century this world was being watched closely by intelligences greater than man" (qtd. in Cantril, *Invasion* 4); a Parlemonium, with whose aid even the "Music of the Spheres" can be translated into human discourse (again the German is significant, *Menchenrede*), in effect, a universal translator of the sort presupposed by most if not all science fiction narratives, but one expressly capable of "converting" all sound, including the most, as it were, "ethereal," into language; and, perhaps most enchantingly of all, an Oneiroscope, with which the dreams of observed aliens can be known. So as to render the obvious explicit, the speaker then points out that it is because of the possession of this device that moon beings share a keen interest in psychoanalysis. They wish to know the meaning of the dreams the Oneiroscope picks up. Significantly, the speaker's preamble ends here without clarifying an obvious question: Where does radio fit? Is it the earthly medium that, as is now said, interfaces with presumably the first of these two machines? Sound cue: gong.

These are more than idle, self-interested questions. If there is an important sense in which *Lichtenberg* models listening and does so *on* the air, then it matters that radio manifests as structure, not content. Specifically, this links radio—the broadcast and reception of its sounds—to the structure of the model. To tease this out so as to clarify the relation between *Lichtenberg* and *The Flight of the Lindberghs* requires attention to the elements of the model that define its structure. As the concept of the apparatus suggests, this involves thinking about the mediation of social relationships. That all such relationships are subject to a massive, preemptive inversion—the speaker, and not coincidentally when elaborating on the appeal of psychoanalysis, uses *Irdischen,* "aliens," to refer to Earthlings, that is, the implied radio audience—is structurally decisive. It establishes that listening is modeled in *Lichtenberg* so as to place listeners, as it were, outside themselves—and not just anywhere, but outside in precisely that which is "alien" to them. Radio, then, effects an interplanetary delocalization. In receiving its signals you know that you are not where you think you are.

Instructive here is consideration of what gets said about the moon in the entry devoted to it—indeed, the entry Adorno thought to contain the philosophy missing from Benjamin's Baudelaire study—in the oft-revised "Berlin Childhood around 1900." There, as if predicting the organizing conceit of Alex Proyas's *Dark City,* Benjamin writes: "The light streaming down from the moon has no part in the theater of daily existence. The terrain it illuminates so equivocally seems to belong to some counter-earth or alternate earth. It is an earth different from that to which the moon is subject as satellite, for it is itself transformed into a satellite of the moon" (405). This "alienation" effect reaches its apotheosis when, after being "unhoused," Benjamin explains: "Thus, each sound and each moment came toward me as the double of itself. And when I had endured this for a while, I would draw near my bed gripped by the fear of already finding myself stretched out upon it" (406). This is written but a scant two years after *Lichtenberg,* and even allowing for the additional temporal displacement of childhood—a childhood very much soldered to radio, as Jeffrey Mehlman has proposed—it seems obvious that interplanetary estrangement is intimately part of the moon for Benjamin, especially, one might add the "light" (*Licht,* of course, in German) streaming from the moon. This suggests, does it not, that Lichtenberg is much more than simply the subject of the listening model bearing his name. He is something like its metonym *en abîme.* Gerhard Schulte has reminded us that this light, this lunar light, is also the dark side of the Enlightenment (36).

Consider, in this light, the several ways in which Lichtenberg as a character, as a subject, is positioned within the model. In all cases, the positioning is reflexive. Clearly with an eye toward underscoring his Anglophilia, Lichtenberg is first paired with the influential British actor David Garrick, who not only thematizes the dramatic dimension of the radio piece but does so in the context of playing Hamlet, that is, in a deft evocation of "The Mousetrap" (the mode of reflexivity by which Hamlet plans to catch the conscience, *sans* Oneiroscope, of the king), whereby Benjamin uses Lichtenberg to stage the play about the play within the play. Then, through the Spectroscope, we actually witness Lichtenberg at his writing desk writing the letter that Benjamin gathers under the title "German Men and Women," the wrenching tale about his dead bride to be. This effectively exposes a link between radio and the newspaper (the letters were published in the *Frankfurter Zietung*) as conflicting modes of *Öffentlichkeit,* but it also extends the logic of reflexivity into Benjamin's corpus, where he appears to be reiterating his own work, or, to call up the uncanny image from the "Moon" entry in "Berlin Childhood," coming upon his own corpus in the cradle of his texts. Lastly, Lichtenberg figures in an intricate juridical proceeding in which his own writings on Lavater's concept of physiognomy are invoked to compare the reliability of signs deployed in puppet theater (yet another instance of staging the play about the play within the play) as opposed to those that appear on the human face and body. And all this in the context of a Korzybski-like meditation on the relation between a map (in this case Lichtenberg's map of the moon) and a territory (in this case the moon as lived by its inhabitants, where a crater is being named after the German dielectrician), a meditation that casts reflected light on the relation between colonialism and naming. Not quite the menacing inflection of *Lebensraum,* but close.

Clearly then, Lichtenberg radiates powerfully through the structure of the model because his is the name for or of the structure of the model, what in Derrida's study of Francis Ponge is called the name for the name. Insofar as this informs us about radio as the medium of this structure, it pairs reflexivity and alienation, suggesting through this pairing that a structure's capacity to double over and act upon itself is indissociable from a reversibility effect whereby the inside and the outside exchange places (the earth can become the moon's satellite). As if to underscore just this feature of the model, Benjamin adds two more elements. First, through the apparatus of the Oneiroscope, he effects the Lacanian reversal whereby the other scene of the Unconscious is outside. Put differently, once Earthlings become alien to themselves they enter their dreams. They do not have dreams, dreams have them. Second, and this appears in the array of apparatuses, the hierarchy of the senses is overturned and leveled. Recall that the Spectroscope allows one to see and hear everything. The Parlemonium allows all sound to be rendered intelligible. And the Oneiroscope allows dreams to be known, if not understood. Wedged, as it were, between two properly scopic regimes is the Parlemonium. As it is used to pick up and carry sound, the name invites comparison with the English word *harmonium,* a small (hence the Greek diminutive suffix) generator—in fact, an organ—of harmony, or, pronounced in Attic Greek, *harmos,* that is, "joint," or "joinings." Indeed, the device flattens the distinction between music and speech while at the same time fulfilling the mediating function between a scopic regime in which "everything" *(alles)* subsumes the difference between seeing and hearing and one in which dreams, precisely to the extent that they are known but lack meaning, are rendered inarticulate, even silent—in effect, seen but not heard. This might imply that Benjamin's listening model traffics in a familiar synesthesia, were it not for the properly ethereal detail of the "Music of the Spheres," with which, by the way, *Lichtenberg* concludes. As Joe Milutis has stressed, this music—precisely to the extent that it was thought to be ethereal—was really more about a breakdown, albeit mystical, of the relation between the interior and the exterior of the subject than about any mere celebration of the (con)fusion of the senses (39). Moreover, as an aestheticized but resolutely secular figure of transcendence, the "Music of the Spheres" thematizes the motif of the limit, of that which falls into the unknown. As such it points beyond synesthesia to the more specifically discursive, or even disciplinary, effects of leveling, or dedifferentiating what can be recognized as sound and what can be recognized as sight. This figures centrally in Benjamin's model, joining to reflexivity and alienation the decidedly epistemological problem of how knowledge mediates and thus orders the relations among the senses in general, but between hearing and seeing in particular. Thus, in his understanding of radio, as a position *on* radio, Benjamin situates the acousmatic—perhaps paradigmatically rendered in the "Music of the Spheres" and the mute soundscape of the dream—squarely within the orbit of the moon as illuminated within *Lichtenberg*.

What light does this cast on the relation between *The Flight of the Lindberghs* and *Lichtenberg*, or between Brecht and Benjamin "on" radio? We know, of course, that in "Theater and Radio" Benjamin declares both his awareness of and his allegiance to the "learning plays" presented at the Baden-Baden Music Festival in 1927, which included *The Flight of the Lindberghs* and *The Baden-Baden Learning Play on Acquiescence*, (both incidentally about air travel, or being as much *in* as *on* the air). But in terms of how this awareness might be said to engage the detail of *Lichtenberg*, two points will suffice. First, Benjamin shares his interest in Garrick with Brecht, and what made Garrick matter to Brecht is not uninteresting. In "Building Up a Part: Laughton's Galileo," Brecht, after commenting on the tendency to over value theatrical works as opposed to the work required to bring them to the stage, writes: "Above all it is that we seem to have lost any understanding and appreciation of what we may call a *theatrical conception* [*theatralischen Gedanken*, plural in the German]: what Garrick did, when as Hamlet he met his father's ghost; Sorel, when as Phèdre she knew she was going to die; Bassermann, when as Philip he listened to Posa. It is a question of invention" (163; "Aufbau einer Rolle" 1117). The second version of "What Is the Epic Theater?" (published in 1939) establishes that Benjamin was indeed familiar with *The Life of Galileo*. True, we cannot know for sure whether in the many discussions that transpired between 1929 and 1940 the two men discussed Garrick, but the epic function of "theatrical conceptions," is active in all of Benjamin's discussions of gestural, or interrupted, acting. It is especially significant that in *Lichtenberg* Benjamin channels one of Garrick's more widely recognized contributions to acting—his resistance to pantomime and bombast, in short, his "realism"—as if to present this as what Brecht understood as the theatrical conception at work in Garrick's portrayal of Hamlet's encounter with the ghost of his father. The listening model aggressively foregrounds the status of Garrick by setting up a deflection in which an initial attempt to reach Lichtenberg by Spectrophone fails, followed immediately by the establishment of a link to Garrick playing Hamlet in London at the Drury Lane Theater. Surely, it is relevant if not decisive that the very scene interrupted by contact from the moon is the scene singled out by Brecht, the scene of Hamlet's encounter with his father's ghost. Thus it would appear that Garrick is deployed to give further depth to the reflexivity of the model by pushing beyond the play about the play within the play, to the relation between Brecht—described by Jennings et al. as having "encouraged Benjamin's efforts in radio" (Benjamin, *Selected Writings* 2: 833)—and Benjamin. That this encouragement came to fruition in a listening model that joins two important moments in the history of acting—the development of the sort of realism then to be opposed by Benjamin to the New Objectivity and the concept of the "theatrical conception"—is a clear indication of the wireless connection between the two men.

The second Brechtean signal in *Lichtenberg* achieves distinctness upon a rereading of the following passage from "The Radio as a Communications Apparatus." In elaborating what is to be understood by a re: working of radio, Brecht writes: "Hence, any attempt by the radio to give a truly public character to public occasions is absolutely positive. Our government needs the activity of radio as much as our court system does. If government or justice resist such activity, they are afraid and suitable only for the times prior to radio, if not even prior to the invention of gunpowder" (42). What might otherwise seem like a passing remark assumes greater import when one realizes that this sentiment, stated in a somewhat more emphatic register, also appears in a statement of Brecht's on radio from 1927, "Suggestions for the Director of Radio Broadcasting." This coupled with a formulation previously highlighted—"a certain caste was able to tell the whole planet [specifically, *dem ganzen Erdball*] what it had to say"—suggests that the scene at the core of *Lichtenberg,* the courtroom drama, if you will, is directly inspired by Brecht's call for a re: working of radio. That Benjamin appeals directly to the motif of the "apparatus" and wires it to a court proceeding at virtually the same time that Brecht is theorizing radio as a *Kommunikationsapparat* may well be the decisive sign that the lines of communication between the two men are, if not crossed, certainly touching.

This last point invites a more speculative hypothesis whose outline can be phrased as a question: Is there an answering absence in *The*

Flight of the Lindberghs to the one that appears in *Lichtenberg* once one realizes that the radio as such does not figure among the apparatuses at the disposal of the Moon beings? And if so, what does this teach us about radio, or, for that matter, listening? Were one simply to consult what Brecht has said about his play—see, for example, "Explanations"—it would not be difficult to answer such questions negatively. No, there is no corresponding absence. Radio appears as both character and prop. However, listening to the play, one comes upon the puzzling line, spoken by Lindbergh(s), "Ich fliege in einem Apparat ohne Radio" (I fly in an apparatus without radio) (*Der Flug,* section 3, line 15). In "Explanations" we are told that Lindbergh(s) is cast not only in the role of listener but also as a figure set on the *opposite* side of the stage from the radio.

Taken together, not only do the line, "I fly in an apparatus without radio" and its staged negation complicate our conception of the apparatus (at once plane, play, and radio), but, as in Lichtenberg, radio drops out of the content of the play, leaving a version of the liar's paradox as its trace. The radio listener is here invited to learn something from the structure of the apparatus. Brecht states the content of the lesson thus: "'The Flight of the Lindberghs' is not intended to be of use to present-day radio but to *change* it" (*Film* 39). Put differently, the radio that Lindbergh's apparatus lacks is the radio that listeners (in the plural) must bring into existence through the practice of transformative listening, through the work of re: working. Perhaps then, between Brecht and Benjamin, on a back channel, there is between the two pieces a communication about the very nature of the apparatus, a communication intimately, even indissociably, patched into radio. But what must radio be if it operates like *this?* Like Sartre, Brecht and especially Benjamin encounter radio as a signal, a signal whose significance scrambles the familiar outlines of their thought. Unlike Sartre's airplane (at least the only one he mentions), which is equipped with a two-way radio, Brecht's airplane has a radio that isn't one. Its structuring of this solitude is, however, instructive. So too is the fact that while *Lichtenberg* fades to the strains of Pythagoras's "Music of the Spheres," *The Flight of the Lindberghs* concludes with a Hindemith and Weill set piece—the alpha and omega of ethereal alterity.[5]

It should come, then, as no surprise that Benjamin's most sustained meditation on radio, "Theater and Radio," deals squarely with Brecht and the problem of education in the context of the mass media. As the earlier citation from the Benjamin-Scholem correspondence established, albeit in passing, this meditation belonged to an engagement with the medium that was largely commissioned, a fact that invites one to recognize the sign of Saturn (first, a failed professorship and then exile) suspended above all of Benjamin's radio work. Mehlman's analysis of the radio plays for children might have opened up more probing questions about radio and psychoanalysis had it struggled more directly with such "sins" of commission. This said, it is important not to overemphasize the power of Brecht in Benjamin's concept of the educational possibilities of radio. One of Benjamin's oldest friends, Ernst Schoen (a student of Varèse's and later the program director of Radio Frankfurt), to whom Benjamin owed many of his radio commissions, worried often and loudly about radio's status as a "gigantic machine for mass education" (Benjamin, *Selected Writings* 2: 585). In 1929 Benjamin published a piece in *Die literarische Welt*, "Conversation with Ernst Schoen," in which his attention focuses on the vexing interplay between instruction and indoctrination. Indeed, these matters figure often in "Theater and Radio," where it is clear that for Benjamin the project of "re: working," in which radio and drama apply transformative pressure on each other (both become differently instructive), is precisely the way beyond or through the instruction/indoctrination deadlock. Here as well, the political and theoretical intricacy of the "on" achieves something of an apotheosis. Working *on* or at the radio station generating "countless talks . . . which are of no interest except in economic terms" (Benjamin, *Correspondence* [1992] 29) helps to sustain precisely the "gigantic" scale of the indoctrination machine. Writing *on* or about radio, whether with Schoen or Brecht, is conceived as a transgression meant to disclose the limit of the indoctrination machine and, without succumbing to the overrated performative contradiction, triggering the effect of re: working. This dialectic, if such a traditional contrast between mental and manual labor can be one, culminates in the telltale alienation effect of Benjamin, in "Theater and Radio," writing *on* his own listening models in the third person. It am another?

Most of "Theater and Radio" is given over to a rehearsal of points familiar to readers of Benjamin's "What Is the Epic Theater?" and the general line of argument regarding technique and tendency in "Author as Producer." More distinctive is its frank consideration of the importance of "live people" ("Theater and Radio" 584) in assessing the political and cultural difference between radio and theater. In elaborating what he calls the reactionary and progressive accounts of the matter, Benjamin teaches us something interesting about alienation and radio.

The reactionary lives in denial and assumes the universal and presumably obvious value of living subjects. The progressive, attuned to the crisis inflicted upon art/theater by technology/radio, must from, within the space and practice of denial, debate it. The living subjects in this debate are "debarred" (*kaltgestellte,* more literally, left out in the cold) (585), caught up in an experiment where they are on trial—not as defendants or plaintiffs but as inquirers concerned to expose and subject to reflection the routines of practical existence. In short, the absence of living people from an articulation of an unlivable situation—the cultural and political crisis of Weimar in the 1930s—is certainly less "harmonious" but infinitely more vital. This suggests, does it not, that in becoming "it" or "he" Benjamin enters the debate already deeply implicated in its terms.

Written the year before *Lichtenberg,* "Theater and Radio"—which makes direct reference to the listening models of one "Walter Benjamin"—would appear to belong, however anachronistically, to the structure of the model set forth in *Lichtenberg.* As we have just seen, both the short article and the model worry over the drama of courtroom proceedings, not just as scenes, but as ways to set before listeners their relation to their listening, to their ears (as Nietzsche had earlier insisted). But more suggestively, the relation between the two pieces again points, albeit from a slightly different angle, to the complexity of the "on." Precisely when instruction comes into (air)play, the psychogeography of pedagogy—when and where instruction takes place—achieves an intensity of articulation that allows us to hear the "on" of "about" and the "on" of "at" as if sounded simultaneously. "Theater and Radio" is both on and at *Lichtenberg,* each confronting the other with lessons to be drawn, both about the radio now and about a radio to come. Although unfinished, "Reflections on Radio" from the year before had developed even further the problem of the "on" by confronting it with its equally complex antonym, the "off."

In many respects, "Reflections" is an oddly physiognomic study. It dates from the earliest of the pieces commissioned by Schoen and is marked by themes of their "conversation." But it is also about the voice. It opens by deploring the separation radio has institutionalized between speakers and listeners, a separation that is characterized as being at odds with radiophonic technology. Whereas in the Soviet Union this separation has been thematized and addressed, in Germany (and the West more broadly) the failure to do likewise has fostered a debilitating lack of critical expertise. Under such circumstances critical listeners are left with one option: sabotage (same word in German): in other words, with the act of "switching off" *(das Abschalten)* (543).[6] It is clear that Benjamin's concern here is with what in "Theater and Radio" will become the instructive capacity of radiophonic technology, emphasizing here the importance of developing radio so as to overcome the separation between speakers· and listeners by teaching both how to criticize and criticize expertly. In this sense, switching off falls back behind the cutting edge of radio both as a device and as the name for a philosophical and political problem. "Off" is not simply not "on"; rather, it is not the interplay of the two "ons." The physiognomic profile of this state is drawn out later in the piece when, in attempting to put his finger on the present pulse of the institution, Benjamin writes:

> No reader has ever closed a just–opened book with the finality with which the listener switches off the radio after hearing perhaps a minute and a half of talk. The problem is not the remoteness of the subject matter . . . . It is the voice, the diction, and the language—in a word, the formal and technical side of the broadcast—that so frequently make the most desirable programs [in terms of subject matter] unbearable for the listener. . . . Accordingly, it is the technical and formal aspects of radio that will enable the listener to train himself and to outgrow this barbarism. The matter is quite obvious. We need only reflect that the radio listener, unlike every other kind of audience, welcomes the human voice into his house like a visitor *[einen Gast]*. Moreover, he will usually judge that voice just as quickly and as sharply as he would a visitor. ("Reflections" 544)

Urging broadcasters to draw public attention to the "arsenal of impossibilities" or "comic errors made by speakers" (in effect, what not long ago were known as "Bushisms"), Benjamin concludes by reiterating that the treatment of listeners as experts *(als Sachverständigen)* remains decisive.

The physiognomic elements in the preceding passage emerge as we are invited to accept the notion that we might make a decision about a broadcaster's voice (and presumably what it has to say) with the same decisiveness that we would decide whether a visitor to our home should stay. It is a question, not of what the visitor says, but of the way voice and visitor converge in a sign-to-be-judged. Behind this lie two other relations, between the book and the radio and between switching off and judging. Book and radio, as instances of two historically charged cultural technologies, are contrasted as devices whose undesirable or unsatisfying effects are differently controlled. The book can be closed with finality, while the radio must be switched off. In being more decisive, the latter is likened to an act of sabotage, a characterization that, though having been applied to Brecht in an early radio talk ("Bert Brecht"), is here set *opposite* critical expertise. Thus "switching off" and "judging" are contrasted as actions laden with political meaning. In effect, sabotage is the equivalent of what is construed as Rimbaud's bohemianism, a position deemed irreconcilable with Marxism. Although reasonably straightforward, these distinctions are not easily applied to the voice/ visitor matrix. What would it mean to sabotage the visitor? To welcome "him" under false pretenses? To refuse the gesture of hosting? In short, what or where exactly is "off" with regard to the radio voice?

In Sartre, "off" was serialized solitude. To end a radio broadcast was, as has been argued, tantamount to collaboration (or in his parlance, *devenir un salaud*) in the sense that in withdrawing from collective life one accepted and indeed condoned its political, cultural, and economic priorities. Benjamin shares with Sartre the notion that switching off is politically compromised, but the matter is not filtered through the problem of seriality or collective solitude. It is important that in his analysis, however sketchy, Benjamin insists upon the fact that the radio audience *(Publikum)* is unlike *any* other. By this unelaborated statement one is left to assume that Benjamin is referring to the fact repeatedly drawn attention to in the greeting that headed each of his children's radio plays—*Verehrte Unsichtbare,* or, "My invisible listeners"—namely the acousmatic structure of separation between the broadcasters and the listeners. Radio, unlike other apparatuses, is reduced to the signal of a voice articulating reciprocal invisibilities. True, as the "stage directions" of *Lichtenberg* make plain, sounds other than the voice "appear" on radio, but voice calls up visitor, guest, foreigner in ways that other sounds, including *musica universalis,* apparently do not. It is as though sabotage is politically problematic under precisely these conditions, conditions where one is hailed by a visitor who preemptively renders visible what is typically invisible. As Benjamin puts it late in "Reflections," at issue is the difficult matter of "the way the voice *[Stimme]* relates to the language *[Sprache]* used" (544). Of course, this difficult matter partakes of a general, even familiar difficulty, so one is entitled to wonder how it articulates distinctively if not exclusively with the radio. Although Benjamin does not confront the matter head on, it would appear that the relation between language and voice functions as an analogue to the visitor/voice pairing, both restating and elaborating its content. This speculative elaboration of the relation between voice and language links the invisibility of the listener to the face of the visitor, prompting the physiognomic thought, "What does it signify? Is the face the sign of a visitor to be welcomed or shunned?" In effect, language becomes the invisible backdrop against which the voice emerges. It is like, to invoke Saussure's reluctant metaphor, the warehouse tucked away in the speaker/visitor's mind. Thus switching off forecloses the critical instruction that might otherwise be carried out by an apparatus capable of piquing public inquisitiveness about its technological limits, especially as these participate in the way the relations between sound, voice, and image are lived within a particular social order. In short, switching off is, for Benjamin, more like "dropping out," in the sense of abandoning the project of re: working, a project whose pedagogical significance derives from the work of radio in putting the expertise of the listener to the test at every moment in every broadcast. To the extent that one of the ways this expertise might express itself is through "going on the air" while thinking aloud about this very location, switching off implies that for Benjamin the intricacy of the "on" must *include* recognition of the political possibility wired into the radiophonic medium itself. While both Sartre and Benjamin (and, for that matter, Brecht) see clearly the political stakes of the medium, it seems plain that the movement from "on" to "in" (in the sense of "in struggle") takes place in human consciousness for Sartre and in pedagogical practice for Benjamin. Indeed, as we have seen, Benjamin is deeply attracted to Brecht's "debarring" of living people from radiophonic expression. In this sense, he might be said to share Heidegger's reservations about the broad philosophical utility of a true humanism, although it is clear that, in ways that irritated Scholem and others, he shared Brecht's urgent passion for "the new man," a being who, like the visitor, is destined to be either welcomed or shunned. Radio, as the visitor's mode of public access, is thus no longer primarily the vehicle for the articulation of a progressive politics but rather the apparatus in relation to which the articulation of politics, here specifically Marxism, and philosophy is lived. From our vantage point, from the moment of radio studies, perhaps this is what allows radio to fly under the theoretical radar. It delocalizes philosophy from within.

CHAPTER 3

Stations of Exception

Sabotage versus *self-negation*. These terms—the first Benjamin's, the second Sartre's—are two names for the condition that results when one turns off one's radio, when one goes off the air. Although the objects of these gestures are different, both are expressly, but also perhaps therefore traditionally, political. Indeed, they politicize the click (as Ponge called it), the flick, that effects the transition between on and off. Moreover, these gestures lean heavily on any more traditionally political consideration of radio broadcasting, especially broadcasting practices that struggle to keep what partisans refer to as "the voice" on the air. In this chapter, various articulations of this struggle situated in Africa and North and South America, especially as they have been antagonized by colonialism and more recently neoliberalism, will be sounded. The purpose will be to consider whether radio—dependent as it is on what Joe Milutis describes as the becoming-property of the ether, that is, the domain of the air—opens up new channels of political reflection: not simply new means by which to circulate political statements, however vital such activity is, but new encounters *with* and *in* the field of politics, encounters that compel reflection on the very concepts and terms used to communicate political statements. Put differently, does the use of radio in the context of political conflict and/or contestation not only help prosecute that conflict but also jam the significance of that conflict in ways that, as it will be put here, oblige us to think outside the vox, that tenacious yet no longer even residual fetish of liberation? Do we, the increasingly globalized arbiters of significance, in other words, academic intellectuals in the North, have a hand in this, and if so, which one?

Before the "end of theory" is taken to the point of no return, that is, to the point of idiocy, it will be crucial to have redeemed those conceptual possibilities that, as Benjamin warned, flare up in the moment of danger that precedes their historical loss. One such possibility, and one carrying an intense political charge, is that of the concept of resistance, especially as it has been agitated in the wake of Michel Foucault's meditation on the "spiral of power." This is a concept that has been debated in the literatures of many fields—few will have forgotten Edward Said's early assault in "Traveling Theory"—but not, to my knowledge, in a way that has delineated with sufficient care the points of contact, perhaps even the common ground, between Foucault's concept and that of Freud, specifically, the concept of *der Widerstand*. Doubtless, Foucault's own redistricting of the Freudian break has had a hand in this.

As many have noted, although none more systematically than Jacques Derrida in his late rejoinder/homage to Foucault, "To Do Justice to Freud," Freud deploys resistance in three importantly different analytical contexts. In one, resistance is used to understand the biophysics of neuronal synapse, what in "The Project for a Scientific Psychology" is captured under the heading of the "contact barrier." Indeed, it is the very operation of resistance that places memory at the core of perception and repetition at the core of consciousness. Resistance is also fundamental to the twisted logic of transference and countertransference, where what it designates is the vexed spot in which the object of the cure shuttles anxiously between the analyst and the analysand. It is the sign, in this setting, that the Real is near. And third, Freud consistently appeals to resistance, not simply to characterize his reception everywhere but in America, but to validate preemptively the critically scientific character of his project. In other words, resistance demonstrates that Freud and psychoanalysis are indeed, as we might now say, onto something.

Those familiar with Derrida's essay know that in the midst of this proliferation of resistances he discerns a fourth modality of resistance, an immanent resistance to meaning figured in what Freud called "the navel" of the dream. Although the insight is certainly not without interest, of more immediate consequence is Derrida's procedure. Specifically, in propagating a fourth resistance he is obliged to draw out the iterative logic of Freud's concept, the fact that resistance, in whatever application, is structurally conditioned by power. The point is not the trivial and familiar one that there is no resistance without power, or power without resistance, or even that all resistance belongs to and thus protects power (the open secret of Foucault's "repressive hypothesis"), but that the *relation between* power and resistance derives from a different, one might even say more fundamental, level or process. For Derrida, of course, sooner or later, this requires recourse to the nonconcept of *différance*.

However familiar the conclusion, what startles in this discussion is the extent to which Derrida's reading of Freud becomes, almost seamlessly, a discussion of one of the central motifs of the late Foucault. Indeed, the terms of my own reading have sought to bring this out. Perhaps because Derrida's rejoinder to Foucault is fraught with a delicate anxiety, he makes no effort to play out his hunch. He proceeds as if Foucault's relation to Freud were such that it blinded Foucault to what Derrida discerns as the resistance to resistance. But the matter is not so simple. Indeed, recall that his homage to Foucault, presented at New York University in 1988, was titled "Au-delà du principe de pouvoir," an unmistakable calque of Freud's transgressive foray, *Beyond the Pleasure Principle*.

For example, in the *Psychiatric Power* lectures from 1973–74, Foucault himself evokes the level or process from which the relation between power and resistance derives by appealing to, of all things, a "system of differences," or "imbalance of forces." Although he avoids delineating the causal mechanism, it is clear that something he refers to as a "dangerous force" produces this imbalance that in turn sets in motion the confrontation between power and resistance. In a sense, danger (and perhaps it is the same as force?) menaces both power and resistance by provoking their confrontation, their propping or leaning on each other. Moreover, and Foucault's anticipation of Derrida's reading could not be clearer, in fleshing out the implications of this for his approach to disciplinary power he writes that said power is "a quite specific modality of what could be called a synaptic contact of bodies-powers *[le contact synaptique corps-pouvoirs]*" (*Psychiatric Power* 40). Only the obtuse would fail to see here Foucault's explicit evocation of Freud's account of the "contact barrier" in "The Project for a Scientific Psychology" and therefore the importance of its structural dynamic, its logic, in his rethinking of the relation between power and resistance. Nor should one, whether obtuse or not, overlook the fact that these lectures as a whole take as their explicit theme the need to separate

Foucault's then current thinking about "madness" from the angle taken in *The History of Madness*, that is, the text at the crux of the debate Derrida anxiously rejoins in "To Do Justice to Freud."

Aside from reminding us that, at times, our received notions about French theory can be pretty silly (to wit, Foucault was "against" Freud and psychoanalysis), my point here is to stress that, especially as we seek to gauge the implications of the rampant if fraught diffusion of neoliberalism in our hemispheres, we need to extend further the resources of the concept and practice of resistance. So, not to put too fine a point on it, the link between Foucault and Freud is not merely of bibliographic interest. It is of theoretical and political interest as well, but in a way that calls for elaboration.

The "Stations of Exception" of my title is a formulation that invites one to proceed along this front in two directions. First, it suggests that Giorgio Agamben's meditation on Carl Schmitt's conception of "the state of exception" promises to carry out an important extension of the concept and practice of resistance. Second, in replacing *state* with *station*—and, to clarify, by this I mean radio station—my titular formulation invites us to spell out both the important structural role of the mass media in contemporary neoliberalism and the matter of how this structural role might bear on the concept and practice of "real" political resistance.

Agamben's *State of Exception* (2003) is the last of the trilogy that begins with *Homo Sacer* and includes as its textual middle *The Open*. All three mull over the motifs of sovereignty, bare life, and the structure of the zone of indistinction. This last is especially relevant because, in articulating the empty point shared by the sovereign and unlawful violence, the law and its suspension, it points directly and unmistakably at the "synaptic contact" between power and resistance, that is, the volatile and unstable relation that derives from something that escapes, subtends, and provokes it. In the penultimate section of *States*, Agamben summarizes the key issues thus:

> From the real state of exception in which we live, it is not possible to return to the state of law . . . , for at issue now are the very concepts of "state" and "law." But if it is possible to attempt to halt the machine, to show its central fiction, this is because between violence and law, between life and norm, there is no substantial articulation. Alongside the movement that keeps them in relation at all costs, there is a countermovement that, working in an inverse direction in law and life, always seeks to loosen what has been artificially and violently linked. That is to say, in the field of tension of our culture, two opposite forces act, one that institutes and makes, and one that

deactivates and decomposes. The state of exception is both the point of their maximum tension and—as it coincides with the rule—that which threatens today to render them indiscernible. (*States* 87)

Here, the zone of indistinction arises precisely where the countervailing movements of instituting and decomposing stand in "maximum tension" with each other. As Agamben says, this is the state of exception, the profoundly political scene in which sovereignty succumbs to the very violence it cannot live without, or, in Agamben's terms, where *auctoritas* submits to *potestas*.

I am certainly not the first to recognize the common ground here between Agamben and Foucault (indeed, Agamben calls attention to it), but surely it is worth stressing that despite Foucault's persistent and sustained interest in the theory of sovereignty (in *Psychiatric Power* he expressly counterposes disciplinary and sovereign power and indeed claims to be unable to think the former without the latter), his still-resonant formulation from *The History of Sexuality,* "We still have not cut off the head of the king" (1: 88–90), makes clear that Schmitt's perspective is far from his own. Indeed, nowhere does Foucault show any sustained awareness of Schmitt's work. Despite this, what is clear is that the structural dynamic teased out of Schmitt by Agamben and formalized as the state of exception is precisely how Foucault approaches the problem of what escapes and thereby conditions the spiral of power. All parties are interested in jamming the "machine that is leading the West to global civil war" (*States* 87) while keenly, even soberly aware that no straightforwardly partisan concept of resistance is truly up to the task.

An obvious point is worth making explicit. What Agamben brings to the Foucauldian meditation on resistance is an urgently global political dimension. In this he anticipates the argument of Michael Hardt and Antonio Negri's *Empire,* where Deleuze's fecund distinction between discipline and control is bent to a similar task. And while one might speculate as to whether Foucault's lack of engagement with Schmitt explains the constraints of his discussion, more urgent is recognition of the contextual implications of Agamben's reading, implications that, as I will suggest, rebound upon his own textual practice.

In principled opposition to the Iraq War and the surveillance systems required by the U.S.-led "war on terror," Agamben, upon learning that he would be required by Homeland Security to provide its computers with a fingerprint should he pass through U.S. Customs, simply refused to accept an invitation extended to him to lecture in the United States. In publishing a statement explaining his position, "No to Biometrics,"

Agamben made it clear that he occupied the very globalized state of exception he was seeking to theorize. In fact, "we" all do, hence the importance of his small but defiant act of refusal. Less clear was the extent to which he recognized the fingerprint of that very state of exception in his theory of it, and it is precisely this that I want to evoke in the notion of the contextual implications of his argument. For that matter, it is not clear that Foucault—an obvious intellectual mentor for Agamben—ever really understood the nature of this challenge. Does, for example, his concept of the "specific intellectual" adequately confront the finely reticulated work of the spiral of power? Is the very specificity of the power/knowledge matrix conditioned by the ontology of thought that arises as discipline gives way to control?

Put differently: How might we begin to think the network of articulation—Lucien Goldmann's "world vision" or Fredric Jameson's "cognitive mapping"—that allows one to recognize the inscription of the theory of exceptional resistance within the social institutions that constitute the state of exception? My title signals the way. In particular, it signals—through the figure of the station—to the institutions and practices of mass communication, as a way to think the materiality of a globalized state of exception, what Lee de Forest—the self-baptized "father of radio"—called an "empire of the air." Stated more directly, what needs to be thought through in terms of delineating and practicing resistance are the material conditions of its exercise. What incites or otherwise enables it, but also how does thinking this state of affairs belong to the very same conditions? The argument that follows will seek to show that the discourse network of mass communications—and here specifically radio—necessarily even if insufficiently constitutes the core of these conditions, conditions whose core has been radically voided, or, as I have argued earlier, "delocalized" by the apparatus that radio is.

As there are various ways to pursue the point here, let me be clear. Emphasizing Kittler's notion of the discourse network commits one to seeking the conditions of resistance in the structural character of the mass media, not in the ethnographies of the agents of resistance, or at least not in some pretheoretical notion of agency devoid of structure. When approached in relation to the history of sound broadcasting, what counts as such a fundamental structural transformation is the shift from radio telegraphy to radio proper, that is, from point-to-point transmission to broadcasting proper. The latter term derives from farm labor, where it refers to the scattering of seed from a centralized point, the body of the planter. It is in that sense decidedly *not* a form of dissemination. The element of continuity that tells one that we are indeed dealing with a transformation of structure is what Hans Magnus Enzensberger usefully, if derivatively, called the "two-way" character of electronic media: as is obvious in radio telegraphy, the passing of information along a line or channel that is organized around two terminals, those of (to use Roman Jakobson's vocabulary) the addresser and the addressee. The whole design of the apparatus is to facilitate remote questioning and answering, in effect, to displace and disperse the intimate and politically charged vivacity of the "face to face" or "I-Thou." With the advent of radio proper, the irreducible reversibility of this circuit became more fraught. One might even say that the premium now placed on the "face to face" is retronymic, that is, developed in the wake of printing and its more contemporary sublimations.

To specify how and with what consequences, it is useful to recall one of the crucial arguments of Walter Benjamin's essay "The Work of Art in the Age of Its Technical Reproducibility," where among other things he tries to establish the immanent link between communism and the cinema. At the core of his discussion is the notion of "aura," the experience of the work of art that secures its cult value. Crucial to this effect is the idea of secular pilgrimage, the idea that prior to the era of technical reproducibility artworks had to be experienced at their own sites and on their own terms. One traveled to the work and invested it with the very distance traversed, the exertion, to enter into its presence. This is one important way to make sense of Benjamin's contention that "aura" registers the presence of distance, regardless of how close an object may be. The cinema, by reversing this circuit, that is, by coming to, as promotional discourse routinely declares, a theater near you, promises to break down the cult status of artworks whose location is comparatively fixed. Regardless of whether one is persuaded by the patently utopian aspects of this discussion, what radiates as theoretical insight is Benjamin's sense of the intimate relation between structure (the relation of access) and meaning in the event of cultural communication.

Radio differs decisively from the cinema in being, strictly speaking, a broadcast medium. Yes, the artwork (the program) travels to the site of reception, the terminal of what in all its guises are iterations, more or less recognizable, of domesticity, but whereas a film is received in public, a radio broadcast was and still largely is received in private (think Sartre); indeed, the early dependence on a headset has, in the guise of the ear bud, returned as a reactive innovation. The ear has become the niche of niche marketing. In this precise sense radio facilitated television, both of which structurally reprivatize a public encounter with sights and sounds. Clearly, reprivatization engages the reversibility of the radiophonic circuit in a decisive way. On the one hand, there is the canonical event of the "live feed," reporting an event in "real time," as when David Sarnoff (future head of RCA) relayed the distress calls from the *Titanic*. This, as we have seen, is the mode of reversibility celebrated by Brecht in his "Radio as a Communications Apparatus" (1932). On the other hand, there is the institutionally mediated circuit of car, telephone, and radio made equally canonical in George Lucas's *American Graffiti* (1973). In the course of the 1980s—with the Reagan/Fowler gutting of the Fairness Doctrine—the circuit of "the request" gave way to a feedback loop in which caller-listeners would, as if miming the physics of the audion tube, repeat back and amplify the incendiary rhetoric of "shock jocks" in what was lived as a form of two-way, participatory cultural democracy. That Howard Stern is now coming to us from among his kind in the firmament suggests that the problem—let's call it the spreading thin of democracy—is fast assuming galactic proportions.

Clear, and there is ample scholarship testifying to this, is the decisively closed character of this information traffic, and this is perhaps the key effect of reprivatization on the radiophonic system of two-way communication. Perhaps predictably, this has placed a high premium on controlling the production and transmission of broadcast signals, a premium that has been realized in the accelerated fostering of alternative or even pirate stations, but also in the more aesthetically driven one-watt revolution in which, as part of a performance piece, Tetsuo Kogawa—or someone like him—teaches participants how to build one-watt transmitters and then dispatches them to broadcast from the micropolitical field of everyday life. What such innovations indicate is that maintaining the closed character of two-way communications networks, in effect the channeling of reception through production, is vital—so much so that one can almost feel the danger thought to lurk just out of range, or, as the rhetoric of predation would have it, on the open system of the Internet. This is a danger, precisely like the one theorized by Foucault, thought constantly to pressure the balance of power and resistance oscillating between the sender and the receiver, the radio transmitter and the radio set. Although it has long been at issue within sound broadcasting, this danger has been given a new significance by calls for the neoliberalization of the media. This is because technical features of what I have been calling structure find their complement in institutional practices. This has been true of radio since the founding struggles between and among Marconi, de Forest, Armstrong, and Sarnoff, as Tom Lewis and others have argued. With the advent of satellite and Web radio, it is doubtless even more the case.

Formulated in institutional terms, reprivatization accords directly with one of the key neoliberal policy objectives as formulated by John Williamson in what has come to be known in policy discourse as "the Washington Consensus," that of systemic privatization. Although Williamson concedes that certain forms of public ownership are to be tolerated, it is clear that in general centralized, or nationalized, forms of production—because they blunt market discipline and, therefore, the putative motor of social and moral responsibility—are understood to be part of the problem in the developing world, and especially in Latin America, to which he was especially attentive. This applies explicitly to the modes of information production: the press, radio, and television. Of course, the status of the mass media in Latin America is profoundly complicated by the North-South geopolitical dynamics of cultural imperialism, a wrenching problem that has attracted the critical attention of everyone from Armand Mattelart to Nestor García-Canclini. Yet as important as it is to acknowledge this complexity, it is equally important to break down the distinction between public and private, or national and corporate on the northern side of the border. It is easy, of course, to insist that U.S. radio and television are private, that is, commercial in distinct and exemplary ways, but this ignores the decisive national dimension of state regulation, the Federal Communications Commission.

Reconstructing the originating myth of the FCC is instructive. It is, and this will come as no surprise, a story about power and resistance. The FCC was brought into existence by an act of the U.S. Congress, specifically, the Communications Act of 1934. It synthesized and displaced the Federal Radio Commission (FRC) of 1927 and the Mann-Elkins Act of 1910, which regulated U.S. telephone service. It is important, even crucial, that this act derived its necessity from a variety of debates and practices that posed openly the question of public versus private ownership of radio. Specifically, public school educators—as staunch Brechteans?—wanted to have access to radio frequencies for broad educational purposes. So as not to place an undue burden on the public treasury, the legislative representatives of said educators offered to seek advertisers, thereby privatizing a public service. In formulating the FCC, Congress explicitly formed a standing, regulative body and instructed it to sort out the tangle of issues here. It also weighed in decisively on what has come to be known as the Brinkley Act, from our listening post a decisive piece of this legislative package.[1]

Dr. John Brinkley, who made his fortune by inserting goat testicles into the impotent scrota of U.S. men, owned and operated a radio station, XERA, on the U.S.-Mexican border, specifically in Villa Acuña in the department of Coahuila. The programs on XERA originated from studios in the United States. In addition to advertising various forms of "snake oil," they advocated a fascist politics of the sort that Leo Lowenthal and Norbert Guterman later discerned in the broadcasts of George Allison Phelps. What brought this to the attention of the U.S. government was not Brinkley's politics but his use of telephone lines to send his programs to his radio transmitter in Mexico, technically avoiding U.S. regulations as codified in the FRC. The FCC and the Communications Act of 1934 expressly prohibited this arrangement, a decision that has persisted to this day, as the Brinkley provisions were continued in the Clinton administration's 1996 revision of the 1934 legislation.

Although the details of this situation are certainly worthy of scrutiny—notably, the "impotence, animal, sound broadcasting, electoral influence" series—its broader implications are of more immediate pertinence. First, it is important to recognize here the extent to which national regulatory policy intimately structures private radiophonic practice, a logic that now reaches down to the physical level of sound waves and bandwidth frequencies. Indeed, in more contemporary quarrels National Public Radio has directly opposed smaller, local broadcasters, arguing that their signals may well interfere with its own if a certain bandwidth frequency interval is not maintained. Also important is the fact that this recursive articulation of the national and the private is codified through an invaginated border, the now much-fraught, indeed overwrought, frontier between the United States and Mexico. In ways that are utterly consistent with the critical insights of postcoloniality, the Brinkley provisions draw attention to the way a certain abject incarnation of U.S. ideology, anti-Semitism, returns from the South, linking in a volatile hybrid or *mestizo* structure the One and its Other. Fundamental to this, of course, is precisely the two-way structure of radiophonic communication—further, perhaps even conclusive confirmation of the intimate continuity between the technical and the institutional dimensions of the radiophonic apparatus.

The history of media regulation complicates Williamson's call for "privatization" in a rather conspicuous way. Namely, and the matter touches on the vexed theme of the state's role in a capitalist economy, if the private is always already both established and disestablished through the public—through state intervention at the regulatory level—what precisely constitutes *re*privatization? After all, even ownership is defined and protected by the state. Although the issues at stake here are twisted indeed, certainly one thing accomplished by the call for privatization is a deliberate fixation of the discursive frame within which policy is debated. In the field of information this may well be the decisive victory, and in that sense the primary objective of the neoliberal initiative. Changing the conversation is not irrelevant, but how does this bear on the problem of political practice, on the relation between power and resistance? Moreover, what do we gain in approaching this relation under the titular rubric of "stations of exception"?

Analogous to the securing of the closure of the circuit of two-way communication, the fixation of discourse operates to oppose power and resistance in a way that obscures both their relation and what conditions it. As a consequence, other iterations of this opposition enter into supportive association with it: for example, the relation between production and reception. At the risk of brutally summarizing a significant and complex episode in recent intellectual history, one way to recognize the degree to which the production-reception relation reiterates the power-resistance relation is to recall the spat that erupted around the emergence of reception aesthetics. An important version of this is to be found in the famous face-off between Hans Robert Jauss and Paul de Man over Keats's *Hyperion.* Another, framed in terms a bit closer to the immediate concerns of this chapter, is the way practices of cultural consumption—think here of Dick Hebdige's study of subcultures—were invoked to outflank the premium placed on cultural production by critics inspired by the Frankfurt School, critics committed to the idea that standardized mass culture so determined its terms of address that only a "Just Say No" abstinence coupled with creative self-affirmation made sense as a progressive political response. In this context, reception became the locus of resistance, not immediately, in the sense of speaking truth to power, but in the sense of turning cultural contents to community purposes. In its most systematic formulation—I am thinking here of Tony Bennett (not the ageless crooner)—the productivity of reception was extended to the point that it displaced the moment of textual production altogether. As with Roland Barthes' distinction between the "readable" and the "writable," radicalized reception—in the case of literature, reading becoming writing, where the text is *nothing but* the reading that puts its possible meanings in play—preempts and usurps the agency more typically attributed to the act of creation. Indeed, it is through agency that reception finds its essential and intimate connection with resistance. And, lest it pass unremarked, this intimacy arises in and is sheltered by the box of the vox.

To unravel what such formulations have to teach us about political practice and to move toward a more sustained treatment of radio, closer consideration of the status of reception and resistance in Frantz Fanon's "Here Is the Voice of Algeria" ("Ici, la voix d'Algérie") is called for.

As is generally known, this essay appears in 1959, in a collection of essays entitled *L'an cinq de la révolution algérienne*. Both the essay and the collection are rallying cries. With the revolution hanging by a thread, Fanon is clearly seeking to snatch victory from the jaws of defeat, a situation largely obscured by Fanon's English translator, who renders the title with the retrospectively confident *A Dying Colonialism*. The title of the essay on radio, with its direct appeal to the voice, anticipates with almost uncanny directness Aimé Césaire's eulogy on the pages of *Présence Africaine* in the wake of Fanon's death in 1962.

> This, then, is the final lesson of Fanon [that the anticolonial struggle is properly international]. There is nothing stronger than this final lesson which he wrote on his death bed. It is already a matter of a voice from beyond the grave *[d'une voix d'outre tombe]*. But what a voice! And it is to the Third World that it addresses itself. It is not a voice of the vanquished, a voice of the resigned. It is, at the edge of the chasm *[au bord du gouffre]*, a strong "Onward!," a call to invention, to creation, a leap across the chasm. (121, my translation)

As in the allegorical chapter that opens the volume, "Algeria Unveils," the chapter on radio, produces through the reliable and resonant metonymy of the voice the national subject of Algeria, and it does so in the mode and mood of anticipation. "Here" is the voice of an Algeria that is no longer French Algeria, where the deixis of the shifter "here" clicks back and forth but certainly ahead to a condition that, in a quasi-performative gesture, is being called into existence but that strictly speaking does not yet exist. In this sense another translation of the title might well be, in keeping with Césaire's gothic rhetoric, "Hello, Algeria here . . ." (as if answering a call from the beyond).

However, Césaire's remarks foreground another aspect of Fanon's title. Stated first in the genre of cliché, "Here Is the Voice of Algeria," or, as the English translator has it, "This is the Voice of Algeria"—the matter is made more blatant in the second version—what emerges is the myth of Fanon as the "voice of the African revolution." In other words, the shifter "this" situates the radio broadcast both in the context of the struggle and in Fanon's words about that struggle. "This" is spoken/written by Fanon and cannot but reference that. *His* is the voice of liberated Algeria. But the shifter also does something more challenging. In effect, it situates the revolutionary confrontation on the split stage of the text and the conflict. *Here,* the word in its idiomatic function, locates the voice of Algeria both on the radio and literally on the page, a page that, unlike the radio broadcast, reanimates the voice whenever and wherever it is read. This is captured, I think, more powerfully through "here" than "this," although as shifters both are messages about codes. Elsewhere I have argued that this broaches an important political, and perhaps distinctly postcolonial, aspect of the Algerian War, but here what matters is clarifying how this "shifty" dynamic radiates throughout the form and content of "Here Is the Voice of Algeria," producing, as it were, a frame for its reflections on resistance.[2]

What, then, is the form of the essay? It begins on a didactic, utterly formulaic note. The verbs are in the future tense and are used to describe what the chapter will be about. The text is talking about itself, about what is coming. In its long "middle," the text clicks back and forth between several pasts—the remote past of Algeria (when radio broadcasting was first introduced), the moment immediately prior to the revolutionary war ("before 1954," as Fanon anaphorically chants), and the past of the book itself (typically captured in the thematically overdetermined formula "as we have seen."[3] As it concludes, the text again turns to the future to characterize the role of the radio in teaching the fully mutated Algerians how to construct the nation their actions have liberated. This too would be utterly formulaic were it not for the fact that the future anterior arrives to complicate things. Its function is to fold idiomatically the future ("will") and the past ("have been") into one another in a way that repeats Fanon's shuffling of the past of the conflict with the past of the book. In the penultimate sentence of the text, he writes: "For many years the radio will have been for many one of the means by which to say no to the occupation and to believe in Liberation" ("Here" 97).[4] As if to stress the "shuffle," the last sentence is written in the simple past. We thought we were looking forward, moving ahead, but instead we are left before the limitless horizon that radio has opened for us. What is significant about the way Fanon's use of the future repeats his use of the past is that the ontological and political questions posed by the deixis of the essay (its where and its when) are expressly echoed in its exposition, in its enunciation. In short, the question of "where" the radiophonic voice of Algeria is to be situated can be heard to recur as a question about the "when" of its emergence, both questions that organize the language and the shape of the essay. This "where-when" of the voice tells us something crucial about both radio and the voice, a point made clearer by amplifying what, apparently, the essay means to say.

The content of the text can be plotted in relation to the formal arc of its argument. In tracing this, it will be my concern to draw special attention to the way it brings resistance and reception into a relation that complicates the stability of both concepts, reminding us to think twice about them both.

As we have seen, Fanon moves directly to establish that because the radio was understood by Algerians to be central to the projection of French colonial power it was, as he specifies, "refused" (70) by most sectors of the indigenous population. In support of his contention that economic reason cannot adequately account for this refusal, he goes on to point out that Algerians aware of the content of French radio (Radio-Alger) refused to purchase receivers because of the sacrilegious content of much broadcasting. Emphasizing the collective character of radio listening in the Maghreb, Fanon specifies that French radio addressed parents and children in ways that undermined the codes governing their relations largely as defined within a local variant of Islam. This matters to his argument because it allows him to advance one of the key themes of his analysis, namely, that anticolonial struggle *necessitates* some sort of negotiation with secular modernity—hence, his opening stress on the refusal of radio receivers, or, to scan forward only one click, reception. Conceptually and politically, the essay thus begins by establishing reception as the object of what later he will refer to as the "no," the refusal of colonialism. This is a refusal grounded, not in reception itself, but in a traditional defense against receiving what might well call tradition into question.

Significantly, the vocabulary of resistance is *not* deployed here, as if to set up a signal distinction between resistance and what he calls refusal, or, at other times, rejection (the "no" with which the essay concludes), a decidedly more psychoanalytically inflected concept. In fact, Fanon later insists that the refusal to purchase radios was *not* an explicit act of resistance. Equally significant, however, is the fact that when resistance *does* enter the essay it does so as a characterization of the *French* reaction to what he designates as, presumably echoing French pundits, creeping "Arabization." After calling Radio-Alger an "instrument of resistance" (Fanon 72), Fanon goes on to specify: "Among the European farmers, radio is for the most part lived as the link to the civilized world, as an effective instrument of resistance to the corrosive influence of an indigenous society that is immobile, lacking in perspective, backward and without value" (72). The decisive observation about the role of the radio in overcoming the urban/rural divide notwithstanding, what juts into the foreground here is the notion that the French *resist the Algerians* by receiving broadcasts characterized by Fanon as the French speaking to the French. Radio-Alger is the "voice" of France in Algeria, an appeal to the voice that, in an essay titled "Here Is the Voice of Algeria," crackles with significance.

The text confronts us, then, with a founding conceptual and political distinction between refusal (on the part of the Algerians) and resistance (on the part of the French). Both pivot warily around reception. In the Algerian case we have a refusal to receive, while in the French case reception serves as the very medium of resistance. In addition, both refusal and resistance pivot around power and, perhaps surprisingly, in both cases a power perceived to be capable of calling into question or otherwise undermining traditional values. Predictably, the French see themselves threatened by the very absence of values, the Algerians simply by values other than their own. This monotony of power, its lack of differentiation in either substance or orientation, soon gives way, however, as does the convenient logic whereby the distinction between refusal and resistance is indexed directly to the intentions giving "voice" to one or the other. Put differently, we are presented here with a standoff, a confrontation between two voices intent on circling around a homogeneity they are concerned to shelter from each other. Resistance, apart from indicating the stance of the colonizer, is here structurally conservative. Because it expresses a structural apartness, indeed the very apartness that in the essay distinguished culture from nonculture, it is marked for reconstruction.

This transvaluation is set in motion by the revolution itself. Specifically, as events begin to unfold throughout the country and Algerians increasingly realize that distorted information is better than none, the refusal to consume receivers is reversed. Algerians discover that the radio, precisely to the extent that signals obey neither linguistic nor national boundaries, can bring international perspectives to bear on the conflict, a conflict whose representation would otherwise be utterly subject to the colonial control of information. This movement away from a preemptive and largely religious refusal of reception is decisively accelerated with the advent of "La Voix de l'Algérié Libre," the radio broadcast of the FLN, that is, the anticolonial resistance. Primed by their discovery of the political and military importance of information, Algerians, beginning in 1956, start to demand more radios—especially battery-powered sets—than suppliers can supply. These are listened to eagerly both at home and in public. As a result, and Fanon is keen to emphasize this, the radio is deprived of its status as a modern, even "evil" object. In becoming the channel through which Algerians attune with the revolution, the radio becomes "a unique means *to resist* the ever increasing psychological and military pressures of the occupier" (84, my emphasis). In short, the radio is taken up as the weapon the French have made it.

This is the decisive shift. Stated succinctly, refusal gives way to resistance, receivers are consumed, and reception is valued as a site of political practice. It is interesting here—and the significance of my opening reflections on Foucault, Freud, and Derrida should now become apparent—that Fanon presents us with, and not merely at the conceptual level, a confrontation between two resistances, a confrontation that, in challenging us to consider whether they are identical, provokes us to recognize the potential importance of resisting resistance, of sensing that something within resistance endangers it. This is not about abandoning resistance but about using "the weapon of theory" (to cite Amical Cabral) to pressure assumptions prematurely sanctified by "real" conflict: for example, the assumption that resistance is resistance and that as such it opposes power at once directly and remotely (i.e., from another, radically separate, ontological location). Radio as the transgressor, the delocalizer, voids this location, urging partisans to gauge carefully the cost of what resistance repeats—in the case of the radio, the nonindigenous modernity of its technological conditions of possibility—in speaking truth to power. Fanon renders the matter with compelling clarity in his extraordinary deconstruction, yes, deconstruction, of the voice of free (at times also "fighting" [*l'Algérie combattante*]) Algeria.

This occurs in his discussion of the war of the airwaves *(la guerre des ondes)*, as his argument is beginning to turn toward the future, a future in which the persecutorial, superegoic voice of the radio is transmuted into an inspiring voice of national consciousness. As the relevant passages have much to say about voice, resistance, and reception, they are worth citing at length.

Here is situated a phenomenon sufficiently original to retain our attention. The extremely advanced French technical services, with experience acquired in the world wars, and familiar with the practice of "airwave warfare," were quick to pick up the wavelengths of the transmitters. The programs were then systematically jammed [brouillés], and the "Voice of Fighting Algeria" became inaudible. A new form of struggle was born. Leaflets counseled Algerians to keep tuned in for durations of two to three hours. In the course of one broadcast, a second station, transmitting over another wavelength would relay the first jammed station. The listener, thus incorporated into the battle of the airwaves, had to figure out the tactics of the enemy, and in a manner almost physical, muscular, outmaneuver the strategy of the adversary. Often, only the operator, his ear glued to the apparatus, would have the unanticipated chance to hear the Voice. The other Algerians present in the room received the echo of this voice through the device of a privileged interpreter, who, at the end of the broadcast, was literally besieged. Precise questions were then posed to this incarnated voice. (85)

Half a page further on, Fanon continues his characterization of the voice, further delineating the rigors of its reception.

Poorly heard [entendue], blanketed by the incessant jamming, obliged to switch wavelengths two or three times in the course of a single broadcast, the Voice of Fighting Algeria could hardly ever be heard in a continuous fashion. It was a chopped, discontinuous voice. . . . Under these conditions to affirm having heard the Voice of Fighting Algeria was, in a certain sense, to alter the truth, but it was above all the occasion to proclaim underhandedly one's participation in the essence of the Revolution. It was to make a deliberate choice, even if not explicit in the first months, between the congenital lie of the enemy and the true lie [proper mensonge] of the colonized that suddenly acquired a dimension of truth. This voice, often absent, physically inaudible, that everyone felt welling up from within, founded on an interior perception of what was the Homeland [la Patrie], materialized in an undeniable fashion. Every Algerian, for his part, broadcast and transmitted [émet et transmet] the new language. (86–87)

Where to start? In the first passage we are presented with the obstreperous clash of resistances, one seeking to tune into the anticolonial struggle, the other seeking to interrupt this attunement. Contact barrier indeed. Both are struggling for power with power, in this case wattage, and the capacity to project one's message. Out of this a new form of confrontation arises, the war of the airwaves, a key feature of which is the "incorporation" of the listener within the conflict. Fanon insists on this vocabulary, clarifying that listening was motivated not simply by curiosity but by the inner need to fuse (faire corps) with the nation.

Important here is the way Fanon is implicating the subjectivity of the colonized in the revolutionary struggle, drawing out the deep structure of the metonym of the voice. Indeed, as the passage concludes we are presented with the figure of the incarnated voice, not the word made flesh (at least not simply this), but the broadcast *materialized* in the receiver, that is, the operator whose ear has fused with the apparatus. As Fanon specifies, this figure "echoes" the voice that is then drawn out of him by his interrogators. The full implications of these rigorously formulated details are spelled out in the second passage.

Here the voice is properly described as chopped *(hachée)* and discontinuous. The obstreperous clash of resistances, in spacing out the voice, in separating the voice from itself, produces a reception context composed of a collective charged with the urgent labor of filling in the tears in the voice. It is not simply that the operator is asked for details but that the entire listening audience is called upon to piece together the shreds of the jammed broadcast. Aware, somehow, that this discussion has wandered onto the terrain of what Derrida, only eight years later, called "phonocentrism," Fanon draws the epistemological conclusion that the "Voice of Algeria" is grounded, not in truth, but in what Plato, in explaining his distrust of poets, called the true or proper lie *(le propre mensonge)*. Precisely because the radiophonic voice requires the active supplementation of reception, it cannot be grounded, nor can it ground itself. It is delocalized and cannot be unified. At a certain level, of course, these specifications are designed to do little more than show in precisely what way the revolution will be produced and sustained through popular support, and one might have expected Fanon to settle for that. But, as Césaire reminded us, he goes on. He goes on to transform the subjects who have incorporated themselves within the national conflict *into radios*. As he insists: "Every Algerian, for his part, broadcast and transmitted *[émet et tramsmet]* this new language," a formulation whose lexical details make it clear that the operator who earlier incarnated the "Voice" has now given way to a collective formation whose nearest conceptual analogue might be a disseminated network. On this construal of the matter, radio is far more than a communication device. But it is also more than a metonym for the *vox populi*, the much maligned *téléphone arabe*, or gossip. Instead, it emerges "here" (again, "where" exactly?) as the event of the revolution, an event structured around a blatant void where resistance is doubled over both inside and outside power, yet where the subject of history, here the Algerian people, is insistently at stake.

Perhaps because of Fanon's principled insistence that the revolution will be made by the subjects it makes (gone is the prior principle of a sheltered homogeneity), his discussion of radio underscores its antemetabolic status as both a site of resistance and a site within which resistance is called into question—not by power as such, but by resistance itself insofar as it lends itself to various articulations and incarnations, and insofar as it is always already conflicted by and over its duel with power. As my sketch of the form of Fanon's essay suggested, a decisive articulation of this conflicted resistance is the one that takes place *in* and *as* his analysis, the "here" where the "Voice of Algeria" somehow takes place. Indeed, the topological complexity of the voice's location(s) seems fully inscribed in the very resistance to resistance, making the essay and the broadcast into terminals in a fully disseminated network. Moreover, Fanon's attentive delineation of the sociohistorical context of reception links the reflexive rigor of resistance to a similarly complex jamming of the opposition between production and reception. Production is not the simple locus of power, and reception is not the pure site of resistance. One might even say that it is bad reception, the failure of reception, that produces resistance, but a resistance about which the subjects of history must lie in order to secure the truth of the revolution and of themselves.

Of course, one may always speculate—given these details—whether the content of Fanon's argument follows mechanically from the form of his analysis (or vice versa), but what should not be buried is the stirring emphasis he places on the dual task of using an implement of cultural domination not only against its benefactors but against the very sense of things circulated by or through its presence: the notion, for example, that speaking out or up—regardless of when, where, why, or how—is the best way to grasp the conditions of one's political subjectivity. In fact, one could argue that the political standard set by Fanon is precisely the one in which a militantly conceptual or theoretical front belongs at the core of anticolonial struggle, as opposed to the more familiar mode of "ideological struggle" where, to borrow Althusser's apotropaic formulation, ideology squares off against a science always already charged with speaking truth to power, but from an undisclosed location. Indeed, it is Fanon's standard that haunts the current standoff between global popular struggles and the Washington Consensus, especially as we in Northern universities think about, not just how to make sense of this standoff, but our complicity with it. Especially striking here is Fanon's problematization of the status of the voice as a way to conceptualize both the vehicle and the meaning of resistance in general but also of resistance in the context of a struggle against and within the means of neoliberal telecommunications.

At no point in his discussion—and this despite the titular theme of his essay—does Fanon have actual recourse to the "speaking truth to power" formulation, where speaking, in Saussure's construal, as the subjective and thus private event of enunciation, becomes the medium of truth's opposition to power. Instead, the voice is subjected to an ensemble of complications: What is its location (on the air or on the page)? What does it say (the truth or a lie)? Who hears what it says (the operator or the listeners)? Where does it come from (the broadcasters— which ones? or the listeners—which ones, the ones who echo or the ones who incarnate?). At no point does Fanon invoke a foundational or grounded status for the voice, yet it is precisely this abstention that gives the voice . . . what, its power? No. Its resistance? No. Its danger? Perhaps. Recall that, pronounced in French, the voice *(la voix)* is also, through the properly acoustic ruse of homophony, the way, the open- ing, the leak *(la voie),* a quality captured memorably when the voice is characterized as "chopped, discontinuous," or even "phantomatic." This is important in two ways. First, as a way to maintain theoretical pressure on the concept and practice of resistance, it cautions against any spontaneous affirmation of the political value of the voice conceived as the agency, medium, or objective of struggle. Second, and here I scan back to an earlier set of questions, Fanon's analysis of the voice—both its form and its content, predicting as it does key features of the analysis in Derrida's *La voix et le phénomène* (by the way voice, not speech, and phenomena)—prompts us to consider precisely to what extent radio, or twentieth-century telecommunications more broadly, organize the so- ciohistorical experience cognitively mapped by deconstruction. Having made a version of this argument in my book *Text: The Genealogy of an Antidisciplinary Object* (see chapter 2, "The Text Goes Pop"), all that I need add here is a more explicit engagement with Agamben's argument about the state of exception that now rules, especially as it might bear upon the "voice, resistance, exception" series.

Recalling that the state of exception assumes much of its political force because Agamben comes to it in his reading of Schmitt on *sov- ereignty,* one might reasonably wonder whether such concerns hover anywhere near Fanon's discussion. They do, but remotely. For example, Fanon writes the following about the epic war of the airwaves: "The cut up and broken acts gleaned by a magazine correspondent more or less attached to colonial domination, or communicated by enemy military authorities, lose their anarchic character and become organized in a form of political thought that is both national and Algerian, take their place in a comprehensive strategy to re-conquer popular sovereignty" (84). One is inclined to read Fanon's formulation as situating the state of exception outside sovereignty, as if the relevant formulation were to "take exception" to the colonial violation of popular sovereignty. Indeed, Fanon actually uses the term *exception* in the final paragraph of the essay when describing the role of the radio in reconstructing the fully mutated, that is, liberated, Algerian. He writes that the radio will have "an exceptional importance" (97) in this struggle, and while this might well lead one to argue that Fanon's discussion has little or nothing to do with Agamben's, it is clear—if we sample these two moments in the text—that for him radio will play an exceptionally important role, not simply in the restoration of Algerian popular sovereignty, but, as it operates from within the restoration, especially in its emergent phase, in resistance to the "sovereignty" (95) of Radio-Alger. If instead of simply counterposing the two modes of sovereignty we grasp that their confrontation, their relation, takes place within the "empire of the air," then one might argue that French and Algerian broadcasting are both thus "stations of exception," outposts of production and reception not simply in competition but in conflict over the future, and— just as important—over the very terms of this conflict. It is as if our current situation appeared on Fanon's radar—a situation in which the globally dominant state of exception is broadcast through and by stations of exception, that is, terminals on a network whose global reach makes struggle impossible outside it. In this, Fanon also cautions us about what resistance might conceivably mean, what its proper scope and scale might be, and in doing so he bequeaths something absolutely vital to us in our effort to grasp what might survive or come after the Washington Consensus. I am concerned that we have spurned this gift. I will say why.

As mentioned earlier, Northern resistance to neoliberalism as articulated within the state-regulated telecommunications industry has realized itself in the embrace of local, community, and especially pirate radio. I find it interesting and certainly congenial to my interests that Pete Tridish—the founder of Radio Mutiny (WPPR) in West Philadelphia—has cited Radio Venceremos, at least as the station's trials and tribulations appeared in José Ignacio López Vigil's marvelous oral history *Rebel Radio: The Story of El Salvador's Radio Venceremos (Las mil y una historias de Radio Venceremos)*, as his inspiration. When the federal and local authorities effectively closed his operations in 1993, Tridish was quoted as having said in relation to Radio V (as it is now called): "These guys—some of them had no education. And they ran a radio station for eleven years without missing a single day" (Karr 25). In other words, the troubles faced by Santiago (the DJ for Radio Venceremos) were far more daunting than those faced by Radio Mutiny, so all setbacks need to be metabolized as hesitations on the road to *la victoria*. Moreover, and this is a more structural version of Tridish's optimism, neoliberal globalization puts resistance movements in contact with each other and allows for the circulation of what Jacques Rancière once called "logics of revolt." Yes, revolt seeks to sustain itself on the energies produced by the spread of its logic, but this is precisely why pressuring the very concept of resistance in the context of globalized telecommunications is so urgent. Again, the point is not to abandon resistance but to make it worth fighting for/over.

Radio Venceremos, quite apart from what value it may hold for Northern radio pirates, belongs squarely within any consideration of the "before" of the Washington Consensus (prepared, one should add, during the first Bush administration) because it belongs to the sociohistorical cusp, the leading edge of what was to become the neoliberal "solution" to economic and political development in the South, or Central and Latin America in particular. In his oral history of the station, Vigil (initially a filmmaker but now a radio journalist working out of Lima, Peru) underscores a number of issues that resonate, if dissonantly, with those pursued by Fanon. Of these I want especially to emphasize the radio's relation to the voice, aware that the tones and textures of an oral history mediate one's encounter with this radiophonic incarnation of the voice in distinctive and perhaps even incalculable ways.

Early in Vigil's study an important frame is set in place. He recounts the establishment and oft-attempted destruction of Radio YSAX, the archdiocesan station used by, among others, Archbishop Oscar Arnulfo Romero, the unlikely liberation theologian murdered by then Captain Roberto D'Aubuisson. Important here—and Vigil skips over the salient detail—is the way Archbishop Romero understood and used the radio. For the three years of his tenure as archbishop, Monseñor Romero used YSAX to broadcast his Sunday homily, a regular feature of which included a segment called "Events of the Week" that gave his broadcast a perhaps fatally journalistic as well as religious character. Only months before he was murdered, Monseñor Romero famously said the following about his broadcast: "These homilies try to be the people's voice. They try to be the voice of those who have no voice. And so, without a doubt, they displease those who have too much voice. This poor voice will find echo in those who love the truth and who truly love our dear people" (Pierce 5–6). As Vigil reports it, the silencing of this voice (a silencing Monseñor Romero himself foretold) directly inspired the activists who formed the initial broadcasting crew of Radio Venceremos. In effect, Radio Venceremos sought to restore the voice of *los sin voz,* a point made crystal clear in its first broadcast from Morazán, when Santiago said: "Brothers of El Salvador and the world: at this moment Radio Venceremos, the voice of the FMLN, begins broadcasting from somewhere in El Salvador to accompany the Salvadoran people step by step in their march toward final victory over centuries of oppression" (Vigil 21). The metonymic, perhaps even catachrestic chain is not difficult to follow: the radio is the voice of the guerilla organization, which in turn is the voice of the Salvadoran people. Vigil himself takes the final step, fusing the radio voice with the voice of Santiago: "His voice is a symbol, it's everyone's voice, the voice of the revolution" (86).

While on the face of it such a formulation would appear to belong to a rather different world from that of Fanon's "Voice of Algeria," one cannot miss the distinctly diectical signs at work within the broadcast. At "this moment" the voice of those without voice is restored, a "shifty" moment if there ever was one, especially when, for obvious reasons, the "where" of the broadcast (the broad national coordinates suffice) is left unspecified, at the very moment when the radio broadcaster says that the radio voice is "accompanying" the march of the people. As Vigil spells out, this accompaniment could take rather direct and immediate forms when, for example, a broadcast might directly inquire of a presumed listener whether a certain task had been completed, as it were, in the field. In the inaugural act, however, the word *accompany* functions to place the voice at once alongside and yet decidedly remote from the people.

In fact, the temporal dispersion of the voice, the "this" and the "somewhere," is, perhaps not surprisingly, what brings it into the closest orbit of Fanon's critique of phonocentrism. But this provocative proximity is not sustained. Of the many fascinating, even heart-wrenching stories told by our Salvadoran Scheherezade—defeats, triumphs, affairs, and even an ingenious act of bricolage in which a barbed-wire cattle fence was used as an aerial—perhaps the most striking is the dramatically narrated episode of a desperate struggle to be "on the air" at broadcast time—in effect, not under any circumstances, to be off the air. As should be apparent, once Radio Venceremos was in existence it became a military target. Not only was it constantly contradicted, interestingly *not* jammed, by VOA (the Voice of America), but the broadcast team was aggressively sought after by the Salvadoran army. Goniometers were routinely used to locate the signal source, and forces would descend upon the specified coordinates. In the story that interests me, Radio Venceremos has been flushed from the mountains and effectively silenced. Taking advantage of this, state-controlled stations and the VOA begin to broadcast that the station has been destroyed. Symbolically, of course, the revolution is itself at stake. Vigil's narration then traces, indeed essentially plots, the frantic effort to move the equipment, set it up, prepare the content, and commence the broadcast precisely at 6:00 p.m., the then customary time. Against all odds, they make it.

What interests me here is the way the speech of the voice, its power, is fully subordinated to the punctual event of enunciation. The diurnal rhythm of sound and silence produces within the voice something that separates it from itself, an absence that provides the fullness its presence is thereby deprived of with deeper significance. Here we brush up against Fanon's discontinuous voice directly, but here too we encounter most immediately the mediating force of Vigil's text and the ball and chain of catachresis: voice, FMLN, nation. For in his reconstruction of the oral history, in his explicitly stated preference for showing and not telling, what takes precedence is the motif of continuity, as if he felt it urgent to protect the voice of the revolution from the time, the event of its transmission. At some level, of course, this is humility—he wants to diminish the importance of the shower's role—but it is also a betrayal of some of the more provocative conceptual features of the political phenomenon that was Radio Venceremos. True, it may be impossible to be frisked for a voice (Vigil 3), but this very quality—the voice's "phantomatic" character—is not inalienable. It can indeed be taken, especially if mistaken for what it is not.

To hasten the chapter to a conclusion, I will observe that what Vigil is wrestling with is the problem of resistance and the temptation to avoid complicating the fact and figure of the voice in order to protect the memory of the revolution. This was perceived to be especially urgent in the 1990s when peace had broken out and elections made it imperative that the FMLN separate itself from Radio Venceremos, thus obliging the station to become the voice of people who, as is said of the vote, had then spoken. But what might we make of what is currently going on—and here I turn briefly to the wake left by the Washington Consensus—in Chiapas? Beginning in February of 2002, one could hear the following echoing through the mountains of the Southeast at four in the morning: "A very good morning. You are listening to Radio Insurgente, the voice of those without voice, the official voice of the EZLN. It is now four in the morning," followed by the playing of the Zapatista "national" anthem. The echoing of Monseñor Romero and Radio Venceremos is deliberate and unmistakable. To this extent, Radio Insurgente seeks to claim for itself a rather specific heritage, a fact that makes Subcomandante Marcos's strategic account of Radio Insurgente interesting, even though the Zapatista "revolution" is an act of defiance or disobedience, not strictly speaking an armed conflict.

This account, in fact one of several, appears in a video message sent to the organizers of the "Freeing the Media Teach-In" during the winter of 1997. In characterizing what he calls "the Fourth World War" (the global spread of neoliberal doctrine and public policy), Marcos specifies that "the giant communication media: the great monsters of the television industry, the communications satellites, magazines and newspapers seemed determined to present a virtual world, created in the image of what the globalization process requires. In this sense, the world of contemporary news is a world that exists for the VIPs" (180). Faced with this, what is to be done? How are we to think about protesting the grip of neoliberalism on the media? Marcos makes the following case. We could, of course, resign ourselves to the North's ability to produce and sustain a way of seeing the world and do nothing. We might also strike a more austere and defiant pose: denounce the lie, the virtuality of the dominant way of seeing the world, and let something like the gentle force of the better argument prevail. Or we could "construct a different way" (181), that is, we could take up the projective weaponry of neoliberalism and fashion an alternative to it from *within* its enabling apparatus. This is the strategy Marcos favors, and he goes on to argue not only that this is the responsibility of the independent media but that this is precisely how he envisions the Zapatista contribution to what he calls a "network of independent media" (181). But this sort of "belly of the beast" logic—however laudable strategically—never quite confronts squarely the vexed motif of independence, a dilemma that becomes acute when, as one should now expect, Marcos appeals to the "independent voices" (181) that will rise up within the envisioned network. In other contexts one might simply let this pass. However, in a context overdetermined by the struggle against neoliberalism and especially neoliberalism as expressed in the field and discourse of communications, that is, in the context of a Brinkley-like provocation of the Telecommunications Act of 1996 (a videographic, hence televisual message *hecho en Mexico,* broadcast in the United States) that questions both the legitimacy and the logic of neoliberal communications policy, one cannot ignore the paradox of privatization as characterized earlier. How precisely are we to bring privatization into productive political tension with independence, the entrepreneur/owner with the pirate, the network with the system?[5]

I will end by observing that "these" questions cannot and should not be primarily directed to Subcomandante Marcos and Radio Insurgente. This is not because we couldn't post them on its Web site. On the contrary, it is precisely because we can post them on such a terminal that our desire to address these questions to "them" is frustrated. Just as we are swept up into the delocalizing force of his address—I still remember finding one of Marcos's early declarations of hostilities from the Lacandon jungles in my e-mail queue one morning—he is similarly delocalized. One of the EZLN's slogans may well be *"Tierra y libertad,"* but the Zapatistas are not true telluric partisans as understood by Carl Schmitt. Indeed, their struggle for the "there" is waged precisely by exploiting the tactical "somewhere" that is always called up by the acousmatic radiophonic voice. We, and lest it pass unremarked, I am thinking now of us, the geopolitical and globalizing academic intellectuals who are positioned to hear in Marcos's voice the discontinuities that, in complicating its political authority, its representational grounding, provoke us to question the disciplinary habits that filter our hearing.[6] Do "we" know what to listen for in resistance? Is there in our listening something that resists it? It is in this insistently interrogative sense that I have stressed throughout the urgency of the conceptual conflict over resistance. La Voix d'Algérie Combattante/Libre, Radio Venceremos, Radio Insurgente are all in some sense putting in a call to us, not to solicit recognition of their resistance, but to implicate us in the struggle to articulate it. From our end, at our terminals, this struggle is about both rethinking this resistance and re: working the disciplinary terrains whose thoughtless accommodation of neoliberal educational policy (interdisciplinarity as the "strip mall," one-stop shopping logic of academic privatization) makes such rethinking more difficult than it needs to be. I repeat: this is not about outsourcing the revolution, or plundering and thereby squandering its energies. It is about the fact that resisting the nearing "Fourth World War" requires an understanding that resisting the resistance offered us, the very grammar of confrontation, is part of it. Indeed, this may be the very least one can do, but it is certainly our part. And while it is important to distinguish between the two fronts of this moment of danger, it is perhaps even more important to refuse to allow the danger of danger to dissipate prematurely.

CHAPTER 4

Phoning In Analysis

The interchanges between and among radio, instruction, and politics invite, perhaps even demand, attention to psychoanalysis and the articulation between radio and psychoanalytic theory quite specifically. As in the analysis of Sartre and Benjamin, this discussion will play up the relation between the two "ons": psychoanalysis conducted *over* the wireless airwaves (the organizing conceit of the long-running television program *Frazier*), and the thinking *about* radio to be found within psychoanalysis, the conceptual benchmark for which is to be found in the formulation from *Dialectic of Enlightenment,* "Radio is a sublimated printing press," discussed in the Introduction. Once again the enabling proposition of radio studies—that radio languished untheorized during the fifty-year span between the 1930s and the 1980s—will be pressured. Once again, the curious crossing between radio and philosophical reflection—in this case philosophical reflection about the implications of Freud's Copernican revolution for both philosophy and psychoanalysis—will be stressed. If in the second chapter much energy was expended in trying to pick up something crucial about the radiophonic apparatus in the clicking back and forth between on and off—asking in effect, "where" something called radio takes place—here, similar energy will be expended not only in sorting through a different way of thinking the off, the punctuation, of radio, but also in posing the question—implicit, for example, in *Frazier*—whether radio is where psychoanalytic therapy can take place, or, put differently, what the radiophonic apparatus must be if something like analysis can occur "on" it.

A different point about Enzensberger's 1971 manifesto, "Constituents [*Baukasten,* closer in fact to Foucault's "tool kit"] of a Theory of the Media," now suggests itself. Earlier it seemed appropriate to underscore Enzensberger's debt to Brecht, but here a particular feature of his critique of the New Left (like the Old Left, it is understood to have an inadequate theory of the media) deserves emphasis. In describing what he takes to be one of the signal failings of the student uprising in May 1968, he writes: "During the May events in Paris the reversion to archaic forms of production was particularly characteristic. Instead of carrying out agitation among workers with a modern offset press, the students printed their posters on the hand presses of the École des Beaux Arts. . . . The ability to make proper strategic use of the most advanced media was lacking. It was not the radio headquarters that were seized by the rebels, but the Odéon Theatre, steeped in tradition" (53). Of course, the risk always taken by formulations that appeal to the concept of "the most advanced media" (modern offset press!) is planned obsolescence. But what remains pertinent about Enzensberger's formulation is the articulation of the politics of popular revolt with radio—broadcasting versus pamphleteering. Virtually contemporaneous with Enzensberger's observations were Jacques Lacan's "impromptu" observations at Vincennes, hurled back into the impatient faces of his audience, to whom he famously quipped: "That is what experience has proved. What you, as revolutionaries, aspire to is a Master. You will have one" ("Impromptu" 126). Although a quite different account of the return of, or the fixation upon, the archaic from Enzensberger's, something here bearing on the link between psychoanalysis and radio calls for attention.

As if channeling Enzensberger's analysis of May 1968, on March 10, 1971, several members of the Front Homosexuel d'Action Révolutionnaire (FHAR), a group whose members later included the now widely recognized figures of Guy Hocquenghem and Christine Delphy, descended upon the Salle Pleyel to interrupt a live radio broadcast announced in *Le Monde* as part of a monthlong nationwide series on March 3, 1971. The show was convened by Menie Grégoire, a broadcaster with station RTL since 1967, well known in Paris as a magazine contributor and the host of an afternoon (3:00–3:30 p.m.) call-in talk show thought to engage in a form of wild and, in some circles, vulgar psychoanalysis. Her topic on the morning in question bore the title "L'homosexualité, ce douloureux problème" ("Homosexuality, This

Painful Problem"). Her guests included, in addition to a psychoanalyst, a priest, a representative of *Arcadie* (the precursor "homophile" organization to FHAR), a musical act (!), and a live audience in which were planted members of FHAR. The published transcript of the broadcast establishes that the interruption begins as the Q&A gets under way. It escalates from pointed questions and a "we're queer and we're here" declaration to the point at which Mme. Grégoire, after protesting the noise interfering with home reception of her show, is forced off the stage as the priest's head is being bounced off the dais table. Many commentators, among them Yves Roussel, Michael Sibalis, and Kristin Ross, give this event mythic proportions. Roussel and Sibalis in particular, by contrasting it with the Stonewall riots of the summer of 1969, see the interruption of this broadcast as the origin of homosexual activism in France, in effect, the birth of the homosexual rights movement there.

While there can be no doubt that Enzensberger would have approved the venue, he might well have demurred on the matter of the objective of this demonstration. Surely the point is not simply to disrupt but, as was once said in earnest, to liberate, to render the radio a two-way apparatus of communication, not just for thirty minutes but as part of a new social order. While the distinction between demonstration and organization is an important one, reducing this episode to its reiteration misses not only the fact that FHAR, an effective if short-lived organization, emerged from it but that radio—and especially radio as a medium, a channel for the dissemination of psychoanalytical knowledge (even if "vulgar"), sits at, even organizes, the core of this episode. Indeed, this last is a point largely overlooked by the many commentaries on this demonstration. To establish what is to be gained from attending to this fact, consider how the broadcast was, to use an overused formulation, structured like one.

In the transcript it is clear that these "live" shows were calculated attempts to reproduce the typical format of Mme. Grégoire's afternoon broadcast, a format that clicked back and forth between conversation in the studio (e.g., reading of letters, some now collected in *Comme une lame de fond* [Like a Groundswell], and chats with guest specialists) and conversation over the telephone with listeners. In the Salle Pleyel, this was reconstructed by substituting a microphone shared with the audience for telephones. Although large, this room did not require amplification for voices to be heard. The point of the microphone was to broadcast the audience's voices to the radio listeners. More than simply a technical substitution, the "live" format was designed to restage the closed-circuit character of the two-way communication typical of talk radio, although here—perhaps even more perversely—the host and her listeners literally shared the same line. It was perhaps predictable, then, that as audience members took up the microphone, precisely here the interruption got started. This was coupled, importantly, with "shouts" (that is, voices from the room not spoken into the microphone) that, regardless of what was said, challenged the relation between the form and content of the broadcast. As the scene unfolded it was doubtless hard to recognize this, but contact was made with the content through the challenge mounted by FHAR members to André Baudry (the head of *Arcadie*), a challenge formulated in terms of a repudiation of his call for tolerance. This challenge was crystallized around a distinction made, in increasingly heated exchange, between the psychogenesis of the homosexual and his or her repression. Maybe not even at bottom but at some profound level, this is also a distinction between psychoanalysis and politics. If tolerance finds its formal expression in turn taking and in sharing the available two-way circuit, then the overloading and transgression of that circuit—literally the physical flushing of the host—is the formal articulation of the repudiation of tolerance. The "birth" of FHAR was thus not simply recorded; it became the recording and its interrupted transmission. To invoke the dilemma of the "on," here was the political articulation of an "off" that is on the air, a sabotage that surrogated all listeners.

Saying this invites an elaboration of the implied link between a certain form and content of radiophonic practice and the enabling distinction between psychoanalysis and politics—and not only in France. It is tempting to treat Mme. Grégoire as a curio, as something like an exception, but this is only a convenience. One does not have to accept her obvious limitations in order to see in her conditions of possibility something more challenging, harder to simply ridicule. Of course she is a "pop" phenomenon, but it is worth recalling that this is precisely what was said of *Anti-Oedipus* when it appeared in 1972. As we have seen, the exception is never what simply proves the rule. In fact, it is the way it both belongs and doesn't belong to the rule that makes it worthy of reflection. Again, Mme. Grégoire does not need to understand this to be interesting; it suffices that she and her audience *believe* that something like psychoanalysis can be conducted over the airwaves. Radio and analysis are *thought,* and are therefore used as if compatible.

At the risk of pathologizing Mme. Grégoire, it is essential to acknowledge in this context Wolfgang Hagen's *Radio Schreber: Der "moderne Spiritismus" und die Sprache der Medien,* a stunning treatment of the spiritualist and techno-medialogical dimensions of Schreber's psychosis, among other things.[1] While in many respects this study teases out precisely the radiophonic mediation of the limits of psychoanalysis (both psychosis as the analytically inaccessible and spiritualism as the dubiously scientific), it is obliged to approach the ordinary vulgarity of psychoanalysis as mediated by radio from, as it were, the outside—way outside. In the Introduction I proposed another tactic, whose elaboration will allow me to proceed toward Hagen in accord with Freud's metaphor in "Three Essays on the Theory of Sexuality" (a text whose treatment of darkness and the voice Hagen has commented on), where Freud describes the movement from pregenital to genital sexuality by saying: "It's like the completion of a tunnel which has been driven through a hill from both directions" (207).

As is generally known, what began as the Princeton Radio Research Project (PRRP) was funded by grants from the Rockefeller Foundation. John Marshall was the foundation officer who took, as we say, ownership of the study from the institutional side. In the small archive of relevant papers in Princeton one comes upon correspondence between Hadley Cantril (then professor of psychology at Princeton) and Marshall in which Cantril is not only pitching the PRRP but doing so by characterizing, as he says in a letter of May 11, 1937, "the exact ways in which Project I [the PRRP was conceived as a sequence of two-year studies] will supplement and go beyond the research now being done by the radio industry" ("To John Marshall"). As Cantril goes on, he somewhat predictably mounts the hobbyhorse of his discipline, stressing that the PRRP will "pioneer" the discovery and use of techniques to "understand the complex problem of why people of various types" listen to radio. As it turns out, one of these pioneering techniques is psychoanalysis. Given, as Hagen reminds us, the vexed scientific status of psychoanalysis, one can see here *ab ovo* what was to explode after the war as the German *Positivismusstreit.* Importantly, radio is at the scene of this disciplinary conflict, the scene of what Cantril, unwittingly to be sure, calls the supplement.

Cantril's assertion came to fruition in the decision taken by his collaborator Paul Lazarsfeld (the then recently transplanted Austrian sociographer) to convene a meeting on December 16, 1939, with a group of psychoanalysts including Harry Stack Sullivan, John Dollard, Karen Horney, and Erich Fromm (who had been affiliated with the Institute for Social Research in Frankfurt since 1931). Two important documents from this meeting have survived: the "talking points" pre-pared by Fromm for this discussion (now archived among his papers at the New York Public Library) and the "notes" taken by Lazars-feld during this meeting (now archived among Lazarsfeld's papers at Columbia University). As neither of these texts is published, I include here my transcription of Fromm's rather ample and suggestive "talking points."

[Page 1]
Radio. [unclear] of discussion not answer the problem.

I *Problem*
1) *Topic:* What is the *reason* for the tenacious grip that *radio* has so swiftly secured on the mental life of men? (Cantril on telepathy).
2 Questions
1) What do we mean by Radio?
2) What is the specific reasoning [over crossed-out "viewpoint"] of psychoanalysts?
2) *What is radio in this psychological sense?*
a) its program. Radio only technical means; one could say this not a new problem, not problem of radio, but old problem of psychology of radio (music, humor, political speeches)
B) but nevertheless radio problem
a) radio gives much greater scope to/in this program [inserted above: other wise people couldn't hear it]
b) radio must create certain types of program
c) radio changes quality
b) the radio experience as such regardless of programmatic communication with the outer world
onesidedness of communication
production of music—easy [crossed-out "perfect"] creation as easy annotation
all are equal before the radio
same problem as with movies and car

[Page 2]
c) Problem meaning of voice. Also old problem, but new because voice isolated and decayed [unclear]
3) *What is particular viewpoint of analyst?*
a) Many answers possible: childhood [above, sexual aspects; below, free association method]
b) essential [above, influence] a) which [crossed-out "co"] unconscious impulses are satisfied, which [crossed-out "fears"] anxieties are allowed. = Dynamics of reaction
c) answer can not be general, namely to every body, but to certain [crossed-out "ch"] personality structure (detached [below, plus and minus] vs. need for affection [below plus and minus])

d) but ["here" inserted] only character structure which is socially relevant, not single peculiar neurotic.

II *The dynamics of the reaction to the program.*

1) depends on specific proposals and only dealt with concrete program.

2) I cannot say anything because I don't know it.

3) an Example [inserted, for problem] of movie where I am more familiar. Mickey mouse. Do *[sic]* which factors does it owe its immense popularity?

[Page 3]

b) Essential point: the big cannibalistic being pursues the female as helpless one but the latter is saved.

c) Interpretation: people's feeling of powerlessness as helplessness toward life, fear of being swallow *[sic]* by the big ones. This fear overcome by [crossed-out "participation"] identification of [crossed-out "in the"] the [crossed-out "sas"] victory of the small ones. At the same time identification with sadistic tendencies, but give satisfaction of security, thrill a *[sic]* excitement. [crossed-out "This only"] Premise: Feeling of powerlessness [crossed-out "of social"] [unclear].

d) Method of studying it.

For example: take 20 very much interested [crossed-out "an"] 20 little, 20 against a study permanently structure. (But problem of defense as reaction formation 1) (Hov *[sic]* in detail later.)

III. *The reaction of the radio experience.*

1) Overcoming of loneliness. Communication with world. [crossed-out "How necessarily?"] Price of isolation and loneliness in modern man. But necessarily: social contracts—seem to express necessary but partly express isolation. [Unclear]

[Page 4]

2) Possibility of letting the voice programmer [unclear] of hostility

3) The solidarity of the audience.

5) [Crossed-out "Problem of"] Producing something. Feeling of unproductivity and therefore insecurity due to opinion of labor and individualistic system.

4) Lack of active response, as in applause, onesidedness. Problem of democracy it seems to be the nature of radio to "encourage people and thus man [unclear] to feel alike" Democracy (development of individual, vs. Fascism (mass suggestion).

6) [Unclear] from tension alone in family.

IV *Method*

1) Usual sampling of specific cases

2) Specific

a) Questionnaire alpha) [crossed-out "spec"] [above, closed] questionnaire to [unclear] leading question, beta) *open questionnaire* with interpretation open answer reveals things [unclear] [Much here crossed out, both in body of outline and in left margin]

[Page 4 *(sic)*]
IV *Method*
1)usual samples of more or less interested
2) Questionnaire
a) closed questions
b) open
a) advantage of better statistical procedures
b) disadvantages:
a) [crossed-out "Does not allow for full express"]
b) leading question (Ex. responsible for fate)
beta) Does not allow full expression
gamma) Does not allow interpretation of most important nuances.
(Ex. Use of [unclear] analytic method of interpretation of important slips)
3) Dynamic personality test
[unclear, over "Handwriting" then in brackets] followed by interview
and compare with behavior to radio.
4) Personal interview [unclear] by surprise effects
what is it? [bracket with "formative" crossed out]
5) Free association—only possible if person is ready to face himself, no
trickery [above, formal disguise] otherwise poor.

Lazarsfeld's notes, which are, alas, both more stenographic and even more difficult to decipher, confirm that several of these points did indeed come up in discussion, although they also specifically mention certain examples introduced into the conversation by Karen Horney. To underscore that Hagen and I are indeed tunneling through the same hill, it suffices to point to the reference to telepathy on Fromm's first page, but it bears acknowledging that at least two of Fromm's specific formulations are in fact cited from the opening page of Cantril and Allport's *Psychology of Radio.* So where Fromm writes, "What is the reason for the tenacious grip that radio has so swiftly secured on the mental life of men?" Cantril and Allport write: "What they do not know, however, and what they would they very much like to know, is the reason for the tenacious grip radio has so swiftly secured on the mental life of men" (*Psychology* 3). Cantril and Allport also presciently compare radio to the automobile and the moving picture. Their evocation of telepathy comes in the form of a "wizard" (Mabuse or Schreber's God?) transmitting commands globally from a "central palace of broadcasting" (*Psychology* 3). Clearly, Fromm prepared for his conversation with Lazarsfeld et al. by boning up on the work of scholars known to be relevant to the thinking of his host, although he may have skipped over the discussion in *Psychology* about repetition and manipulation. This said, there are moments of suggestive sparking.

At the forefront of Cantril and Allport's introduction is the notion that radio is, as they say, "something new under the psychological sun" (yet another Schreberian allusion?), a development that "caught the social psychologist unprepared" even as—in virtually the same breath—they insist that "the really important problems of the radio now are psychological problems" (*Psychology* 4), implying that perhaps the most important psychological problem is precisely the one that probes the fit between radio and the psychological field. In a certain sense this reiterates the pose assumed in Cantril's letter to Marshall, but when we consider the matter in the context of the steps taken to follow through on the assertions made to Rockefeller, steps that included the gathering of analysts, then what is striking is that Fromm, in his talking points, seems spurred to grab the bull by the proverbial horns. He asks, "What do we mean by Radio?" followed by "What is the specific viewpoint/reasoning of psychoanalysis," and then synthesizes the two questions as "What is radio in this psychological sense?" Here we come to perhaps the most fundamental question: Is the difficulty one has in approaching radio due to the difference between psychoanalysis and psychology, or, put differently, are radio and psychoanalysis modes of the same substance, to invoke the vocabulary of Spinoza? If so, to reiterate Fromm, what do we mean by radio? Also, where did this enormous primate stand in the room (apparently a restaurant) where Lazarsfeld et al. had their discussion?

True to his more positivistic orientation, Lazarsfeld scans for research questions, examples, analytical techniques, and the like, but even he seems compelled to underscore the more probing philosophical problem when, under the broad heading of "Quality in Radio," he writes, as if to highlight something clearly noteworthy, "Radio as special exper[ience]." While it is true that this never expands to match Fromm's epistemological concerns, one clearly senses that in this conversation (or at least in its archival traces) the question of what psychoanalysis might bring to radio research is persistently haunted by the sense that a more fundamental, more pressing matter precedes this: namely, do we even know what we are trying to apply psychoanalysis to? Perhaps one way to make sense of the persistent fretting about novel research techniques—grant applicationese, but not merely that—is as a defense against the perplexity opened between radio and psychoanalysis in attempting to bring the latter to bear on the former?

This is more than a hunch. If one thinks about the modes of exemplification that operate in and between the two texts, it becomes clearer.

In Lazarsfeld's notes the example that is adduced is that of Charlie Mc-Carthy, the star of the ventriloquism show that was immensely successful on radio in the 1930s. In Fromm's talking points, the example used is that of Mickey Mouse. As Fromm provides one with more to go on, I take him up first. Fromm turns to the Disney character—not, by the way, a radio personality—on page 2 under the general heading, "The dynamics of the reaction to the program." As if implying that he was not a radio listener (and, in fact, the Fromm archive contains evidence that he was a subscriber to WQXR), Fromm appeals to Mickey Mouse after writing, "I cannot say anything because I don't know it," establishing that familiarity is essential to understanding reaction. He then provides us with a plot summary, "the big cannibalistic being pursues the female as helpless one but the latter is saved," followed by an interpretation.[2] As an account of the dynamics of reaction, the interpretation appeals to an identification both with the feeling of powerlessness, the fear of being swallowed by the big ones, and with the sadism of the big one, the excitement of triumph. Although inflected by the language of psychoanalysis, this reading of Mickey Mouse resonates rather obviously with the line that concludes Benjamin's essay on Disney's character from 1931, "It [the reason for the popularity of Mickey Mouse films] is simply the fact the public recognizes its own life in them" ("Mickey Mouse" 545). In this sense, Fromm's familiarity with this example is as much due to its public popularity as to the institute's account of it. But how precisely does this bear on the relation between radio and psychoanalysis?

Upon reflection one realizes that Fromm is trying to spur a conversation about people's reaction to radio, about—to invoke the reinvoked Cantril and Allport—the tenacious grip of radio on the mental life of men. He starts and then breaks off. He turns to what he knows. It is an animated story of cannibalism, a story of something big devouring something less big, and the concomitant feeling of powerlessness. Aside from film being used—as a medium thought to be more familiar—to make sense of radio, the content of the example stages Fromm's own dilemma. How not to be swallowed by something whose true nature escapes you? If we recall that the work that initially attracted Horkheimer to Fromm was work that obsessed over the character types of industrial capitalism (see, for example, Fromm's "Psychoanalytic Characterology and Its Relevance for Social Psychology" [1932]), then we can also recognize yet another dimension of the familiar, that is, Fromm's familiar way of thinking about the familiar. Thus it would be fair to hear in the example Fromm's effort to brandish his particular hybridization of Marx and Freud to avoid being consumed by the radio, our reaction to which both menaces and escapes us. What seems especially striking is that through the now familiar pairing of mass culture (film) and mental life, Fromm agitates the festering question of the adequacy of psychoanalytic knowing as concerns radio, implicitly conceding that the epistemological advantage of psychoanalysis over other techniques of study is that it knows that *it* doesn't know what radio is.

And what of Charlie McCarthy? Ed Miller, in his provocative reading of Welles's *War of the Worlds* broadcast, casts instructive light on Lazarsfeld's example.[3] He does so first by establishing that *The Chase and Sanborn Hour* was running concurrently with the Mercury Theater broadcast and then by teasing out the decisive link between a thrown voice (a voice thrown from, as the French would say, *le ventre* [the stomach], hence ventriloquism) and a voice from not inner but outer space with searing perlocutionary force. Miller shows convincingly how this programming serendipity contributed deeply to the uncanny impact of "the Invasion from Mars" (as it was renamed by Cantril and the PRRP). My point is simply this. If one recognizes in the example of Charlie McCarthy the motif of the voice from the stomach, then one recognizes instantly the point of contact between the two examples. That is, the anxiety about being swallowed, cannibalized (as we now say of dismantling other machines for spare parts) repeats in its own way the uncanny topography of the radio voice. Where does "it" come from, or, put differently, where is radio (coming from)? In this sense the examples push out ahead of or below all technical or methodological concerns. The question is not whether one hears voices on the radio and how psychoanalysis might approach them but whether radio *is* a voice, and if so, whose. Cantril and Allport put the matter with fitting decorum by describing radio as "the vast inhuman network of the air" (*Psychology* 4), so that the question of our reaction to it assumes acute urgency. Perhaps this is why, in his summary of the deep significance of Mickey Mouse, Benjamin wrote: "In these films mankind makes preparations to survive civilization" ("Mickey Mouse" 545).

Not surprisingly, the matter of the voice is raised insistently by Fromm, and in this his concerns again echo those of Cantril and Allport, who, as we have seen, devote an entire chapter of *Psychology* to the radio voice. As has been repeatedly demonstrated in these pages, this preoccupation with the voice is something of an alibi. It is the way to have the conversation about the "nature" of the radiophonic medium without having it. But here a different point suggests itself. If, as Dolar, among others, proposes to argue, the voice is the quintessential object of psychoanalytical attention, and if, as the preceding points suggest, the voice is the one way to pose the question about the nature of radio without asking it, then have we not stumbled upon a telling encounter between radio and psychoanalysis, one that prompts us to consider whether—beyond the event of origination—the FHAR's attack on Mme. Grégoire's RTL broadcast wasn't striking at the very heart of what radio and psychoanalysis share? Not voice, but voice as alibi, alibi for a form of knowledge that cannot come into existence in the absence of an enabling prohibition against it. In this sense, the FHAR's *prise de la parole* was more than a capture of speech, "taking the floor." It was intervention in the radio voice that engulfed it in queer sounds and, as such, transgressed the limit, the front, along which psychoanalysis and radio support each other.

Even though, as I have argued, one needs to avoid establishing a strict and austere difference between state-controlled and commercial radio, it is important to concede that U.S. radio broadcasting in the 1930s is not the same as French radio broadcasting in the 1970s. Moreover, the PRRP as a privately funded research project comes to the encounter between radio and psychoanalysis in a way that resists easy transposition to the Mme. Grégoire phenomenon. Even so, some of the more philosophical aspects of this uneven encounter ring true and thus survive this unevenness. The voice does appear to point at an intimacy between radio and psychoanalysis whose inner folds deserve further elaboration. With this in mind I dial back to France and to the critique of psychoanalysis, specifically to the radio work of Jacques Lacan and Félix Guattari.

The opening paragraphs of Lacan's much-thumbed essay "The Instance of the Letter in the Unconscious, or Reason since Freud" (originally a lecture delivered in the Descartes Amphitheater of the Sorbonne in 1957) contain an unusual evocation of the term *text,* later worked up and over by his "friends" at the journal *Tel Quel.* Lacan deploys the term to capture the peculiar status of his remarks, remarks that fall, as he emphasizes, midway *(á mi-chemin)* between writing (literally, *l'écrit*) and speaking *(la parole).* At one level he is merely pointing to the fact that a lecture became an essay, but precisely in stressing the motif of the midway, the between, he is not only complicating these facts but also drawing characteristic attention to the mode of enunciation, the means of transmission of what he insistently referred to as his teaching. That here, in a bold interrogation of the Cartesian *cogito,* Lacan insists upon the specifically textual character of that which is neither writing nor speaking is a matter of import to French intellectual history best left for another occasion.

Equally familiar is Lacan's reticence about publishing the writings gathered under the name *Écrits.* Some, Elisabeth Roudinesco among them, have argued that he felt compelled to publish in the context of the institutional quarreling taking place in and around the International Psychoanalytic Association, its French incarnation, and the various schools launched by Lacan, most famously the École freudienne de Paris. Lacan himself, in the "Overture to This Collection," after citing his formula concerning language and the unconscious—"that in language our message comes to us from the Other . . . in inverted form" (3–4)—goes on to suggest that his writings were transmitted in response to a reader, indeed a new reader. They are, presumably, the inverted form of a message sent to Lacan by this reader. They are, in this sense, midway between a reading that took the form of a demand, a speaking, and a writing that replied. Yet they are called writings, indeed writings in which the problem of their enunciation is posed over and over again. While it is always tempting to chalk such tics up to subjective factors— especially with analysts—the deliberation evident in Lacan's "texts" suggests, and suggests strongly, that this is one of those historiographic temptations better resisted. The question of transmission, of enunciation, of asking and answering or refusing to, addresses the very core of Lacan's intervention in the analytical tradition founded by Freud.

Friedrich Kittler, in *Gramophone, Film, Typewriter,* has pursued the matter by mapping onto each of his titular technologies one of Lacan's categorical transparencies—the imaginary (for film), the symbolic (for the typewriter), and the real (for the phonograph)—suggesting, as is his wont, that these categories are conceptual articulations of transformations wrought upon the human being by the advent and operation of the technology in question. As my debt to Kittler is at this point rather obvious, I'll add nothing further except to stress that my point here will be a different one. What is striking about the critical character of the problem of enunciation for Lacan is the way it found consistent expression in his thinking about and engagement with both radio and television. Indeed, it is this engagement that allows one to grasp what is to be grasped in Lacan's answer, doubtless inverted, to the question: What is radio for psychoanalysis?

Three texts will concern me in what follows: "Petit discours à l'ORTF," "Radiophonie," and, to a lesser extent, "Télévision," all now available online as audio files. Of these, "Radiophonie" is the center-piece, for reasons that will become obvious enough.

The "Small Discourse" (or "brief discussion" or tonally perhaps, "Modest Proposal") matters not only because, of these three, it comes first, but because its broadcast coincided with *Seuil*'s publication of *Écrits* in 1966. As underscored earlier, it matters that Lacan's remarks are a "response" to questions put to him by the host, George Char-bonnier (recognized in the Anglophone world as Claude Lévi-Strauss's interlocutor in "Conversations with Claude Lévi-Strauss"—also, by the way, a radio broadcast), a response later published on the pages of the journal *Recherches*. It is thus a text about writings that is itself "mid-way," perhaps even suspended, between speaking and writing. In fact, it is a text about a text about the psychoanalytic import of this midway. What does it transmit on this score?

A scant six pages in print, the essay opens with the trauma of seces-sion. Specifically, Charbonnier solicits Lacan's account of his "Discours de Rome" (the now much-anthologized "Function and Field of Speech and Language in Psychoanalysis" from 1953). This is an appropriate place to start, not only because this sprawling text is one of those writ-ings to be found in *Écrits* (the actual "Discours de Rome," the remarks delivered, that is, spoken, at the colloquium, is now available in the posthumous volume *Autres écrits*), but because it inaugurates on a de-cidedly international scene both Lacan's reading of Freud (his famous "return") and his defense of his teaching, specifically the technique con-demned by none other than Anna Freud, namely, the short session. As if channeling Saussure, who opens *The Course on General Linguistics* by asserting that linguistics can achieve scientific status only by delim-iting its proper object (what will come to be called the sign), Lacan appeals to the concepts of speech *(la parole)* and language *(langage,* not, as the evocation of Saussure might have led one to expect, *langue)* as the means by which to secure scientific status for psychoanalysis. For him, the "Discours de Rome" was the announcement, or better the enunciation, of this challenge to the psychoanalytical establishment. Immediately, in effect with the first deictically unstable *ici* (the third word of the text), Lacan broaches the vexing epistemological problem of psychoanalysis's intellectual authority. Thus Charbonnier is not sim-ply asking him about a psychoanalytic book. He is broaching, however unwittingly, the question of psychoanalysis, that is, what it is. Boldly, perhaps ill-advisedly, Lacan wants to discuss *this* "on the air." Live. The tactic obliges him to assume a pedagogical position and to conceive of his practice as a teaching.

As the program unfolds, Lacan makes the now familiar argument that the facts of Freud's science—the dream, the slip, and the joke—are all facts of language (again, *langage,* that is, not *a* language, but language *in general,* its concept), making sure that when he calls for listeners to "read" Freud, they are likewise charged with engaging the full presence of language in Freud's texts, of, in effect, relearning how to read. It is this precise sensitivity to language and the details of its enunciation that draws attention to the three places in Lacan's remarks where he speaks directly about his text, *Écrits.* He prepares us for this engagement by the rehearsal of some of his "formulas." First, "the unconscious is the discourse of the Other" and in this sense "exterior to the subject" ("Petit discours" 223, my translation). Second, "The desire of Man is the desire of/for the Other." Then, with these out of the way and without prompting from Charbonnier, he turns to *Écrits.*

As if hedging on his earlier claims to scientificity, he follows with the formulation "These propositions simply indicate a line of inquiry" ("Petit discours" 224, my translation), one intended largely for those in the analytical community who can make use of them—until now. In other words, the publication of his writings is conditioned, perhaps even called for, by recognition of the fact that they are no longer meant exclusively for analysts, not simply because they are now meant for everyone, but because the analytic community—as made obvious by the topic of secession with which the interview/broadcast began—resists this line of inquiry and its implications. Here Lacan sheds light on his later assertion in "Télévision" that "analytic discourse should be withheld from the rabble *[aux canailles]*" (43), suggesting that at the head of the pack of dogs are the practicing analysts bent on betraying Freud's science, decidedly *not* the undifferentiated unwashed. Lacan prepares the impact of this statement by saying in his opening remarks, "There's no difference between television and the public before whom I have spoken for a long time now, a public known as my seminar," followed by the impish but telling qualification, "Do not, however, get the idea that I address everyone at large *[à la cantonade]*" ("Television" 3). Strictly speaking, the Godardian character of "Télévision," in which Lacan is being addressed offscreen and more or less from the position of the camera/spectator by a fellow analyst, Jacques-Alain Miller, undercuts the provocative character of the assertion regarding the isotopy of his two audiences. Indeed, the broadcast is exactly like his seminar, but precisely in having little if anything to do with television, a fact, noted by many commentators, that the medium is written off in the exaggerated pantomime of Lacan's voice and gestures (he broaches the matter of castration with his hands stuffed in the pockets of his pants, rolls his "r's" throughout, etc.). What complicates this and brings psychoanalysis back into account is the pun, emphasized by Lacan's English translators, on *la cantonade,* for when it is retyped as *lacan tonade* one sees that the question of audience, the object of transmission, is structured like a language. One's message is sent in response to a message that arrives in inverted form. One is never speaking either simply to oneself or to others. In this, television is exactly like the site of analytic transmission, or teaching.

In the "Petit discours" this cluster of associations gathers in the "*jusqu'à maintenant*" (until *now*). While on the one hand it is clear that Lacan is here referring to the publication date of *Écrits* (the now of 1966) as the moment when his teaching reached a different public, presumably the site of the new reader, on the other, his "now" refers to December 2, 1966, the date of the broadcast, and to the radio audience as such. Together these hands produce the clap whereby the isotopic audiences in "Télévision" flash into view in "Petit discours." Certainly it is important that in justifying the publication of the writings through which Lacan proposed to challenge the psychoanalytical establishment he was moved to stress not simply the question "To whom does this science address itself?" but the question "Literally, in what way is the structure and dynamic of address, of enunciating the one *in* and *to* the many, part and parcel of the becoming scientific of psychoanalysis, of finding its epistemological footing in language?" In this he recognizes the special intimacy between radio and psychoanalysis, implying that one answers Fromm's question—What is radio for psychoanalysis?—by pointing to the way radiophonic transmission embodies—not exemplifies, but embodies—the structure of language sheltered in the repressed core, the burrow, of the Freudian discovery. It seems especially important to have signaled this insight by cuing a distinctly Saussurean but equally ethereal figure, insisting that human beings are "immersed in a bath of language" ("Petit discours" 223, my translation). Although Lacan deploys this figure to secure the naturelike objectivity of language, it works, perhaps even more dramatically, to clarify precisely in what way, and at what level of experience, television and a seminar divvy up a public. Everyone's scalp is tousled by the ether wind in which radio transmission was long thought to take place. This action-at-a-distance is exterior to all subjects, and in this sense the question of what *is* psychoanalysis finds its affective connection in a form of subjectivation—a way of being a subject—held in common by listeners and analysts.

The second explicit invocation of *Écrits,* or, as he calls it, "my book," follows immediately upon a derisive summary of current nonsense about the status of sexuality in what then (that is, prior to the *now*) passes as psychoanalysis. Again, Lacan is keen to underscore the metacritical character of his enterprise. Importantly, as part of this repetition, Lacan also returns to the question of audience, of the reception of his transmission, if in a somewhat "arch" fashion. He says/writes: "What I am saying here [his rejection of the role of unconscious prohibition in sexuality] the whole world knows, but each of us *[chacun]* merely comforts himself with the easy accommodation of the most hackneyed superstitions" ("Petit discours" 225, my translation). On the face of it this is a version of the line from the section on fetishism in the first volume of *Capital* made memorable by Slavoj Žižek: "They do not know this, but they do it" (Marx 88, my translation). In other words, the whole world already knows the truth of what Lacan is saying about language and sexuality, but people cling to their hackneyed superstitions without realizing it. This archly recrafts the isotopic audiences but now in the modality of self-deception: there are the ones in the know that are in fact ignorant (analysts), and the ones not in the know who are made to feel ignorant (the public). Again, the seminar and the public. Then, as if on cue, he refers to his book. Actually, he is more subtle. He says: "My *Écrits* assemble the bases of the structure for a science that remains to be constructed—and structure means language—for which language would furnish the foundations" ("Petit discours" 225, my translation). Contributing to the subtlety of this formulation is the way it both does and does not mention his book. English grammar obstructs the effect of saying in French "*mes écrits,*" where it is possible to say both "my writings" and "my *Writings*" (the book *Écrits*), an effect that extends here to the scene of audition, restating in yet another way the problem of transmission but now in the form of a book that isn't one because it is simply writings in general. This problem, rendered in the code, the language structure of Lacan's statement, now makes the space of the book ambiguous. Put differently, the problems posed *within* it are now indistinguishable from the problems posed *by* it, or, at the very least, by the effects (doubtless, some infelicitous) that arise in speaking about them/it (problems, writings, book?) over the radio. Indeed, radio is itself engulfed in the forking deixis of "*Ce que je dis là . . .*" (What I am saying here/there), where the "here/there" could be any of three places: *Écrits,* the immediately preceding moment of the broadcast, and, as Benveniste would almost certainly stress, the discourse itself.

The final reference to the book occurs as the "Petit discours" concludes. In the penultimate paragraph he returns to the "*mes Écrits*" formulation, but now in the context of a final pirouette on the question: Why am I publishing this material? As if eager to establish that, unlike the betrayers of Freud, he grasps his enterprise in terms of his own analytically charged formulas, Lacan insists that he was compelled to publish by dint of the requests he received, as he says, "from the place of the Other," from "those to whom I listen" ("Petit discours," 226, my translation). In effect, by finding himself at large *(à la cantonade),* that is, in the position of his audience, he was compelled to gather "my writings." To render the full implications of such precise formulations impossible to miss, Lacan makes use of the transitive verb *émettre* (to transmit or broadcast) when characterizing the dissemination of "his *Writings.*" This, wired to his self-presentation as a receiver of that to which he listens, strongly suggests that he sees *Écrits* as a transmitter, as, in effect, a radio. Although the concept of "transference" is not expressly addressed here, it would seem that the formulation from "The Founding Act" (published the preceding year) is on his mind: "The teachings of psychoanalysis can only be transmitted from one subject to another by transference" ("Television" 103), where both transmission (in the French, *transmettre*) and transference are called for with equal urgency.

To seal the deal, as it were, the final reference to the book makes use of the locution, again deictically fraught, "*ces Écrits*" (these Writings). Indeed, the final statement of the broadcast "reads": " It will be necessary for me, with these Writings, to bar [*mettre une barrière*] the covetousness now stirring among the forgers always ready to march under the banner of the Spirit" ("Petit discours" 226, my translation). Those eager to read "negation" into Lacan's reluctance to accept the equation drawn by Freud between knowledge and paranoia might well adduce such a sentence to support this contention, but a different point suggests itself as well. It concerns the barrier. Specifically, it is important to recall that in his *Écrits,* for example, in "The Instance of the Letter," where Lacan throws his full weight behind Saussure's algorithm for the sign, Lacan characterizes the bar, "*la barre,*" as "*une barrière*"

(254) that resists signification. While it is certainly true that Lacan is concerned to tweak Saussure's algorithm (a fact detailed at length in Bruce Fink's *Lacan to the Letter*), it is no less true that this is motivated by the drive to intensify the rigor, the scientificity, of Saussure's contribution. In effect, his approach is anaclitic: he seeks to prop the properly delimited objects of psychoanalysis and linguistics upon one another. Thus, returning to the "Small Discourse," when Lacan says/ writes that his Writings will have to bar the covetousness of his forgers, it is clear that he is insisting not only upon the need to declare differences, to define the terms of a dispute, but on the role that the sign is destined to play in this struggle as well. Indeed, it is this insistence upon the letter (Lacan's contentious rearticulation of the "material support" of the sign), as transferred through the virtual homophony of barrier and banner, that calls for the otherwise unmotivated invocation of the spirit (the mind, the god, the joke, the journal) that concludes the piece. Again, and the reiteration is suggestive in its own right, he links the analytical statements of his book—the theory of signification, or, as he prefers, "*signifiance*"—to its fraught enunciation between, as it were, two audiences: the public at large (here the listening public) and the analytic community, especially those within it seeking to forge, to counterfeit, Lacan's innovations, a task rendered improbable if not impossible by the professional envy obstructing their understanding. The fact that "my Writings" gives way finally to "these Writings," where the pronominal drift away from the possessive situates the event of the broadcast, as it were, midway between speech and writing urges us to recognize, from yet another angle, the implied extimacy between radio and a psychoanalysis worthy of its scientific ambitions.

So much for the "Petit discours." Is it exceptional? Does the relation it stages between the metacritique of psychoanalysis and radio fade with this transmission? My earlier appeals to "Télévision" (the televised exchange with Miller) would suggest otherwise, but to elaborate the point and to tease out further Lacan's response to the "what is radio for psychoanalysis" question, I dial now to his "big discourse" on radio, "Radiophonie," from June 1970.

Those who have read or listened to the seven "responses" that constitute the "Radiophonie" broadcast recognize that it is contemporaneous with Seminar 17, "The Other Side of Psychoanalysis." Indeed, several contributors to the Clemens and Grigg volume *Jacques Lacan and the Other Side of Psychoanalysis,* refer to the broadcast, if only in passing. What brings this feature out is Lacan's persistent recourse to the motif of discourse, or more specifically to the thesis of the four discourses: that of the master, the analyst, the hysteric, and the university. That in a statement enunciated "on" the radio there appears to be no discourse of radio (or mass culture more generally) strikes one as odd, until one understands that this discourse—such as it is—takes place between the explicit, albeit passing, remarks about radio and the considerably less explicit, perhaps even unconscious, remarks made, not about radio as such, but, for example, about Sartre's discussion in the *Critique* of the function of impotence in effecting the movement from the subject to the agent. Interestingly, such remarks occur precisely as "someone named Lacan" (the function of indirection will require explanation) struggles in question 7 with the problem of psychoanalysis's contradictory, perhaps impossible but certainly vexing, attachment to the discourses of which it purports to be critical, underscoring the extent to which "Radiophonie" is also, among other things, a probing meditation on the "nature" of psychoanalysis. Thus radio (maybe even the discourse of radio) is lodged at the midpoint (where else?) of the barrier between the discourse of the analyst and the discourse of the university. In this it assumes a complex and radiant relation to the recurrent motif of "influence," here the carrier of transmission and transference.

The motif of influence comes up quickly. In fact, the first of Lacan's responses is to a question that asks, in reference to *Écrits,* in what sense Freud anticipated Saussure. As if picking up where the "Small Discourse" left off, Lacan frames his response initially by underscoring how the question cuts to the quick of the very pretensions of an interview and subsequently by linking this gesture to the suggestion that reading his book, while better than not reading it, is no guarantee that understanding will arise between interviewer and interviewee. An antemetabolic parallel is sketched between the question of anticipation and the anticipation of the question, a parallel that puts the give-and-take of an interview in play. In what follows, this complication of the temporality of the message, literally of the communicative distribution of sender and receiver, not only raises unsettling questions about the logic of anticipation, that is, who influenced whom, but becomes the matrix out of which a startling, even properly ethereal question about the relation between radio and psychoanalysis emerges.

As Lacan, or someone just like him, elaborates his point, he tries again something put to good effect in the "Petit discours": he complicates the question of anticipation by repositioning both Freud and Saussure. Observing that Saussure's decisive contribution to linguistics—the one that provided it with an object worthy of scientific recognition—was the bar between the signifier and the signified, Lacan, as if slyly exemplifying the concept of metaphor, substitutes for it the term "cut" *(la coupure)*. More than just a separation, this cut is then deployed to problematize the reality of the thing signified (he produces the phonological metonymy, *l'achose,* the not-a-thing, out of *la chose*) in a way that associates the bar with Freud's topography of the psychical apparatus. He can then propose, not that Freud anticipated Saussure, but that the unconscious anticipated linguistics, or, in the terms of the "Petit discours," that analysts and the public at large are in the same lifeboat when it comes to the challenges put before them by psychoanalysis. Put differently, "something" was at work on both Freud and Saussure that affected their disciplinary interventions in analogous ways.

Not content to complicate the relation between Freud and Saussure, Lacan then proceeds to complicate the concept of anticipation by exploring its relation to influence, the first step of which is to suggest that the unconscious is what propelled linguistics outside the university. Strictly speaking, Lacan has in mind here the "discourse of the university," being fully aware that Saussure's formulations were transcribed by students in a university setting, and a Swiss one at that. Because a responsible characterization of what Lacan intends by "the discourse of the university" would take us far afield (see Clemens and Grigg for several useful glosses), I will instead underscore Lacan's proposition that *influence* is a term that circulates in this discourse and does so to secure and protect its functioning. In a dense yet rich passage he writes: "But the university has not had the last word. It will make this whole story [the relation between Freud and Saussure] into a dissertation topic: the influence [same word in French] of Freud's genius on the genius of Saussure. This will show how the one got wind of the other before radio existed. We act as though the university did not always live without this radio that has so deafened us" ("Sign, Symbol," 205, translation modified). The clear implication of his immediately subsequent turn back to the notion of anticipation is that the question about anticipation from M. Georgin is framed *within* the discourse of the university, where what substitutes for anticipation—as if in Greimasian rotation—is the notion of influence. In effect, the question about anticipation has been anticipated, even preempted, by the discourse of the university, where insight into the way the unconscious anticipates all speaking subjects— the "speakers" of linguistics, to be sure—is obstructed, perhaps even repressed, by the dominant concept of influence. In a cutting move, of which Lacan was the master, he implicates Georgin in the deafness promulgated by radio, a deafness that desensitizes both the host and presumably his "listeners" to their collaboration with the discourse of the university.

Deafness, in this context, certainly calls to mind Sartre's "silence," but it sparks differently when thought about in relation to genius and wind. Why is the university interested in both or either? I would argue that these formulations follow from Lacan's earlier remarks on the occult and telepathy. Framing these themes in the context of an attack on the model of communication where language becomes a tool, Lacan takes them up as a way to ridicule the notion of wordless expression, that is, communication from, as it were, soul to soul. Even Freud, as Hagen has drawn to our attention, is not spared Lacan's ridicule on this score. Thus, if the discourse of the university traffics in genius and wind, it is because both belong to the enduring intellectual paradigm in which occult, that is, nonmaterial, forces are understood to permit a uniquely spiritual or psychical form of communication of the sort thought to transpire among the geniuses populating the high ground of what Nietzsche called "monumental history." Wind, of course, when not simply "hot air" or flatulence, is the medium of choice when one refuses recourse to the "little bird" that typically communicates from a source whose location resembles "black space." In the wind, in the air, on the radio: this is the clear channel of associations that prompts Lacan to implicate the very medium through which he is "communicating" in the general deafness that he protests. Although no mention is made of Victor Tausk—Freud's vexed and vexing disciple—it certainly seems that Lacan is here channeling the former's concept of the "influencing machine" *(des Beeinflussungapparates)* in attaching as he does the radio to the university's substitution of influence for anticipation.[4]

One way, certainly, of dealing with what earlier I referred to as Lacan's indirection, his persistent yet inconsistent recourse to the third person when discussing himself, would be as an effect "suggested" by the Moebian complicity at work within his enunciative practice. If radio, precisely in obscuring the limits of the discourse of the university—does it really predate the advent of radio?—sustains a deafness that renders unthinkable the anticipatory structure of the unconscious, and if this last is the meaning of "Lacan" as the carrier of the discourse of analysis, then perhaps Lacan can *never* speak in his own name. His voice must always be set off, rendered as an iteration of itself when heard on the radio. This auto-affec(ta)tion, this positing of an action-at-a-distance within the orbit of his own thought, finds an extraordinary elaboration, indeed one that renders his sense of radio's relation to psychoanalysis far more ambitious than that of Sartre, with whom, nevertheless, he remains in contact, if not precisely in dialogue.

In the final "response" to the first set of interviews (questions 1–4), Lacan takes up the question of Freud's relation to Copernicus, or the Copernican revolution. Specifically, M. Georgin asks Lacan to clarify in what sense the discovery of the unconscious constitutes a second Copernican revolution that subverts any theory of knowledge. Lacan's response is provocative whether taken right side up or upside down, that is, inverted. He begins by reminding listeners that Freud (in the *Introductory Lectures*) had already made the connection between his work and the work of Copernicus. He then adds, however, that Freud himself did not grasp the deep meaning of this association. Specifically, Freud did not recognize that geocentrism and heliocentrism are nonantagonistic models, a point that requires appreciation of the fact that in both models the geometry of the circle as the astro-mechanical inscription of a radiant and perfect god remains unquestioned. Put differently, centrism of whatever stripe presumes a center. To move this forward in the mix, Lacan proposes that both models be seen as versions of "photocentrism," that is, models in which light, whether physical or metaphysical, is understood to emanate from the meaningful order of concentric orbits themselves. What then requires a second Copernican revolution is the discovery of the unconscious, that is, the structure of language in general mediating the subject's relation to *any* model of meaning whatever. The center that cannot hold must be displaced. The circle must be broken.

One finds what amounts to a migratory pattern in Lacan's work with regard to the discussion of Copernicus. He returns to it time and again. Just as compulsively Lacan presents the brilliant historian of science Alexandre Koyré as his guide to and through this material. In fact, when the matter is raised in Seminar 20, "Encore," Lacan explicitly hectors his listeners about whether they have taken any of his many hints to go back to Koyré. It is not hard to see why. In "Radiophonie" Koyré is adduced as Lacan's authority on the "photocentric" dimension of the Copernican revolution, but he is also invoked as the figure who helps Lacan grasp what eludes Freud's grasp of the matter. Specifically, when one consults Koyré's *Newtonian Studies* what leaps out is his fascination with the enigma of gravitation, in other words, the problem of thinking the structural coherence of a system without a center.

In effect, what Lacan is attracted to in Koyré's study is the way that, precisely through the motif of attraction-at-a-distance, it stages what Althusser meant by the concept of "structural causality," that is, the idea that relations among effects can bring their cause into being.[5] This is important to Lacan primarily because it obliges us to recognize the radical agency of structure, or, at the end of the day, the unconscious. But there is something else there too, something that prompts him to write "that nothing plays there [in the Newtonian account of gravitation] the role of the medium in transmitting that force" ("Radiophonie" 422), where the motif of "transmission" reappears at precisely the moment where Lacan seizes upon what is missing from Freud's appraisal of Copernicus: the physical, psychic, and scientific—that is politico-epistemological—danger of the nothing, the electromagnetic vacuum.[6]

Here, however, one must return Lacan the favor he has done Freud. For just as Freud can be said to have underplayed the radicality of his reference to Copernicus (and Darwin, let us not forget), Lacan can be said to have—and he would appreciate the formulation—misrecognized the radicality of his reference to Koyré. Specifically, what reappears in Koyré's discussion is the vexed motif of the occult. This motif arises in Newton's face-off with Leibniz, where the latter accused Newton's concept of gravitation of having necessary recourse to an occult phenomenon, namely miracles, writing, "This lazy hypothesis would destroy equally our philosophy which seeks reasons and divine wisdom which furnishes them" (qtd. in Koyré 140). The sting in Leibniz's charge is not simply that Newton's reasoning is faulty but that it appeals to something that undermines the very concept of reason, or, to invoke M. Georgin, something that subverts *any* theory of knowledge. Not surprisingly, in the context of the seventeenth-century debates, this subversion teeters, as it were, on the edge separating physics and metaphysics in efforts to account not only for attraction-at-a-distance but for the space of the void, its status as an entity, especially one that might support gravitation. If we recall that Lacan earlier appealed to the occult and telepathy in order to dismiss the notion that thoughts can be communicated in the absence of language, one not only sees the parallel between telepathy and gravitation but in that very moment of lucidity also wonders at Lacan's antipathy toward the former. Like Newton, Lacan—who repeats the mantra of Saussure's scientificity every chance he gets—wants faith (and certainly the Christian god), if not out of the picture, then reduced to anamorphic proportions, but what this lets slip is the radicality of the confrontation between psychoanalysis and science. The danger of the nothing as a medium is that it is void of science (of a physics without a metaphysics) but also of religion, which, at the end of the day, is a theory of knowledge, and never more so than when disguised as something else, say, a belief system. The point here is that Lacan, in insisting upon the authority of Koyré, *should* be more sympathetic to what the occult signifies, not so as to abandon his commitment to the structural causality, the material effects, of language, but precisely to recognize the void agitating, we might even say structuring, this structure. Although their dispute was more framed as a philosophical one, here Derrida's challenge to Lacan's phono-phallogo-centrism can be restated in relation to the status of psychoanalysis within the history of science, a history of which Lacan was keenly aware.[7]

Truly interesting is the fact that this is also all about radio, or, more specifically, about the question: What is radio for psychoanalysis? Perhaps the most serious shortcoming of Milutis's otherwise remarkable subtitle "The Nothing That Connects Everything" is that in the course of his study there is insufficient ado about nothing. By the same token, in reminding us that the ether was, somewhat ambiguously, thought to be the medium not only of light but of sound, he prompts us to puzzle over the matter of how to think about radio's relation to the ether and nothing. As if conceding the point made about his misrecognition, Lacan brings radio into his discussion of Koyré through the trope of "deafness." The paragraph immediately following his formulation about the nothing that mediates the transmission of gravitation reads: "For there indeed is the scandal that the conscience of the laity (whose stupidity, conversely *[tout à l'inverse]*, made the parishioners a rabble) ended up censoring, simply by making itself deaf" ("Radiophonie" 422, my translation). Certainly, in one sense Lacan is simply repeating the familiar story about the conflict between faith and reason, a conflict that led Bruno to be executed by Rome and Galileo to recant. However, the necklace of signifiers—medium of transmission, inversion, the rabble, deafness—loops around material that has already been shown to bear on the medium of the radio itself. One thinks of the problem of the two audiences, the message that returns from the other in inverted form, and, of course, the point made earlier in "Radiophonie" regarding the "radio that has so deafened us." In effect, Lacan appears to be setting out a parallel between those caught up in the discourse of the university and the subjects of church censure. To what end, especially since such a parallel would appear to complicate some of the historical aspects of the theory of the four discourses?

Again, the matter at hand treats something Lacan himself treats obliquely at best, but consider that midway between the radio audience and the seventeenth-century flock stands, or vibrates, a question about how the word, or, compressed further, a signal, travels. Who sends signals? How, literally, do they get where they are going? And what are they saying to us? What impressed Lacan about Koyré was the way he recognized that gravitation posed versions of these questions to Newton and his contemporaries. Some of the inverted responses solicited by such questions shook the belief structures that held together not only emergent scientific paradigms but, at the same time, the world of secularism to which those paradigms belonged, as well as the nonsecular world thereby pitched against it. Lacan proposes that to deflect the consequences of this shakeup, this "Lisbon Earthquake," communities resort to deafness, a deafness tuned not to the silence of nothing but to the murmur of the excessively familiar. By associating this form of deafness, an apotropaic deafness, with radio, does he—or someone like him, someone speaking in or from his place—not also invite us to hear on radio, perhaps even in "Radiophonie," its relation to "the nothing that connects everything," but here rendered as our limitless encounter with the void that rushed into our ears when the ether dropped out from underneath radio signals in the early twentieth century?[8] As has been observed by many, the "ether theory" died hard; indeed, Einstein—well aware of the failed Michelson-Morley experiment of the previous century—was attempting to rescue the ether for general relativity well into the 1920s, just as wireless was going live. Koyré, who had relatively little to say in print about Einstein (although they were colleagues at the Institute for Advanced Study), would figure prominently among those urging us to recognize in this agony of the ether more than a mere physical problem. After all, Einstein was still toying with god; he just insisted that god wasn't toying with us.

In ways, then, that resonate with concerns voiced in "Petit discours," "Radiophonie" addresses itself to the structure of the scientific revolution that is the "return to Freud," in effect that, for Lacan, *is* psychoanalysis. Armed here with the question of influence and its complication, Lacan tries to tease out how language in general as structure, as the unconscious that is "outside," is both traced within the second Copernican revolution and active in the very break-in of the nothing, the void, that this revolution heralded without being able to face. By insisting that, under such circumstances, turning a deaf ear emerges as an attractive option, Lacan as interviewee simply continues talking.

Precisely because, after insisting upon the deafness imposed by radio, Lacan remains on the air and continues to speak, it is clear that deafness is not silence, a point made explicit when in his response to question 6 he observes that, given what he has said, he is astonished to have said so much over the radio ("Radiophonie" 442). In fact, as becomes even more evident in "Television," what arises under such circumstances is a now familiar distinction between speech and the voice (in "Radiophone" between listening and hearing/understanding), where voice assumes its value as a way to mark the phatic character not only of a signal whose content is turned down but of a signal whose inaudibility reflects its troubled passage through a vacuum, the void. As Dolar, among others, has argued, this voice is essential to any psychoanalysis worthy of the name, and it is clear that Lacan's studied invocation of deafness is designed to put it in play. Less clear is precisely how he wants us to then think about radio in concert with this voice. Is it, as the occasion, the condition, for "this" performance of the voice, likewise essential to what psychoanalysis is? What would that mean? That radio *is* the deafness inflicted upon human life by the wound suffered when the real menace of heliocentrism, the delayed *(nachträglich)* discovery of the structural unconscious, set up shop in the human universe of the face to face? Perhaps here the tendency within contemporary scholarship on radio, inside or outside radio studies per se, to model radio sound on the voice finds here its warrant, as if the now global embrace of interdisciplinarity expressed itself through a persistent yet "off the radar" allusion to Lacanian psychoanalysis. Or so might one suggest were one to tease out, as I am essaying here, the deafening yet unspoken implications of Lacan's attraction to Koyré as a way to think the "outbreak" of psychoanalysis on radio. To be sure, who or whatever it is that addresses the speaker "Lacan" in the third person leaves a surfeit of clues, including, of course, the very fact of indirection. To take my most recent example: "For there [in the disappearance of the medium of gravitational attraction] indeed is the scandal that the conscience of the laity (whose stupidity, conversely *[tout à l'inverse],* rendered the parish a rabble) ended up censoring, simply by making itself deaf" ("Radiophonie" 422). Midway, as it were, between the scandalized conscience of the laity and the radio-like deafness you have the expression "*tout à l'inverse.*" "Conversely" or even "completely opposite" but also, in a series of responses that have constant recourse to the motif of the four discourses being elaborated in the then contemporaneous seminar "L'envers de la psychanalyse," the virtual homonym between *inverse* and *envers* would appear to insinuate, in the form of interference, the question of psychoanalysis but now in the mode of a reflection on its "other side," its "reverse." Importantly, this does not appear to be the "reverse" brandished decades earlier by the likes of Lowenthal and Adorno—"Mass culture is psychoanalysis in reverse"—where radio is thought to contradict the analytical practice it faithfully opposes. Instead, as if unsure as to how he wants to land on the question, Lacan keeps radio lodged, as it were, in the problem psychoanalysis poses both for itself and for science. It would be fair to say that the question is no longer "What is radio for psychoanalysis?" but "What *isn't* psychoanalysis on radio?"

Clearly, this casts a rather different light on Menie Grégoire and her *differend* with the FHAR, not to mention her approach to radio as a site of analysis. To detail the spectrum of this light, another questioning of psychoanalysis and one attuned to the politics of radiophonic practice solicits attention. I am thinking here of the work of Félix Guattari, as it formed in the context of his radical clinical practice, but particularly as it formed as part of the "free radio" movement in both Western Europe (largely Italy and France) and Japan. Perhaps the two most important statements made by Guattari on this front are his 1978 preface to Collective A/Traverso's *Radio Alice, radio libre,* "Des millions et des millions d'Alice en puissance" ("Millions and Millions of Potential Alices"), and his 1978 contribution to the communist cultural magazine *La Nouvelle Critique,* "Popular Free Radio" ("Les radios libres populaires"). These are formulated prior to his later interest in media ecology, to which I will pay much less attention, even as I retrieve scattered formulations on radiophonic practice from across his corpus.

A late self-characterization of his theoretical and political project is instructive. "My perspective involves shifting the human and social sciences from scientific paradigms toward ethico-aesthetic paradigms" (*Chaosmosis* 10). Published in the year of his death, this formulation suggests not only that Guattari sees his own work turning more to ethics and art but that he thinks about this turn in the terms, circulated by Thomas Kuhn, for explaining the Copernican revolution, among other things. Thus he is expressly thinking about the need for a paradigm shift and in that sense would appear to accept the framework of his teacher and foil, Lacan. The recently published *Anti-Oedipus Papers* (2006) makes clear just how fraught this relation was, but not, as is often the case, because of the narcissism of the smallest difference. Although both men were caught up in a confrontation with the psychoanalytical establishment, for Guattari Lacan was in significant ways part of that establishment, a dilemma Lacan struggled to both acknowledge and deny. As we have seen, Lacan's sense of the relevance of Copernicus to his own project was tied to a complication of Freud's account of the displacement effected by heliocentrism. This complication was indexed to Lacan's concept of the unconscious as the agency of a systemic mode of structural causality, a concept whose practical and specifically thera-peutic implications caused him to run afoul of Anna Freud and others in the international psychoanalytic establishment. Guattari's challenge was pitched differently, no less "cosmologically" but differently. Per-haps predictably, it leads to a different position "on" radio.

Stated perfunctorily, Guattari's challenge was mounted through the strategy of clinical innovation, especially as it might be brought to bear on what is called "institutional psychotherapy." If Lacan sought to re-think the logical time of the analytical session, Guattari sought to re: work the space of analysis. This was approached not simply as an alter-native, an option among several, but as a completely different way to think the condition of possibility for human subjects. Instead of trying to reach the unreachable through the "talking cure," Guattari and his collaborator Jean Oury sought to access troubled subjects, often deeply troubled subjects, by using institutional space and spatial practices ef-fectively to recast them as new subjects. In "La Borde: A Clinic Unlike Any Other" (1977), the English title alone might be said to have said it all. For not only was La Borde not just unlike other such endeavors (the French, "un lieu psychiatrique pas comme les autres," stresses this), but it was unlike any Other, that is, it was an incarnation of the posi-tion of the Other that for Guattari had little or nothing to do with the object cause of desire in the Lacanian sense. If one's speaking, precisely to be full of truth, must seek a response, even and especially when that response is silence, then an inaccessible alterity is the very presupposi-tion of the cure. The point is not that one *is* cured but that the desire for such a condition remains radically possible. Against this Guattari pits La Borde, firm in his conviction that traditional psychoanalysis is con-demned at best to discover the social components of neurosis through the patient labor of the individual case instead of grasping these compo-nents directly, that is, in their immediacy as elements in the very subject-hood of the patient.

It is then far from uninteresting that in "La Borde" Guattari circles back to another key figure in his own formation: Sartre. Describing the broad ambitions of the clinic that wasn't one, he writes: "A word that was fashionable then was 'seriality,' which defined, according to Jean-Paul Sartre, the repetitive and empty character of a mode of existence arising from the way a practico-inert group functioned. What we aimed for through our multiple activities, and above all through the assumption of responsibility with regard to oneself and to others, was to be disengaged from seriality and to make individuals and groups reappropriate the meaning of their existence in an ethical and no longer technocratic perspective" (191).

In an interview given to the *Frankfurter Rundschau* four years earlier (Guattari, "Interview"), Arno Munster reminds Guattari that this is far from the first time the problem of seriality figured prominently in his work. Although Munster points directly to "Le étudiant, le fou et le katangais," a statement issued in the wake of the student uprisings in 1968, he might just as easily have pointed to any number of the pieces in the still largely untranslated *Psychanalyse et transversalité,* where the signature concept of "transversality" is elaborated in direct confrontation with Sartre's lexicon (seriality, totalization, etc.), suggesting clearly that much more than "fashion" was at stake in the legacy of Sartre. Indeed, one might argue that although Sartre was a figure who mattered to Lacan—the opening moves of Seminar 17, "The Other Side of Psychoanalysis," take up *Being and Nothingness* directly—Guattari is the one who succeeds in linking the sociopolitical stakes of the *Critique* to a challenge to the psychoanalytic establishment. Because several of the contributions to *Psychanalyse et transversalité* date back to the 1950s and 1960s (the collection, however, was published the same year as *Anti-Oedipus*), it is not surprising that Sartre's meditation on dialectical reason was still very much in the air. And although Guattari does not take up Sartre's extended discussion of the radio broadcast, it is fair to say that tension between seriality and transversality finds expression in Guattari's embrace of free radio.[9] Or so it will be proposed here.

For Sartre, as argued in "On the Air," seriality belongs to the much larger theoretical and political project of articulating existentialism and Marxism. The *Critique* is deeply marked by the French experience of de-Stalinization. Not surprisingly, Guattari's elaboration of the concept of "transversality," by which he understands, among other things, the process to which the practico-inert is continuously subjected such that it is corrosively menaced or at least provoked from within, is similarly marked by the manifestation of what we have come to call "new social movements," a manifestation crystallized in the gulf widening during the 1960s between the Communist Left, indeed the French Communist

Party, and a field of unaffiliated but unmistakably "leftist" political actors. In other words, like Sartre, Guattari approaches radio in the context of a reflection on the situation of then contemporary Marxism. And while it is true that Sartre was interested in and engaged with psychoanalysis (see, to pick one example from among many, *The Freud Scenario*), his reformulation of it as "existential psychoanalysis" oddly figured little if at all in his struggle to situate existentialism on or before the unsurpassable horizon of communism. Perhaps because, as he puts it in "The Group and the Person" (a piece from *Psychanalyse et transversalité*), Guattari "like[d] Sartre precisely because of his failure" (27), he was freed to approach the relation between Marx and Freud in a resolutely different way, without thereby abandoning the important theoretical and political problems unearthed by Sartre in putting the finishing touches upon his monumental impasse. For both men the problem of the group, and especially the Left's capacity to both think and address it, remained urgent, a fact underscored, if indirectly, in Deleuze's insightful introduction to *Psychanalyse et transversalité*, "Three Group Problems."[10]

In lieu of a thorough presentation of Guattari's philosophical and ultimately cosmological perspective, let me underscore one of its germinal nodes by misquoting Simone de Beauvoir: one is not born but becomes a subject.[11] Indeed, if Guattari was attracted to psychoanalysis, having read in philosophy at the Sorbonne, this was largely because of the way Freud sought to engage the *production* of the individual within the Western familial context. If Freud failed to appreciate fully this sense of "production," it was because he failed to understand the family as a group articulated with other groups, not as emanations of "family complexes" but as distinctive formations spread across, indeed composing, the social field. Resisting this tendency requires fidelity to the notion that "becoming-subject" (a formulation I will risk here out of convenience) depends upon the reproduction of the family as a group designed to stabilize a social order in which its triadic logic ("mommy, daddy, me") can be projected with explanatory and descriptive force throughout. The reproduction of the family is thus a political project, one voluntarily and involuntarily pitched against a multitude of other becomings, of other conditions of possibility for other groups and their subjects, including—to remind us of where this chapter began—becoming-queer. Crucial then for Guattari is the task of understanding the production of the subject, of interpreting the ways it fails or deviates (in this he is profoundly Freudian), and of changing the world organized by this mode of production (in this he is equally profoundly Marxian). For this reason Guattari is politically and theoretically attracted to all sites within a given social order (whether local or global, national or international) where becoming-subject is taking novel or potentially revolutionary forms. In principle, this is taking place always and everywhere, but it is surely this ubiquitous transversality that prompted his impassioned embrace of the student uprisings of the 1960s and also his involvement with the Italian workers' movement of the 1970s (Potere Operaio) that spawned Autonomia, the Red Brigade, and Radio Alice in Bologna. He says as much, and more, in "Why Italy?" an interview—at the time unpublished—given to the French press just prior to the arrest of Antonio Negri in 1979 and two years after he first made direct contact with Franco "Bifo" Berardi and other members of the Radio Alice collective.

To be fair, his attention had been deliberately signaled from afar. Those militants involved with first the magazine/journal *A/Traverso* and then Radio Alice presented their inspirations as "Situationist" but also as "deleuzoguattarian." It is thus fair to say that certain resonances between the politics of free radio and the micropolitical thought of Guattari are, in effect, overdetermined. But for this very reason it is interesting to consider how Radio Alice broadcast this affiliation. In "Radio Alice—Free Radio," a broadcast transcription, one can read the following: "All the 'unstated' *[non-detto]* is emerging: from the *Chants de Maldoror* to the struggles for reducing the work day. It speaks in the Paris Commune and in Artaud's poetry. . . . Desire *[il desiderio]* is given a voice *[una voce]*, and to them it is obscene. . . . Silence *[silenzio]*. The subject *[il soggetto]* has changed" (Collective A/Traverso 131; Berardi and Guarneri 40). Most immediately, this is a broadcast responding to charges leveled against the station by local authorities who proposed that national obscenity laws were being violated by the collective. What is striking, however, is the logic of the response, that is, the notion of setting up a correlation between the unstated (or unsaid) and the obscene. What is achieved here is a distinction between the obscene as a content and the obscene as an act. When the "unstated," earlier "the voice of the body" (Collective A/Traverso 130; Berardi and Guarneri 40), is given voice, it is by definition obscene. That in the formulation "desire is given a voice" a key category of *Anti-Oedipus* slips into the broadcast should make it plain that Radio Alice is deliberately seeking an alliance with the "deleuzoguattarian" tendency. Buried in the mix, however, is a whistler, a crucial point about the specific incarnation of the radiophonic medium that is free radio. In other words, *what* is said here is operating on the same plane as *where* and *how* it is being said. Radio Alice is thus presenting itself as the means by which the "unstated" erupts as the obscene, as the location where desire is given a voice, forging an impossibly intimate relation between a desire no longer structured by lack—in this case, what is here called its voice—and a means of public communication that is, de facto and de jure, free of state licensing and control. As Guattari might well have insisted, this desire—in outline, the factory model advanced on the early pages of *Anti-Oedipus*—belongs to a subject that has changed whether as topic or topos. Not to put too fine a point on it, this becoming-subject is taking place *as* Radio Alice, just as the becoming-schizo was taking place *as* La Borde, just as, we might add, the becoming-Algerian was taking place, in a certain sense, *as "la voix d'Algérie."* Recall that Fanon thought of the *mujahadin* as becoming transmitters of the voice, as becoming-radios.

One finds direct confirmation of this line of argument in a late interview given by Guattari to one of his U.S. interpreters and translators, Charles Stivale. Asked by Stivale what sorts of "collective modes of enunciation" he had hopes for in the decades of the 1970s and 1980s, Guattari responds: "Listen, from 1977 to 1981, a group of friends and I organized a movement, that wasn't very powerful, but wasn't entirely negligible . . . that was called the Free Radio Movement. We developed about a hundred free radio stations, an experimentation, a new mode of expression somewhat similar to what happened in Italy" (Guattari, "Pragmatic/Machinic"). He goes on to explain that it was Mitterand and the PS that actually destroyed this movement, not by censuring it—declaring it obscene, et cetera—but by integrating it into the French telecommunications industry, by, in effect converting piracy into a business force. While it is true that here he is not talking directly about Radio Alice, it is plain that he is doing more than merely citing an example. Indeed, he goes on to cite several, drawing attention to the fact that what is important is what repeats in the examples, namely the impossible intimacy between free radios and the very concept of a "collective mode of enunciation." They are, in effect, the materialization, the embodiment ("the voice of the body") *of* the concept. As readers of Deleuze and Guattari know, "agencement collectif d'énonciation" is a crucial theoretical operator in their project. In my own work I have deployed it as a way to think about the dispersed articulation of signs, practices, and institutions that constitute the cinema as a global phenomenon, but for Guattari in particular it functions to bring out the embeddedness of all production, and first and foremost the production of speech. While Saussure and other linguists (notably Benveniste) are content to place speech somewhere between language and the speech functions of the body and brain, Guattari wants to place speech within a field of systems that reach well below the neuro-somatic and well above the *logos*. And while this may indeed suggest that wherever human communication is involved one is dealing with a "collective mode of enunciation" and that in this sense the example of free radio is pertinent merely in principle, it strikes me as important that *this* is the first example to come to mind. Moreover, there is a political dimension to this example—if it is one—that recommends it.

This dimension emerges fully in Guattari's "position paper" on the movement mentioned to Stivale, the well-known article from *La Nouvelle Critique* translated as "Popular Free Radio." It opens by setting up what is now perhaps an all-too-familiar distinction between two developmental tendencies in the history of mass communications. On the one hand, there is a tendency toward hyperconcentration and control, whose aim is to subject the public to state-sanctioned norms; on the other, there is a tendency toward miniaturization, whose aim is to offer the real means of communication to minorities as well as the masses. The political purpose of this distinction is made clear in a summary paragraph where Gauttari glosses the tendency toward miniaturization by invoking the phrase "new spaces of liberty," the title—imperceptible in English *(Communists Like Us)*—of his later collaboration with Toni Negri *(Nouvelles espaces de liberté),* a collaboration in which a prototype of the geopolitical analysis found in Hardt and Negri's *Empire* is taken for a spin. Although purely implicit, miniaturization and minorities thus find here their cognate in multitude. Rendering all of this even more provocative, Guattari then asks: "How is it that a relatively old technology like radio has set the stage for a breakthrough in this second direction—in Italy and France—through the phenomenon of free radio stations?" ("Popular Free Radio" 73).[12] As his subsequent rhetorical questions make clear—Why not video, why not cable?—this is a question of the sort I have been tracking through the thickets of this chapter: Why radio? or, What is radio such that it can become the materialization of a micropolitical desire?

Because Guattari's statement is a prescient and preemptive strike against the telecommunications agenda of Jack Lang (a friend of Guattari's) and Mitterand's government, it unpacks the question of radio so as to stress precisely in what way popular free radio cannot be protected and fostered through monopolization, whether public or private. As if laying down a winning poker hand, he says, "Just look at what's on television!" But what makes radio, and specifically free radio, different, in fact so different that neither capital nor the state knows what to do with it? Although he makes several specific points, they all orbit in a certain sense around a version of the posture struck in the interview with Stivale. After having restated Lévi-Strauss's distinction between the *bricoleur* and the engineer (here, *spécialiste*), Guattari says: "Now, to be precise, the way opened up by the free radio phenomenon seems to go against the whole spirit of specialization. What becomes specific here are the collective arrangements of enunciations that absorb or 'traverse' specialties" ("Popular Free Radio" 75). In the context of Guattari's statement, the concept of the collective arrangement of enunciation is elaborated in useful detail. As the evocation of the *bricoleur* makes clear, free radio is a collective arrangement because it arises from the desire not only to speak directly to and with others but to diddle (as Poe once put it), to invert the passivity imposed by forms of media whose basic technological mechanism eludes us. In brief, this is his answer to the rhetorical questions cited above. Not surprisingly, he links this becoming-amateur with an distinction first drawn in *Psychanalyse et transversalité*, that between "group subjects" and "subjugated groups," where the clear lesson to be drawn is that collective arrangements of enunciation arise out of and give expression to "group subjects," that is, modes of becoming-subject in touch with their irreducibly collective character. Although apparently subject to the effect Roland Barthes once called "Italianicity," Guattari's insistence upon the term *traverse* (think the journal *A/Traverso*) in this context would almost certainly imply that enunciation produced under the circumstances of a collective arrangement achieves its effects through the breakdown of subjugated groups, in effect, through the confrontation between seriality and transversality.

Free radio then would appear to be a radicalization of Sartre's second radio, the aircraft radio that allows for two-way communication. To think this radicality, that is, to think beyond point-to-point, two-way communication, Guattari calls up as a representation of the direct speech facilitated by the collective arrangement of enunciation something he calls "an immense, permanent meeting place" ("Popular Free Radio" 76). In the French this is rendered even more provocatively through the inclusion of a phrase set off by dashes, "whose dimensions are those of the surface of listening," where speech, as Lacan would have insisted, projects across and addresses itself to an immense surface of listening that conditions enunciation as such. As if to drive home the engagement with psychoanalysis, Guattari is quick to insist that direct speech of the sort he sees active in free radio is "charged with desire" (76). At one level, it is a desire for "new means of expression," "new," even "minority languages," but at another it is micropolitical desire as such. Is this not the significance of the figure of the "surface," the "plane of immanence" where speaking folds into listening and both fold into desire? As before, Guattari moves here to place radio, the collective arrangement of enunciation, and desire on the same surface, that is, within the same social network of production, so that, to pick up an earlier thread, free radio is only an example of micropolitical desire to the extent that the latter can also be said to be an example of free radio. This is, as some readers will recognize, the Peircean critique of representation rendered in the deliberately studied vocabulary of Guattari. What it implies is that free radio has become a crystallization of productive potential active but latent within the archaic technology of radio, one that invites us to recognize the startling symmetry between it and, say, La Borde, another setting of the struggle between "group subjects," and "subjected groups," where miniaturized, customized articulations of desire are subjecting the latter to the corrosive force of transversality. Guattari treats these settings as though they were stations, as once was said, "on the dial," but a dial modulating the functioning of an apparatus that looks and feels more like a *socius* than a device. Here Guattari and Sartre again find one another in that, if the radio broadcast can and should illuminate seriality, the very motor of the practico-inert, it is because Sartre too understands that radio is more than a piece of furniture or, in the discourse of automobility, an option. It is all about how groups form and transform one another through their capacities to affect each other.

But let me suggest that Guattari also re-encounters the Sartre of the "Republic of Silence." This is not meant strictly in the sense that Guattari actually spoke into a microphone at Radio Alice (which he did) but in the sense that Radio Alice sought to appropriate the power of silence. For Sartre this was achieved through a dialectical maneuver whereby the silence imposed by the Occupation amplified, that is, gave political gravity to, the slightest murmur of speech. For Radio Alice the matter orbits around the motif of "the unstated." Earlier I urged that the movement from the unstated to the stated is what lay baffled behind the charge of obscenity. But consider what is added to the matter at hand by the following formulation from the same broadcast: "The silence, the uncanny [il estranietà], the 'unstated,' that which remains to be said . . . frightens," and moments later, "Radio for the participants or radio for the uncanny" (Collective A/Traverso 131; Berardi and Guarneri 40)? Here silence is inserted into a chain, and an interesting one in that it is posited as the counterweight to "the unstated" around the fulcrum of the uncanny. Moreover, as a gloss on "the unstated," "that which remains to be said" folds that which is not *yet* said on top of what is not said, underscoring a double potentiality: that of overcoming censorship but also, even more provocatively, that of language itself. Silence is thus humming not only with that which will be deemed obscene upon utterance but with everything that a language might allow us to say before it dies out. Perhaps this is why between silence and "the unstated" lies the uncanny, that most pivotal, most antithetical, of terms. On the one hand, it functions syntactically as an apposition, a repetition of silence (an echo without report). On the other, it installs a certain antithetical gliding within this appositive repetition, a gliding that soon spills toward the formulation "radio for the uncanny." When in the broadcast "radio for the uncanny" (as opposed to "for the participants") is glossed, the first characterization to be heard is "something continues to flee from language," followed soon by "stammering, silence". (Collective A/Traverso 131; Berardi and Guarneri 40). By setting up the contrast between participants and the uncanny, the broadcaster suggests that these are various ways to think about audience or even, more generally, reception. However, the gloss "something continues to flee from language" suggests something rather more surprising, namely, that radio, when, as in the case of Radio Alice, broadcasting "the unstated," becomes a site *for* the uncanny, for silence, for what continues to flee, or, translated back into French, *une ligne de fuite*. Radio, and specifically, free radio, as a line of flight/vanishing point on the surface of listening. Bad reception.[13]

If, as I have proposed, free radio is not merely an example of a collective arrangement of enunciation, then a decisive feature of the silence that frightens is the fact that what will have been deemed obscene, the stating of "the unstated," is the dispersion, the collective proliferation, of transmitters and receivers ever ready to articulate that which flees language, not in the guise of the repressed, but as the more, the pure enunciative potential of an as yet undead language. Even Saussure in theorizing the evolutionary spiral of speaking and languages recognized this. And while one might insist that what is at stake here is even better realized in the low- or one-watt FM radio movement (think here of Tetsuo Kogawa's Radio Home Run in Japan or his "workshop" at Radio Rethink in Canada, or, perhaps even better, the work of the Neurotransmitter Collective), it seems fair to say that free radio frightens because it distributes "the unstated" and what "the unstated" puts at stake, not just potentially everywhere, but in the everywhere of an uncanny potential. This is a different nothing, indeed one with a political valence indexed less to the ethereal and haunting medium of transmission than to the collective ownership of the means of transmitting and receiving. Or, if we are still here speaking of haunting, then it is decisively in the mode of the spectral haunting that Marx and later Derrida linked to the spirit of communism, a presence absent everywhere that the steady thump of the gravediggers' shovels is being frantically jammed. Such a qualification prompts one to revisit the title "La Borde: A Clinic Unlike Any Other, for what it underscores and amplifies is the psychoanalytical side of this discussion.

To put the matter bluntly, free radio as theorized by Guattari is to psychoanalysis—the interrogative anaphora of this chapter—what La Borde is to L'École freudienne. Important here is not so much the conceptual isomorphism of free radio and La Borde (or what Guattari will also call "Labordian logic")—both being factories machining the parts for group subjects, for postserial subjectivity—but the specific character of the theoretical and practical tension between two challenges to the psychoanalytical establishment, Lacan's and Guattari's. In an interview suggestively titled (by Sylvère Lotringer) "Everywhere at Once," Guattari characterizes the tension in terms of what he calls "a systematic demolition of Lacanism" (30), drawing our attention, I think, especially given his now well-documented ambivalence regarding Lacan, less to the substance of this dispute than to its fact. It is as though transversality, when expressed in the framework of analysis, whether clinical or not, required a certain accentuation of rivalry, an insistence upon the absolute difference separating the two. While all the "sons of Freud" (as Catherine Clément famously called them) would be quick to point out the Oedipal character of this articulation of transversality, my point is different. What seems striking is the way radio, yet again, figures centrally and intractably in a field's self-understanding, here psychoanalysis. Moreover, this self-understanding appears coiled with, indeed seems inseparable from, critique, as though the field of French psychoanalysis in the 1950s and 1960s *were* the problem of how properly to hate it, to appeal to one of Adorno's many zingers.

This would suggest that between Lacan and Guattari there arises yet another variation on Fromm's question, "What is radio to or for psychoanalysis?" Specifically, radio is the resistance within psychoanalysis to itself, to its limits—not, I hasten to add, to the device of the radio (what Guattari might call "a gadget") but to the apparatus, the cultural technology of subjectivation that radio transmits and receives, even if in inverted form. The point is not that this is what radio truly is but that this is what radio comes to be figured as in the encounter between it and psychoanalysis. This is its specific gravity within the convulsed field. Turning back, in concluding, to the beginning of this chapter, does this reformulation of the question not imply, first, that Menie Grégoire, however confused she may be about analytical practice, is not wrong to believe that therapy takes place "on the air"; and second, that what the FHAR sought to interrupt in her live broadcast was its homophobic content only insofar as that content was correctly perceived as obscene, that is, an irruption of the "unstated," not as the deep truth of queer identity, but as the shallow truth of a medium aggressively if futilely turned against the tendency toward miniaturization, minority and multitude? In this sense I earlier proposed that more was at stake in this attack than prejudice. Guattari, I think, gets at this in "Anti-Psychiatry and Anti-Psychoanalysis" (1976) when, in response to a question about the current function of the psychiatric hospital *(l'asile)*, he writes: "Almost everyone nowadays trashes *[cartonne]* the psychiatric hospital—which is good, but not enough. What is at issue is an overall problem, not just the hospital but public sector psychiatry, and the different forms of psychoanalysis: you can't make a slip of the tongue nowadays without happening upon some concierge who will interpret it for you wildly *[sauvagement]*. Worst of all, someone like Menie Grégoire is part of the new psychiatric outfit" (48, translation modified).

As his title implies, Guattari is concerned here to further distance himself (see, for example, his essay on Mary Barnes in *Molecular Revolution*) from Laing and Basaglia, and to do so by taking up the critique of psychoanalysis directly. In this iteration his concern is less the status of Oedipus in Anti-Psychiatry (although the matter comes up elsewhere in the piece) than the broad social diffusion of psychoanalysis. Although it is clear that he has little but contempt for Grégoire, he nevertheless places her on a continuum that includes all the "different forms" of psychoanalysis, as if to say: while her call-in therapy represents a certain extreme case *("A la limite . . . ")*, it is merely the crystallization of what psychoanalysis, regardless of school, has become, namely, a mode of hermeneutic policing where nothing escapes the labor of interpretation, the conversion into meaning, where nothing, finally, flees language.[14] It is interesting to note the rather deliberate and certainly conspicuous way that Guattari, at the risk of attempting to hide behind an open declaration of complicity, associates through the adverb *sauvagement,* whether freely or not, the concierge with the subject of Freud's 1910 essay "'Wild' *[wilde]* Psycho-analysis," Theodor Reik. This short piece, which never mentions Reik by name, defends psychoanalysis from the charge of quackery by proposing, first, that Reik's patient was less harmed than psychoanalysis itself and second, that psychoanalysis was fully capable of monitoring these sorts of excesses through the executive body of the International Psychoanalytic Association. Here Freud himself seems to be authorizing the mass diffusion of wild analysis coupled with the self-monitoring function of the IPA. Why not let the concierge interpret your parapraxis as long as the effects of doing so are, when all is said and done, subject to review before a professional body ever poised to intervene when necessary? Doubtless this is what Gauttari means when moments later in the interview he bemoans the fact that the "super-ego will invade everything" ("Everywhere at Once" 48). By draping this necklace of signifiers around Grégoire's neck, he would appear to be making radio the medium of this invasion, implying that radio facilitates, even echoes, the diffusion of psychoanalysis. To this extent, Gauttari answers the question "What is radio to or for psychoanalysis?" with one word: everything. Against this, he comes at it from everywhere, from precisely the collective arrangement of enunciation, the rhizomatic (decentralized or Labordian) network that is free radio. Surely this response is so inverted as to become entirely alien to Fromm and Lazarsfeld, but it is, just the same, a response to *their* question, only one their receivers could pick up badly if at all.

CHAPTER 5

Birmingham Calling

In preceding chapters much has been made of the way reflection on radio has confounded not only distinctions among philosophical tendencies—say between Adorno and Heidegger—but distinctions between philosophy and other theoretically charged practices, for example psychoanalysis or sociology. The repeated argument has been: radio is not simply the occasion for such effects, it also stands in a relation of contingent necessity to them. Here, this argument will be repeated but by passing more directly over the recurrent motif of education from the angle that opens up when one recognizes the insistently pedagogical spread between Brecht, who thought of radio as an apparatus by means of which a public might be informed about the conditions of its social existence, and Lacan, who thought of radio as producing the conditions under which his seminar at the École normale and the so-called "listening" public might be superimposed. Specifically this chapter turns its attention to the university as an educational institution and seeks to tease out the instructive relation between radio—both as an object of reflection and as an apparatus of communication (like everyone from Adorno to Guattari, most of the leading figures at the Centre for Contemporary Cultural Studies [CCCS] were no strangers to the radio broadcast)—and the structural transformation that galvanized the emergence of the field of cultural studies. The intimate relation between this transformation and the mode of knowledge production we call a discipline will serve here as a way to repeat or reword what has already been said about the various confoundings of philosophy in the preceding chapters. Virtually every recounting of the emergence of cultural studies worries over its distinctive interdisciplinary formation, often in quite sophisticated ways (as in the case of Stuart Hall), but without satisfactorily locating radio in the plot of this emergence. This is what will be essayed here.

Many if not all the scholars who have reconstructed the origins of CCCS at Birmingham—whether insiders like Richard Hoggart, Stuart Hall, Richard Johnson, or Michael Green or outsiders like Alan O'Connor, David Morley, or Kuan-Hsing Chen—stress the urgency of not situating the center in textual sources. This is done, often explicitly, so as to show that cultural studies has indeed transformed the practice of institutional historiography. Yet with equal tenacity, commentators, once they have finished gesturing to the annual reports in which the founding acts of the center have been textually inscribed, consistently turn to five originating texts: Hoggart's *Uses of Literacy;* Raymond Williams's *Culture and Society* and *The Long Revolution;* Edward P. Thompson's critique of Williams, "The Long Revolution Parts 1 and 2"; and Thompson's *The Making of the English Working Class.* However theoretically or politically fraught, this gesture nevertheless invites one to consider what gets said in the public lecture "Schools of English and Contemporary Society," delivered by Hoggart on the occasion of the opening of CCCS in 1964, especially because the event could be said to have articulated the textual and the institutional. Its status as a fourteen-page, and in that sense belabored, performative is thus not without interest.

The body of Hoggart's text is broken into three sections, each given a particular forensic task. The first seeks to establish that "schools of English" need not compromise on their core aesthetic values—the "tempering of mind and imagination" ("Schools" 247) through the cultivation of respect for language—in order to engage with "contemporary society" (246). Here Hoggart sounds his signature theme of speaking, the persistent, everyday use of language, as he labors to distinguish between the modern and the contemporary, this last a decisive adjective in the name of the new center. The second section sets out to describe the status of these core aesthetic values within contemporary society. Here he introduces, *pace* Galbraith, the notion of the "articulate society," that is, a society in which considerable attention is devoted to speaking, while the faculty of speech nevertheless decays. Although his focus here is not on the Hunslet neighborhood of Leeds, he is repeating the concerns of *The Uses of Literacy* from 1957 by concentrating on the impact of mass communications on speech and stressing that academic intellectuals ought properly to care about this impact. The third section opens with the sentence: "The approach I have been outlining may be provisionally called Literature and Contemporary Cultural Studies" ("Schools" 254), and it justifies the center his remarks call into existence by showing how this sort of institutional innovation—to be sure, more evoked than described—is the way to bring "English Schools" into the right sort of contact with "contemporary society." It appeals directly to "radio criticism" (257) only once and in passing, but there is more here than meets the ear.

As with the earlier *Uses,* this text is concerned with the social transformation of subjectivity, a transformation thought to be comprehensive in scope—it affects all subjects in the groups to which they belong (families, neighborhoods, classes, etc.)—and, for the most part, deleterious in consequence. Hoggart is always careful not to succumb to a Leavisite condemnation of all present trends (indeed, as Michael Green has suggested, this is key to the insistence on "contemporary" in the center's name), but he is cagey about precisely how to evaluate what is happening. This would appear to be because he recognizes that he is a subject and that everything *he* is saying would thus properly belong to the contemporary fate of speaking. In *Uses,* this situation expressed itself in Hoggart's declaration of his class affiliation.[1] Here, perhaps because of the very force of the historical argument in *Uses,* the matter is handled at a more philosophical level. Its effects are telling, particularly because they radiate around "love."

In the second section of his talk, Hoggart spells out in some detail what about subjects in the "articulate society" concerns him. In his lone explicit mention of Leavis, Hoggart wonders "whether in any previous period so many words were being used inorganically" ("Schools" 251), explaining that by *inorganic* he means speaking on behalf of the concerns of others as opposed to saying something about one's own experience. On the face of it, this would appear to characterize political speech—insofar as it involves representing the concerns of others—as inorganic, but what Hoggart is expressly pointing to is the speaking undertaken by commercial advertising. He does not say as much, but one might think here of a celebrity endorsement of a commodity where whatever the celebrity might say must be understood as spoken on behalf of the (marketing) concerns of others. Think Bill Murray's character in Sofia Coppola's *Lost in Translation.* In other words, the issue for Hoggart is not just that there is so much of this kind of talk—hence the centrality of radio, television, and the press, all those "quieter voices"—but that it produces a gap within the subject between his or her experience and, to invoke Marie Cardinal, "the words to say it." In keeping with the motif of organicism, Hoggart sees that this plunges us into a "high nervous pseudo-life," a state in which many words become "unusable" (251). He produces a short list of such words, the last of which is *love*. Of course, any of the words on this list raises epistemological issues—What does it mean to use an unusable word as an example for itself?—but in this text *love* plays an important role. Before tracking it, let me complete Hoggart's account of the then contemporary destitution of the subject.

Perhaps the very nadir of inorganic life lies in the fact that the "endlessly working, conveyor-belt productiveness of modern communications" ("Schools" 252) not only introduces a gap between our words and our experience but transfers this gap into the structure of the subject. As he says, the writing one finds in the press, "addresses us as parts of men"; "we are addressed as bits, bits who belong to lopsided blocks" (252). It is not, then, just that we have difficulty expressing our experience but that, even more insidious, we have difficulty having experience at all. We cannot, to use a Kantian formulation, bring unity to our manifold of sense impressions because we lack the requisite unity. Today, such formulations read as quaintly pretheoretical, but the point here is to appreciate both the detail of Hoggart's brief account—remember, he is here publicly inaugurating a research center—and its scope. "*We* are addressed as bits," that is, all of us who might be potential recipients of these remarks, including, of course, Hoggart himself. He too is a bit from a lopsided block, which is why his list of such blocks ends with the words "or redbrick [not "stone," that is, Oxbridge] professors" ("Schools" 252).

If I insist upon this, it is because it illuminates the instructive role of love in Hoggart's remarks. We have seen that *love* is marked as a word whose use lies in its ability to exemplify, with relevant pathos, the unusable. For reasons that may well have to do with the vexed hierarchy of British postsecondary education, Hoggart does not avail himself of Austin's stony distinction between *use* and *mention,* a fact that puts even more pressure on a formulation that occurs in the first section of his remarks. Characterizing what it means for writers to avoid using words as tools, Hoggart writes: "A writer always wants to pick them [words] up and make them fresh again by the power of his love" ("Schools" 247). A mere five pages later we are told that *love* has been rendered unusable by the ravages of "articulate society." This is not inattention. Perhaps it would be if this invocation of the power of love were not the counterweight to words spoken on behalf of the concerns of others, but the invocation *is* precisely this counterweight. Moreover, it is this very account of the writer's labor that Hoggart appeals to in section 3 to establish in what way the CCCS knows what it means to privilege, as Hoggart insists it must, literary critical methodology. In fact, his final explicit use of *love* occurs in the waning paragraphs of his talk. Advocating on behalf of a sociologically inflected attention to reception, he writes: "A little more humility about what audiences actually take from unpromising material would be useful. Perhaps no one should engage in the work who is not, in a certain sense, himself in love with popular art" ("Schools" 258). And, as if responding to a suggestion made by his own word choice—here, "in a certain sense"—Hoggart adds: "One kind of 'love' is a disguised nostalgia for mud" (258). This is a welcome complication, for it holds open the prospect that there is a usable and an unusable "love," a prospect dashed when one recalls that "the power of love" that refreshes words picks them up out of what Hoggart earlier called "the mud of life" (247). Odd. Does this mean that Hoggart is not someone who can conduct reception research, a fact contradicted by the very existence of *Uses?* Does it mean that a writer's redemptive love of words is merely a disguised nostalgia, that is, a love that isn't one? And what precisely is happening here to the use of the unusable, and with what, if any, consequences for the CCCS at Birmingham?

Aware that everything set up in the talk is beginning to cave in around him, including, presumably, the center thus "chewed up" by the contemporary society whose culture the center is proposing to study, Hoggart plots a way forward, a line of flight, through the fraught field of reception. He writes: "Of course, this art [bastardized mass art] is being increasingly machine-tooled. . . . But even with these [soaps, women's magazines, westerns, and commercials], there are sometimes spaces between the brittle voices, in which a gesture sets you thinking in a new way about some aspect of human experience" ("Schools" 258). Spaces between the brittle voices. If, as has been argued, Hoggart's voice falls of necessity within the field of brittle voices, then perhaps either it echoes in the space between them, or, within his own voice, a brittle voice that cannot effectively separate the usable from the unusable, spaces open up that call to listeners, inviting them to hear gestures that while sonic are not, strictly speaking, vocal, to, in effect, hear the conditions of receiving speech. Such reformulations might seem a stretch were it not for the interesting and quite unremarked fact that Hoggart, in detailing the cultural work performed by English schools, describes them as "active transmitters" ("Schools" 246), in effect, bookending his remarks with the distinctly radiophonic rhetoric of a transmitter (the center) and a receiver (the audience of the "articulate society").

It is in this sense that the passing reference to radio criticism ought be seen as a distraction, or perhaps more a deflection, of our attention away from the more profound and intimate way in which the inauguration of the center is spoken from within a space of communication organized by radio. It is not, in the end, a matter of the insistence of radiophonic communication, the fact that its ubiquity ceaselessly solicits scholarly attention; rather, the questions whose answers the center is established to provide are put to it by the effect of radio—here the unstable proximity of the usable and the unusable word—within academic speaking. Despite appearances, this is not, however, a war of transmitters. What Hoggart, perhaps unwittingly, gestures to is the strategic value of jamming the signal transmitted by the "articulate society," by transmitting on or through the spaces between the brittle voices, relying on the gesture of reception to amplify and thus radicalize the work of the center. Here, without saying as much, Hoggart emphasizes the activism of the center's project, suggesting that cultural studies—when done properly—is a field that engages its objects of attention deconstructively, that is, on their own terms but as if read from the inside out. Activism is thus not simply or primarily a way of intervening within daily life; it is also about building an institutional structure cut to the shape of such an intervention and consistent with its aims. Thompson and others were never happy with this cozy, port-sipping relation between cultural studies and the university, but this never stirred them to produce as provocative an account of the sociopolitical character of the contemporary university either.

Hoggart's capacious account of speaking allowed him in *Uses* to mention more than to use radio. But to conclude from this that he had little specific interest in the medium is to do him a disservice. In fact, he was so recognizably concerned with "wireless broadcasting" that he was called upon to participate in the Pilkington Report on Broadcasting from 1963, one of whose charges was consideration of whether commercial, that is, private, radio ought to be permitted to flourish in Britain. Hoggart's defense of this report, "Difficulties of Democratic Debate," figures prominently in Raymond Williams's review of the two volumes of *Speaking to Each Other* for the *Guardian*. Indeed, Williams treats the piece as something of a metonymy for the collection as a whole. It is therefore worthy of our attention.

Williams begins his review thus: "At the time that Richard Hoggart and I were inseparable, we had not met" ("Practical Critic" 9). This whimsically implicates Williams directly in the problem he praises Hoggart for thematizing so effectively in the piece, namely, the difficulty of "speaking to others," especially on matters concerning the media of such speaking. Most directly, Williams is drawing attention to the fact that his review will be received by readers who, in believing that there is a Raymond Hoggart who wrote *The Uses of Culture* (Williams reports this parapraxis with obvious relish), may well doubt the objectivity of the reviewer. Thus his speaking is distorted by a reception context in which it will be heard as both by and about him. Rendered explicit, the matter is set aside, and Williams proceeds to his evaluation.

There would be two ways, at least, of thinking about how Hoggart in "Difficulties" characterizes the difficulties. On the one hand, and this line of reflection dominates Hoggart's rejoinder, democratic debate is hindered and thus made difficult by interests, especially—but not exclusively—commercial interests. So, precisely because the report openly reflected upon the habitual association of serving the public good and serving it for private profit, it made the possibility of speaking to each other more tenuous, more vexed, because the report dislodged people. It obliged them to consider that interests, when allowed to normalize speech, often make it difficult to resist the temptation to, as Jacques Rancière has more recently said, hate democracy, that is, to resent the demand to justify private opinion in public. Hoggart's critique of the press on this score ("Difficulties" 190–91) is deliciously scathing. In effect, one of the chief difficulties besetting democratic debate was, in the narrow sense, ideological.

On the other hand, and this might be said to express Hoggart's "literary critical" perspective, democratic debate about the Pilkington Report was rendered difficult by a more linguistic, even epistemological problem. Hoggart puts it thus: "There is not even a moderately precise vocabulary for discussing the cultural questions raised by the study of broadcasting. There is no adequate terminology, no adequate sense of the history and process of this kind of cultural change, and no adequate language for discussing the popular arts" ("Difficulties" 199).

Here the difficulty reaches below interests to the very language, the words, in which those interests might be conceived, formulated, and expressed. This rather decisively ups the ante in a report charged with formulating policy recommendations on broadcasting. Here, one of the authors of the report, in seizing upon the most difficult difficulty of "speaking to each other," risks a version of the Cretan's paradox: we do not have the means to speak about what we are speaking about. Although nothing in what Williams says in his review of this chapter points directly to this dimension of the problem, his own passion for terminological clarification (think, for example, of *Keywords,* or the first chapter of *Communications,* "Definitions") might suggest that this is precisely what leads him to value the chapter as a metonymical condensation of Hoggart's achievement. Is it irrelevant that in setting up these self-defeating but theoretically challenging formulations Hoggart affirms the committee's struggle to find a "plain voice" ("Difficulties" 199) and that what Williams underscores time and again in his review is the "reasonable" quality of Hoggart's voice, the measured consistency of its tone? I think not, but the important matter here is something slightly different. What leaps out of Hoggart's chapter—also written in 1963—and his second, more provocative, characterization of the difficulties besetting democratic debate in particular is its strong resonance with his contemporaneous, inaugural lecture of CCCS, "Schools of English and Contemporary Society."

There Hoggart introduces the dilemma of terminological precision through a long citation from, of all people, Ezra Pound. He turns to an early newspaper article of Pound's, "Books," to flesh out an assertion made about the "life of language" ("Schools" 249). More specifically, Pound is adduced as someone who helps us understand whether "contemporary society" values the "life of language." It does not. Not only does it despise the literati, those charged with maintaining the "cleanliness of the tools" ("Schools" 250), but it embraces a "slushy and inexact" (250) relation between words and things. As Hoggart summarizes: "They [the members of articulate society] are often talking nonsense—but they do so in whole sentences" (250). In effect, contemporary society traffics in imprecision, sustaining the very difficulty besetting debate over the Pilkington Report, that is, sustaining a broad epistemological framework within which the absence of adequate terminology is neither noticed nor missed. While it is certainly true that Hoggart strains to separate himself from Pound's version of the aesthetic aristocracy, it is no less true that cultural studies and CCCS emerge in the inaugural lecture as what must fill the void left by its repudiation. In this precise sense, Hoggart's two texts converge in linking broadcasting (both radio and television) to the institutional innovation that was, up until 2002, the CCCS at Birmingham. Put differently, what emerges in the relation between Hoggart's two texts is a bold, even risky claim about the way contemporary society solicits, in effect calls for, the emergence of cultural studies as the institutional means by which to produce a vocabulary, a voice, perhaps even a tone (a term rich with radiophonic resonance) through which to make sense of the impact of broadcasting on our ability to speak to each other.

That Williams zeroes in on this chapter invites reflection. Specifically, it invites us to consider whether radio, or sound broadcasting (a retronym formed in the wake of the advent of television), is taken up by Williams in a way consistent with his praise for Hoggart's insight. It does, but in texts—as the partisans of radio studies might have predicted—largely eclipsed by his book-length study of television. Most of the texts in question are occasional pieces written during the mid-sixties for venues such as *Politics and Letters* (not the collection of interviews with Williams later gathered under this title but the review) and *Tribune,* a socialist magazine of news commentary and cultural analysis. Before we turn to them, though, it is worth calling to mind the six pages devoted to radio in the opening chapter of *Television.*

This discussion, published in 1975, although brief, is important because it essentially crystallizes the logic of his earlier, more dispersed statements about sound broadcasting. Two features of this logic invite emphasis. On the one hand, by narrating the history of the relation between technology and society and plotting radio within it, Williams shows that so-called mass communications (and I put it this way because Williams spent a career troubling the very rubric of "mass" communications) oscillated between two models of communications: one, of the sort to be found in the cinema, namely a form of distinctly mass distribution earlier examined and championed by Benjamin (as discussed in chapter 2), and the other, a form more properly described as broadcasting, an institutional practice that goes beyond the press in transmitting content directly into homes, eliminating entirely the movement into or across public space for the purpose of coming into contact with this content. Despite his keen and abiding interest in the press, Williams begins his story of "mass" communications with the changes in reception wrought by the cinema, thereby drawing attention to the subsequent and signal achievement of the radio in being the first articulation of cultural technology and society that relied on the structure of broadcasting. This belongs crucially to a social history of television because radio provides the former with the content-neutral, abstract form of broadcasting. In developing this insight, Williams, with no apparent awareness of Sartre's concept of seriality (he reviews Sheridan's English translation of the *Critique of Dialectical Reason* for the *Guardian* two years *after* the publication of *Television*), appeals to the concept, later described as an ugly phrase, of "mobile privatization," a form of communications technology that is "at once mobile [and he means here to invoke the automobile] and home-centered" (*Television* 26).[2] This, let's call it, *heimlich* maneuver is vital as an abstraction, not because of its generality, but because of its formal, I think we would now insist, structural character. This is because as a structure the *heimlich* maneuver allows one to grasp the historical connections between different materializations of communication, say, traffic and information, but also allows one to isolate a more ontological matter, namely, the means by which a property of radio repeats itself as a residualism in any and all subsequent materializations, say, television, that, in a sense, puts the moving image in the place where nothing but sound haunts the later medium. As Williams formulates the matter: "Unlike all previous communications technologies, radio and television were *systems primarily devised for transmission and reception as abstract processes, with little or no definition of preceding content. . . . It is not only that the supply of broadcasting facilities preceded the demand; it is that the means of communication preceded their content*" (*Television* 25, italics in original). Brecht's own formulation about the radical prematurity of radio might well appear to be the residualism haunting Williams's remarks, an extravagant formulation whose warrant will later appear.

As his remarks on radio come to a close, Williams draws attention to the second key aspect of its logic. Splicing together a broad claim about the essential link between communication and power with the fundamentally contradictory form of radio—"centralized transmission and privatized reception" (*Television* 30)—Williams broaches the political question of ownership, precisely the matter agitated so directly by the Pilkington Report. Already in "Communications and Community" (1961) Williams had cast his lot with Hoggart's sympathetic treatment of the BBC's "paternal" (24) resistance to the commercial ownership of broadcasting, so there is certainly nothing new in his emphasis on this feature of the logic of radio broadcasting. And while it might be interesting to tease out the resonance between Foucault's later concept of "pastoral power" and what Williams means by "the paternal," what the occasional pieces on radio invite one to note is the altogether compelling stress placed by Williams on the link between radio and socialism. In other words, the matter is not just the policy question of whether or how to commercialize radio but the far more provocative question of whether one can have a coherent theory of radio that isn't at the same time a theory of socialism. As the preceding reading of Hoggart implies, this is also a question of the if not essential then certainly indispensable role of cultural studies, and the CCCS more particularly, in articulating (joining through enunciation) the fates of radio and socialism.

This matter is joined in one of Williams's early forays into radio criticism on the pages of the *Tribune,* "Just What Is Labour's Policy for Radio?" Published on February 18, 1966, the opening paragraph throws down the proverbial gauntlet: "There are persistent reports that the Labour Government may, in the near future, introduce plans for some kind of commercial local broadcasting. At first hearing, these reports seem incredible. . . . Is it possible to believe that Labour could respond to these [commercial] pressures by surrender or compromise?" (8). Twice Williams motivates his polemical tone by appealing to belief. Is it possible to believe, is it credible, that a ruling party calling itself a Labour Party would support the commercialization of sound broadcasting at the local level? Rhetorically, of course, the answer is no, but it seems urgent here to tease out the more ontological dimension of the point, namely, that for Williams what Labour *is* as a political formation is a party for which the question of the commercialization of communication is, or should be, obvious. Thus the strategy of Williams's intervention is to challenge Labour to recognize precisely how intimately its politics and radio press upon each other.

Perhaps this is what dictates the distinction drawn, almost immediately, between "traditional Socialist answers" and a "contemporary Socialist answer" ("Just What" 8), a distinction mobilized both to produce a fragment, perhaps even a miniature, of political memory and to approach without quite embracing the tone of shaming his interlocutor, as if to say, Have you forgotten who we are? Because Williams clearly aligns himself with contemporary socialism, his characterization of traditional socialism is instructive. In particular, not only does he stress the link it grasps between mass communications and what he calls "a continuing social education" (8), but just as emphatically he writes, "It is wrong to allow this most human of needs—the need to speak to each other in a large and complex society—to be treated as a by product of the need to sell transistors and records" (8), a formulation that slyly cites Hoggart ("speaking to each other") and thus prepares us for the turn to "contemporary Socialism." Although it almost passes unnoticed it is vital to stress how attentive Williams is to the tenacity of the problem: transistors, which might well be deployed as the very technical means by which members of a complex society might speak to each other, are not to be deployed so as to reconfigure this most human of needs. It is as though "traditional Socialism" were here cast as too quick to separate the human and the device, whereas the deeper problem lies in the distinctly commercial articulation of this relation, an articulation in which need becomes an afterthought or by-product.

What, then, of "contemporary Socialism"? A full account of what it means for Williams would require discussion, not just of the anti-nuclear New Left of the 1950s, but of his decision to abandon the Labour Party in the very year "Just What Is Labour's Policy for Radio?" was published. This moves us out of range, but certainly under the circumstances another title of his *Tribune* piece suggests itself: "What Is Labour for Radio?" That said, Williams announces the decisive relevance of "contemporary Socialism" thus: "We have been learning, in recent years, that the systems and models set up in communications, and the consequent ways in which men talk and listen to each other, are among the most powerful of all social relations" ("Just What" 8). The emphasis falls here on education, not just in general, but on recent learning directed at the systems and models of communication. Because this would, at a certain level, appear merely to reiterate the traditional socialist point about the human need to talk to one another, it seems clear that the evocation of recent learning is meant to suggest that this need is being grasped in a fresh way. In the cited passage the difference that leaps out is that Williams insists upon the pair *talk* and *listen*, as if stressing the fact that there is an irreducibly intersubjective and asymmetric dimension to human need. In this he would appear to be channeling Marx and Engels in *The German Ideology* where they insisted upon the originally practical character of human consciousness. However, in describing the last of his four systems or models, the democratic, he introduces a fraught and highly charged juridical rhetoric: "Or you can have, finally, a democratic [as opposed to authoritarian, paternal, or commercial] system in which the right to speak and to listen is established on the basis of a genuine equality of access, publicly and practically guaranteed" (8). The *right* to speak and to listen: that this is stressed in the context of an elaboration of "contemporary Socialism" would clearly imply that recent learning has established, among other things, the juridical character of two human faculties, an insight that presumably undergirds Williams's insistence upon the significantly powerful character of the social relations conditioned by these faculties. Here it appears that what he is seeking to break with is a socialism of production, a politics of speaking, in favor of a socialism of producing *and* receiving, a socialism geared toward crafting innovations in the juridical sphere of the superstructure in response to recognition of social relations whose power is not economically derived.

Likewise apparent is his decision to cast "contemporary Socialism" as committed to a democratic system or model of communication, and while this leaves his most trenchant critique of Labour stated with uncomfortable baldness, it decisively reverses the interrogative flow of his piece. Readers now want eagerly to know what radio policy, in espousing a democratic model or system of communication, is indeed true to the tenets of "contemporary Socialism." Tellingly, in providing his answer, Williams says something vital about radio while also clarifying his insistent appeal to recent learning in the *Tribune* article. His answer refers immediately to the notion of local broadcasting and the political support for it. It is introduced and fleshed out in the following paragraph: "Fortunately we now have in print a detailed and imaginative account of what local broadcasting could really do if it could be, from the beginning, unambiguously a social service. The Centre for Contemporary Cultural Studies at Birmingham has published a pamphlet by Rachel Powell, *Possibilities for Local Radio,* which lifts the whole argument on to a new plane" ("Just What" 8). He goes on to summarize some of her key findings and proposals. Before we turn to these, it is worth pointing out that when earlier Williams emphasized the importantly democratic character of "a genuine equality of access" he was thinking directly of what local radio comes to mean in Powell's study. Moreover, not only does his direct appeal to CCCS make precise what was meant by his reference to "learning in recent years," but perhaps even more provocatively this gesture would appear to place CCCS at something like the pivot between two moments in the history of British socialism. Radio, and state policy regulating it, appear to articulate this pivot in ways that resemble the importance that Hoggart attached to this medium when, as has been argued, he laid out the intellectual and political agenda of the center.

As if in anticipation of Williams's invocation of Powell's pamphlet, the latter contains a deft headnote signed by Hoggart and Stuart Hall that, after announcing the inauguration of the now highly regarded

"Occasional Papers" published by the CCCS (Powell's was, in December of 1965, the very first), goes on to clarify:

> Rachel Powell has not "edited" this statement for the Centre; it is her own. But the Centre is, of course, in general agreement with her arguments. More, we think that Rachel Powell gives a new depth and detail to the idea of local radio, and shows what could be meant by the imaginative use of broadcasting within small communities. Essentially, she is asking us to dare to think about creative amateurism. . . . The contrast with the looseness and generality of the ideas for local radio put forward by those who are seeking commercial franchises in this field is considerable. (Powell 1)

The closing formulation in particular marks Powell's pamphlet as an example of what earlier in the headnote is characterized as a statement "about aspects of social and cultural change on which it seems necessary to speak soon and in practical terms" (1), but the insistence upon her independence (her remarks not having been "edited") is surely meant to give this intervention at least the appearance of independence, an effect heightened, one should think, by the fact that it is Williams, down the road at Cambridge, that "amplifies," one might also say "broadcasts," Powell's remarks. Given Williams's desire to engage Labour, perhaps even to explain his abandonment of the party, it is clear that what matters to him about Powell's statement, independent or not, is that it supports what are, in effect, two interventions: one in the commercial dispute over local radio but another in the dispute over British socialism in the 1960s.

In approaching what Powell has to say, it is worth recalling Hoggart's troubled assertion about the absence of a proper vocabulary for analyzing media, an absence to be rectified, as has been proposed, through the work of the CCCS. In light of this, the headnote's distinction between "depth and detail" versus "looseness and generality" is clearly meant to underscore Powell's key contribution to specifying "what might be *meant*" by radio broadcasting at the local level. Aside from her practical suggestions, this more linguistic issue is clearly a vital aspect of her and the CCCS's intervention. Although it does Powell something of a disservice, one might usefully think of her text as a ghosted entry in Williams's *Keywords* where the aim is to produce something like an analytic vocabulary—in this case, a vocabulary that seeks to formulate and thus grasp what it means to modify broadcasting with the adjective *local*. Williams's own "private mobilization" (all his protestations regarding its ugliness notwithstanding) is another such analytical formulation, one whose relation to Powell's "local broadcasting" invites, and will here receive, attention.

Powell's *Possibilities for Local Radio,* like Hoggart's inaugural lecture, is broken into sections, twelve in all, each designed to realize a certain stage in her argument. Seen from above, however, the slim twenty-one-page pamphlet splits in two (almost at the staples), shifting from a witty, detailed polemic against the commercialization of local broadcasting to a series of likewise detailed, extremely practical proposals regarding the public control of local radio broadcasting. It is this last that Williams invokes enthusiastically in "What Is Labour's Policy for Radio?" At the pivot point, and here the comparison to *Keywords* is irresistible, sits a section titled "Culture." As it is here that Powell really attempts to ground the meaning of the local in the phrase "local broadcasting," it calls out for scrutiny.

Picking up on an earlier insight—"there is no fixed nature of broadcasting" (Powell 6)—the "Culture" section of *Possibilities* turns immediately to the task of separating local radio from "the tired and rigid framework of commercial thinking" described earlier (6), establishing that Powell has something like a theory of ideology. Thus whatever the local might be made to mean will become cognizable once the commercial means by which to think the local is neutralized. In the pamphlet, Radio Caroline serves as a metonymy for the commercialized local, that is, a broadcasting practice serving assumed local interest in popular music by providing an audience—even if illegally (hence "pirate")—for the products of the British phonograph companies.[3] To get at what is needed, Powell asks that we approach the decommercialized local through two urgent questions: "How far are the majority of people enabled to participate in a real community?" and "How far has culture, as an energetic and meaningful way of life, any substance in most people's experience?" (12). It would be difficult to pack more CCCS buzzwords—*people, participate, real, community, culture, energetic, meaningful, way of life, substance, experience*—in a tighter space, and it is clear that Powell is keen to shift the meaning of the local from the framework of commercial thinking to the framework of cultural studies thinking. This is why "culture" is the pivot: if we first clarify what is meant analytically by this concept, then we can state with fresh analytical precision what local radio can mean. Indeed, summarizing her early points, Powell writes: "The argument about local radio, then, is an argument about culture" (12).

Of course, this lexicographical loop requires Powell to be clear about what she and the CCCS mean by the term *culture*. Invoking for her own purposes the Pilkington Report, Powell distinguishes sharply between culture as "esoteric art-works" and culture as something of a necessary evil, as "essentially *the* term for the quality of life as we live it, . . . for what happens when people pursue activities with passion and discrimination" (12). Although the second phrase is cited from one Geoffrey Bantock, it might just as easily have been cited from "Culture Is Ordinary," Williams's *parti pris* from 1958. The source here is not as important as is recognition that this is a war of words and that Powell, confronted with something like the tenacity of the signifier (she concedes that *culture* will be variously "translated"), can neither avoid this essential term nor control its meaning. This imports into the pamphlet, if not a certain hollowness, then certainly a structural instability, one whose effects on the concept of local radio will have to be attended to. Consider first, though, what Powell has gained in decommercializing the local through her translation of culture.

Differentiating between four levels of description—the social, the educational, the cultural, and the political—Powell advances the following proposals about local radio. It could serve as the means by which the people of a town talk to and get to know each other. It could teach people, especially youth, the skills of communication—in effect, how to talk to each other. It could provide "democracy with a voice" (12–13); indeed, the very existence of local radio could prompt community members to "regard access to public media as a democratic right, like literacy" (13). The pattern here is plain. Powell grasps the local on Hoggart's model of "speaking to each other." As she says in turning to launch her practical suggestions: "I am asking then for a local station that can be used by the community both at the listening and talking end. We have a habit of forgetting that people need to speak just as much as they need to listen, and have far less opportunity for it. . . . The point about communication is that it can develop only where the channel exists" (13). Setting aside, for the moment, the precipitous and now familiar reduction of radio to voice, it is clear from her appeal to the need for and the "right" to verbal and auditory experience that Williams found more than Powell's practical suggestions regarding local broadcasting of import to his own intervention. Her language was attractive too. It is equally clear that, given the interdependency of communication and channel, the local and radio conceptually lean upon each other. Radio—not television—is the channel through which the local can produce itself as the form of communication out of which or through which radio assumes its proper cultural meaning. Needless to say, cultural studies is fully in the loop of radio and the local. That is, its ever-emerging account of the cultural is what the properly radiophonic local derives from or rests upon. As such, contrary to Williams's later remarks in *Television,* radio, precisely by being thus twisted together with the culture of the local, here loses its *purely* formal structure.

In light of this, how might one think about the precise relation between "private mobilization" and "local broadcasting," as two ways to generate a precise, nonslushy meaning for radio? Of course, the immediate temptation is to stress that Powell is describing a mode of radiophonic practice that is the direct opposite of what Williams is seeking to render in his "ugly" phrase. This is true, but only to a point. To indicate what this truth misses, it is worth returning to the "Culture" section of *Possibilities,* where one finds the following "example" adduced to defeat a certain argument for commercialization. Responding to the notion that only commercialization could divide up bandwidths in a rational way, Powell writes: "Clearly, all cannot broadcast at once, but neither can every car occupy simultaneously the same position on the road. We don't therefore forbid cars, or restrict them to professional mechanics; we make traffic laws instead" (13), a formulation whose direct appeal to the automobile as a communicative analogue for the radio clearly anticipates Williams's formal concept of "mobilization." In other words, while there may indeed be no "nature" of broadcasting, Powell at various points in the pamphlet—her discussion of "familiarization," her discussion of "homework," the appeal to Dr. Himmelweit's research—characterizes the local as a rearticulation, a reconfiguration of the home-centered circuit of broadcasting later analyzed by Williams, implying, one would think, that, *qua* broadcasting, the local and the commercial (even in its paternal guise—the BBC or "Auntie") share something very much like a structure—if not a nature, surely a second nature. As a matter of fact, Powell concedes the point when, as if stringing together essences (culture is essentially *the* term, *supra*), she defends the importance of teaching radio literacy in schools by saying: "Why not radio? So far, partly because radio is one monolithic lump, of course, and, while you can get something of the effect from a tape recorder, it doesn't have the essence of radio, the actual broadcast" (16). Here, *lump* and *essence,* while referring to precisely the same thing, read quite differently. This difference invites us then to concentrate on the two machines, that is, the distinction between a tape recording and a radio broadcast. It is not hard to discern that for Powell radiophonic literacy involves more than speaking into a microphone attached to an apparatus of inscription. It involves speaking into a microphone while aware that invisible listeners are listening to one's speech—not that those listeners can *in principle* listen to it but that they are *in fact* listening to it, and listening acousmatically. Learning to do this is developing radiophonic literacy. Why? Because broadcasting is *the essence* of radio, whether commercial or local.

What is striking here is not Powell's self-implication in the dubious sin of essentialism (how tedious) but rather the precise configuration of tensions that link and trouble her key words, specifically *culture, local,* and *broadcasting* (or, as we have just learned, *radio*). Earlier, attention was directed to her anxious handling of the term *culture*. Its use, although crucial to any argument about local broadcasting, is not only immediately divisive—it connotes both aesthetically ("esoteric art-works") and anthropologically ("way of life")—but structurally exposed, through translation, to endless reception and connotative elaboration. More than simply a necessary evil, "culture," perhaps even especially when rooted in the "cultural" of cultural studies, lacks a ground. Culture, to push the point if only slightly, cannot be localized. It may be ordinary, but it cannot be local. This resembles, to some degree, E. P. Thompson's critique of Williams (that "culture" in both *Culture and Society* and *The Long Revolution* ends up being a tautological abstraction), except that the matter involves not logic but language. Powell's problem is not that culture and the local logically presuppose one another but that they together resist the effort to bring lexical precision to the analysis of radio, that they "essentially" and therefore irremediably complicate and thereby sustain the work of cultural studies.

The same can be said of broadcasting, the essence of radio. One picks up the problem by listening carefully when Powell says, "Towns are different; so should their radio be" (13), coupled with, "It [a radio station] could initiate a real revival of the sense of living in a society, not only locally but nationally" (19) or "The radio channel could be used deliberately as a means of making otherwise unimaginable ways of life seem accessible" (15). The distinctions between "radio," "a radio station," and "a radio channel" are negligible compared to the impact that this series—"town, society, nation, way of life" (and "unimaginable" at that)—has on the local, an impact likewise manifest in Powell's repeated agitation of the "national" versus "regional" distinction. To be clear, I do not disagree with her critique of commercial broadcasting (her reading of its necessary link to journalistic sensationalism is prescient indeed) or even with her embrace, ultimately, of BBC paternalism. Rather, my disagreement arises precisely at the point that one seeks to modify broadcasting with some precise or even generally reliable notion of the local. Put differently, "local broadcasting" is an oxymoron, and as such it exhibits the same lexical and conceptual looseness, the same necessary evil, as "culture" does. If the essence of radio is broadcasting, then radio is radically delocalized, so delocalized in fact as to interfere with this very characterization of its essence. Thus, even as Powell moves to proclaim "a new concept of radio" (14), her signal breaks up, the drive for "precise words" falters.

Described in her pamphlet as someone who has taught English (Powell was a "reader" at Birmingham), it is clear that she is certainly capable of precision, and while she deplores a certain "hysteria" that has crept into debate about mass communications in Britain, it is likewise clear that her faltering is due to something other than either idiocy or incapacity. To begin thinking about what may be at stake here, it is useful to return to Hoggart's and Hall's headnote where they both embrace and distance themselves from Powell's pamphlet, insisting that she has not "edited" it for the CCCS but that everything she says is consistent with the views of the CCCS. Taking their own turn with the rhetoric of essentialism, Hoggart and Hall distill the gist of her argument by writing: "Essentially, she is asking us to dare to think about creative amateurism, which is neither parish-pumpery of a narrow kind nor the professionalism which is so easily a form of patronage" (Powell 1). What is striking is that this translation of "local broadcasting" would strain with considerable difficulty to find its warrant in the pamphlet. Powell uses the word *amateur* only twice and certainly never proposes the virtues of creative amateurism in any conspicuous way. Williams, in referring us to her work a scant year after its publication, likewise never characterizes its position in these terms. We might explain this discrepancy as proof that the pamphlet was not "edited" for the CCCS—although it might also be interpreted as the opposite, namely, that in the corridors at Birmingham everyone "knew" that this was what Powell was "really saying"—but why not read it as a sign of the restless emergence of cultural studies as an academic discourse? In other words, why not read this discrepancy as the trace of a field in the process of trying to figure out what it will and will not, can and cannot say about what its partisans acknowledge to be a phenomenon that resists lexical precision? That Hoggart, Hall, and Williams all see Powell's text as an intervention suggests strongly that at issue here is not simply local broadcasting but the field of cultural studies itself insofar as it seeks to emerge in a space that is neither "merely" academic nor "fully" political, a space that then flashes into appearance within what I am here calling the more than rhetorical discrepancy between "local broadcasting" and "creative amateurism."

Stressing this, of course, invites one to think more carefully about the methodological or disciplinary constraints that surface in Powell's pamphlet, since these might then be read as the pressure put on academic practice by radio, pressure that subsequently precipitated into the debates, the speaking to each other, that was becoming cultural studies. With this in mind, what one notices immediately about Powell's study is that it is profoundly textual. She cites repeatedly from a wide range of sources: the Pilkington Report, the press reception of same, the parliamentary record (notably the cited comments of select MPs), various authors and scholars, several different newspapers, journals, and magazines, and on and on. I do not mean to suggest that her pamphlet is a "mere" tissue of citations, far from it, but its disciplinary profile is unabashedly literary, much as Hoggart's inaugural lecture might have led us to expect. To be sure, there is a strong sociological aspect of the study—Powell is deeply attentive to the institutional and practical dynamics of what she calls "community," where differences of location and therefore perspective preponderate—but this too is largely defined by Hoggart's approach to the social bond as a relation mediated by language, a "speaking to others." In fact, it is clear that radio recommends itself as an urgent object of inquiry not simply because of the Pilkington Report but perhaps even more directly because its "essence," broadcasting, at once thematizes the sociology of speaking—what Mikhail Bakhtin earlier called "dialogism"—and displaces from within the ideology of the face-to-face encounter the directness of the "to" in "speaking to others." If earlier I stressed that Hoggart's influence at CCCS waned in the course of the 1960s, it now seems appropriate to point out that this is because his very way of thinking the social modeled on the "organicism" of the face to face (by the way, within the discipline of political science, a persistent touchstone of so-called direct, or representative, democracy) could not be sustained. If, moreover, one thinks about the form and content of Powell's text, one sees instantly that it is fully situated in the disciplinary movement agitated by the sinking of this particular ship. The whole pamphlet stages a series of debates, teased out of textual sources, so as to affirm a vigorous form of "speaking to others," a form that then serves as the vehicle for an argument about the need for a national policy to organize radio broadcasting (and by extension the entire domain of mass communications) so as to keep it as close as possible to a local incarnation of the face to face—in a sense, to keep radio as close as possible to radio telephony but supplemented with something like a speaker phone.[4]

This is a bit unfair—remember, Powell is keen on bringing those "unimagined" others into the local conversation—but the disciplinary, even interdisciplinary, profile of her overall project is thrown into useful relief by a comparison to the work of Dorothy Hobson, another woman affiliated with the CCCS doing inspired and innovative work on radio. In 1978 Hobson completed an MA thesis at the CCCS titled "A Study of Working Class Women at Home: Femininity, Domesticity, Maternity," a portion of which was included, as "Housewives and the Mass Media," in *Culture, Media, Language,* a volume of CCCS papers that she edited with Stuart Hall, Paul Willis, and Andrew Lowe. As her title suggests, Hobson was very much part of the "major rethink" (to use Hall's phrase) effected within the CCCS by its encounter with feminism. Less evident, but no less important, is the fact that Hobson's study opens with a long and rich consideration of the role of radio in mediating the working-class woman's relation to the home, a consideration framed boldly in ethnographic terms. In concentrating on the home as a site of media consumption, of course, she is embracing what I have called the *heimlich* maneuver, but, unlike Williams or even Powell, Hobson is keen to deploy the disciplinary resources of ethnography to, as it were, *actually* speak to others. Much of her thesis is given over to transcripts of taped interviews with working-class women, transcripts that in an important, if not altogether convincing, sense give those involved the "right" to speak and to listen to each other. Like Powell, Hobson—who, in effect, is working in the wake of the failed efforts of Powell, Williams, and others to resist the commercialization of local broadcasting—devotes much energy to *reading* the transcripts of her taped interviews. In this she repeats Powell's and Hoggart's reliance on the literary interpretation of texts, and this despite the fact that her material obliges her to develop an entire code for registering and then interpreting nonlinguistic sounds on the tapes (pauses, laughs, etc.). This said, the social in Hobson's thesis is reduced with difficulty to the dialogic model of social interaction. Yes, she is talking to women as a working-class woman, but her study insists upon situating this talk in the homes where her subjects live, near the radios they listen to, among the objects that constitute the texture of their domesticity. Granted, Powell's approach is about making a case for as she says, "a possibility," but the inflection of her literary hermeneutic is limited by a rather diminished encounter with the social. Put differently, as the issue is not primarily an empirical one, Powell never thematizes the version of the social embedded in her disciplinary allegiances. To be fair, Hobson is no more metacritical than Powell—the entire circuitry of her study, the trajectory from university to community, retraces the *heimlich* maneuver, thus repeating what Williams might well characterize as her problem in its analysis—but what is quite apparent in the contrast between Powell and Hobson is that a different account of the social has emerged to pressure the theorization of radio at the CCCS. One could even say that as Hobson recognizes a sense of "collective isolation" ("Housewives" 108) in the remarks of one of her informants, what Hall characterized as the absence of an encounter with the late Sartre exacts its theoretical price on the ethnographic construal of the social. This is yet another way, now in the guise of a missed encounter, in which Hobson's study "belongs" to the debates that *were* the CCCS. The point here is not to judge the theoretical merits of her study but to stress how radio—the effort to study it academically and as part of a transformation under way within British academia—insistently emits contrasting ways not simply of grasping society but of the very logic of social inscription, a fact that, I will propose, agitates the core of Williams's appeal to—as if deliberately echoing an essential emphasis in the title of the CCCS— "contemporary Socialism" in his own article on Labour's radio policy.

A final observation about Hobson. Those familiar with her thesis, or even that portion of it reprinted in *Culture,* know that the analysis of radio—as if mimicking Williams's virtually contemporaneous study— gives way to an equally ambitious ethnography of television reception. It thus seems important to justify the importance I am attaching to the theoretical significance of radio. At bottom it would appear to find its warrant in the absent presence of Brecht, and Brecht's writings on radio in particular. Given the enduring centrality of Hoggart's dialogic model of the social bond, the emphasis insistently placed not simply on speech but on speaking to others, radio looms large because of what Brecht grasped about its potential status as an apparatus of "two-way" communication. This possibility of reversing the circuit of broadcasting, of clicking back and forth—even amateurishly or inexpertly—between the modes of sending and receiving, radiated from radio in a way that television seemed almost designed to foreclose, if not technically, then certainly economically, but politically in either case. It is precisely this potential, the significance of its possibilities, that puts radio in the vanguard of mass communications. It is certainly not the earliest form, but it is the form where it is broadly and immediately sensed that the political fate of mass communications, the very sociality of society, is, as it were, up for grabs. It is this that prompts Powell to grope for its "new concept" in a statement otherwise devoted to the prudent rhetoric of pragmatics, and it is this, I would argue, that prompts Williams to brandish Powell's pamphlet in his quarrel with the Labour Party. Yes, the debate is framed in terms of "policy," but clearly it is Williams's conviction that radio poses *the* burning question: What is socialism today, and what, therefore, must the Labour Party believe today?

In light of this, it seems difficult indeed to think that radio was left untheorized at the close of its Golden Age in the United States. If the critical character of "Critical Theory" derives in part from its distinctive engagement with its conditions of possibility, then the CCCS encounter with sound broadcasting urges us to recognize the apparatus of radio at the core of these conditions, interfering with and thus structuring their self-reception.

But what of "contemporary Socialism"? As intimated above, Williams gives us little to go on in the *Tribune* pieces, and while one might certainly comb his immense corpus for any number of incisive and sustained elaborations of his thinking about socialism (think here, for example, of the entire final section of *Resources of Hope*), it is worth recalling that a central charge leveled against Williams in Thompson's influential critique of the early work was that Williams had effectively severed himself from the intellectual traditions of British Marxism. Wary himself of the intellectual risks of Left orthodoxy, Thompson is far from unsympathetic to Williams's project, even if he does not put the central question as directly as one might: Is cultural studies the needed re: working of British Marxism that can "listen to" that tradition while speaking differently, that is, speaking with a vocabulary up to the task, to the political and theoretical needs of the labor movement? In attempting to make sense of Williams's recourse to Powell's pamphlet, I have answered, on Williams's behalf, in the affirmative. More needs to be said, particularly about my insistent recourse to the concept of re: working, especially as put to work in a discussion earlier said to be "haunted" by the present absence of Brecht, a figure who had his own ax to grind with really existing socialism.

To pursue this within range of the radio, it is useful to turn to what appears to be Williams's earliest publication on radio, a short but trenchant piece titled "Radio Drama" from the British journal *Politics and Letters* (1947). As the title might suggest, the encounter with Brecht could not be more direct—except that it isn't, a detail that signals our attention.

"Radio Drama" appears in a section of *Politics and Letters* called "Commentaries," and while it devotes much attention to Louis Mac-Neice's recently published collection of radio plays *The Dark Tower*, it is not exactly a review of the text. Instead, it treats the collection as an occasion for a compact reflection upon "drama in English" (106), one of Williams's most enduring aesthetic and political preoccupations. The question at hand is whether radio constitutes a revitalizing and thus important stimulus for the theater. Because answering such a question necessarily involves saying something decisive about what radio is such that it might or might not revitalize theater, Williams's remarks carry considerable weight in this context.

As one might expect from someone Williams characterizes as the "most eminent exponent of radio drama" ("Radio Drama" 106), Mac-Neice takes the view that radio is in certain respects the ideal vehicle for theater, precisely because it removes the distraction of the visual from what MacNeice clearly regards as the essence of theater, namely "calculated speech." Key here, although it is not formulated as such, is precisely what is meant by the acousmatic character of radio sound, and while it is true that this generates distractions of its own, it is vital that Williams accepts this formulation as the basis for what, in the end, will turn out to be a gentle but firm disagreement with MacNeice. This is the first of four broadly theoretical claims made about the nature of radio. The remaining three are looped through the disagreement between Williams and MacNeice, a disagreement that bears on the precise question of where and how drama and radio connect. More specifically, at issue are two entwined propositions: first, that drama suffers as an aesthetic practice when its relation to that which constitutes it as literary art is compromised, and second, that what constitutes drama as literary art is what MacNeice refers to as "calculated speech," or, as Williams later has it, "spoken language" ("Radio Drama" 107). While at first hearing this might suggest that this disagreement is hobbled by a narrowly "textual" account of drama, the matter is really more complex, for both men are concerned with something like the cultural or aesthetic force of language and whether drama blunts or sharpens it.

Teasing out the problem brings Williams to his second broadly theoretical insight about radio. Agreeing that radio creates an opportunity for re-elaborating the relation between drama and speech, Williams decisively qualifies this agreement thus: "The first general point which seems worth making is that radio drama, like all broadcast programs, does not depend on language to anything like the extent which a cursory examination would suppose. Its total effect depends in practice on all kinds of other sounds" ("Radio Drama" 107). This "vital point," as Williams later puts it, adds to the notion of the broadly acousmatic character of the radiophonic medium, the decisively antiphonocentric proposition that speech, that is, spoken language, is only part of what constitutes the full spectrum of radio sound, and crucial here is Williams's specification that this bears not simply on radio drama but on "all broadcast programs"—in other words, with radio as such. These two theoretical propositions are stitched together through the logic of supplementation, or, to use Williams's vocabulary, "compensation." That is, for Williams what MacNeice omits from his discussion is the fact that radio, in practice, does not and cannot exploit fully its acousmatic character, because it "compensates" for the suppression of the visible with the sonic supplements of sound effects. In effect, the distractions of the visible return in the "evocative noises" (107) that claw radio drama back into the aesthetically challenged maw of theatrical naturalism. Although Williams appears to be unaware of the research reported on in two of Roman Jakobson's statements on visual and auditory signs—research conducted in the Soviet Union in the 1920s by Aronson that sought to generate the "storehouse" (to invoke a Saussureanism) of the sonic signified by cataloguing radio sound effects—his emphasis on this provocative feature of radio's encounter with language is remarkable, if underdeveloped.[5]

The general point established by foregrounding the presence of "evocative noises," namely, that MacNeice approaches radio drama without really thinking first the specificity of radio, is fleshed out further in the third and fourth of Williams's theoretical propositions. Countering the suggestion that MacNeice (or, for that matter, his colleagues Auden and Isherwood) is revitalizing drama by using radio plays to produce "new dramatic conventions" ("Radio Drama" 108), Williams situates radio within a theory of mass culture. He writes:

> The characteristic institutions of expression in our time are mechanical in quality. Consider the newspapers, with their headlines and other devices of emphasis; or the cinema, with its use of super-imposition, montage, and

flashback; or popular songs, with their catch refrains; or political campaigns, with their use of repetition and slogan. These institutions are mechanical in the two senses that they usually depend on technical invention in the way of new machines and processes, and that they function by mass-producing a standardized product which has no organic connection with, and which does not depend on participation by their consumers. These are the characteristic institutions of our culture, and it is to their modes of expression that the mass-mind has been conditioned. Radio broadcasting is a similar institution. (108)

As a repudiation of the claim that NacNeice is developing new dramatic conventions, this argument proceeds by agitating a distinction—familiar enough across the entirety of Williams's corpus—between the mechanical and the organic and proposing that the mass mind has become so wholly subject to the former that it would not and could not recognize what properly deserves to be called a convention if it had to. Why? Because conventions, perhaps especially dramatic, that is, aesthetic conventions, are organic, they require the participation of consumers. Or, to play the Brechtean card, they require "two-way communication," and radio, as a mechanical institution, is anything but. In failing to recognize this, MacNeice et al., perhaps tragically but certainly inevitably, confuse mere devices for conventions and squander whatever revitalizing power the radio might be said to bring to drama.

To put the nail into the box, as it were, Williams concludes with his fourth and final theoretical proposition about radio: that as a mechanical institution it has generated characteristic devices of its own, devices it seeks to promote as conventions, that of the announcer and the commentator. Bringing these broad theoretical claims about the nature of radio to bear decisively on the quarrel with MacNeice, Williams writes:

> Radio is itself a mechanical institution, and has its own devices, of which the announcer and the commentator are the most important. What has happened in radio drama of the experimental kind is that these devices have been elevated into conventions, alongside the other conventions of the slogan, the headline, montage, flashback, and the popular song. A documentary feature by Mr. MacNeice employs the same technique as one of his plays. In the plays themselves, the devices are prominent. . . . The effect is clearly considerable, but it is not an effect which aids the literary expression. . . . Out of it all nothing very precise emerges. ("Radio Drama" 108–9)

If I have characterized such formulations as theoretical, it is because Williams appeals frequently to turns of phrase like "radio itself is" while simultaneously neutralizing the relevance of generic distinctions between drama and documentary. He, like Hoggart, is seeking to speak with the precision he faults MacNeice for lacking and appears thus to be prosecuting a theoretical argument whose arc might be parsed as "While MacNeice writes interesting work for radio, he has no conceptual grasp of the medium itself." As a result, MacNeice's aim of restoring and revitalizing the link between "calculated speech" and contemporary drama misses its mark. In effect, MacNeice fails to realize that a third radiophonic device, implied by the announcer and the commentator, is that of the consumer, and as long as one writes drama for such a construal of the audience, the literary character of such drama is decisively undermined. Or, put with maximum concision: radio drama is a contradiction in terms, at least in 1947, for Williams concludes by holding open the possibility that radio "may become" something different, a qualification that presumably sheds light on his eager embrace of Powell two decades later.

The problem with all this—and like others, I share Williams's reservations about *The Dark Tower*—is that once the dispute is cast in theoretical terms one is urged to probe whether Williams has achieved the theoretical precision he is calling for. If one argues that radio is a conflicted acousmatic medium precisely because, as a mechanical institution, it belongs to mass culture and the consumers unidirectionally addressed by it, then it would seem that the theoretical reflections and innovations of Brecht—especially as they bear on the matter of re: working the relation between radio and drama—acquire a distinctive urgency. Indeed, I earlier played the "Brecht card" both to foreshadow this development and to designate a problem. How are we to make sense of what is going on in "Radio Drama"? Is Williams using Brecht without mentioning him, and if so, why? Or, equally improbable, is Williams unaware of Brecht's "learning plays for radio"? Recall that Thompson chastised Williams for not drawing on the Marxist tradition, he did not accuse him of being ignorant of it.

While a full accounting of the relation between Williams and Brecht falls outside the service area of this chapter—note that *Drama from Ibsen to Eliot* becomes *Drama from Ibsen to Brecht* in the fifteen years separating the two texts—something like answers to the questions posed above appears in the texts that register the abrupt appearance of Brecht on Williams's radar. The two texts in question both appear in 1961: one is a lengthy contribution to *Critical Quarterly*, "The Achievement of Brecht," and the other is a review in the *Guardian* of his colleague Ronald Gray's contribution to the Writers and Critics series, *Brecht*, a review auspiciously titled "Creators and Consumers."

Interestingly, both texts open with a frank, but enigmatic exposition of Williams's encounter with Brecht, much as though Williams felt compelled to make sense of his own prior reticence. The first of these—reprinted with some emendations as the concluding chapter of the first version of *Modern Tragedy*—frames the encounter thus: "It quite often happens that a writer's reputation reaches us before we have any close knowledge of his work. It was so with Ibsen in the England, in the 1890s; it has been so with Brecht in the 1950s. Ideas can travel faster than the literature from which they are derived" ("Achievement" 153). As though not quite satisfied with this formulation, he writes in the *Guardian* review: "In our own time, Brecht is the most obvious victim of our consumers and their attendants. He was a name before many people knew anything at first hand about him, and the same is still true of Ionesco" ("Creators" 15). It is not hard to discern a certain sharpening, a distinct politicization of Williams's rhetoric in the second formulation. In the first, he seems content to index his experience against something like the perennial vagaries of reputation. In the second, precisely by insisting upon a term put in play in his disagreement with MacNeice—*consumer*—Williams sets aside the motif of reputation and stresses instead a dynamic whereby "creators" are essentially victimized by the circuits of consumer culture. Name and firsthand knowledge substitute for ideas and the literature from which they derive. Either way, what Williams seems compelled to reiterate is the notion that Brecht—whether a name or an idea (philosophically not an uninteresting distinction)—became detached from his work and arrived, somehow telecommunicated, in England during the 1950s. As if describing the reception of a remote signal, he writes, "A reputation reaches us." Behind this he presents two self-justifications. In the first, he characterizes his reticence as a gesture of prudence: like so many he lacked "close knowledge" of the work and therefore held his uninformed tongue. In the second, prudence gives way to politics: aware that creators are routinely victimized by the cultural mechanism through which we encounter them, he refused to participate in what he later calls "the endless circling and the chatter of Brecht-selling" (15).

Striking here is not simply the way Brecht brings out a political accent or tone in Williams—in his many subsequent treatments of Brecht he is keen to engage and evaluate this very dimension of the work—but rather the way this discussion, precisely on the matter of his encounter with Brecht, repeats a theoretical proposition about radio in the disagreement with MacNeice, namely, the notion that radio as a mechanical institution willy-nilly places the work of creators before consumers with whom it lacks all organic connection. It is as if, with an entirely apposite faintness, Williams in some sense *feels* the presence of the radio in his inopportune encounter with the rapidly approaching name "Brecht." If earlier I invoked the Derridean motif of "haunting" to describe the place of Brecht in "Radio Drama," it was to prefigure this enigmatic quality of the encounter that took place somewhere, a term I chose deliberately, at the close of the 1950s between Williams and Brecht. Although he certainly does not say as much, perhaps *this* is Brecht's "achievement," that is, the capacity of his work to influence in the absence of direct, firsthand contact, or, as Williams describes in the concluding paragraph of "The Achievement of Brecht," Brecht's ability to touch "the next stage" ("Achievement" 162).

This double entendre on "stage"—where historical phase and performance space restlessly converge, an effect that repeats in miniature the structure of telecommunication—bounces us back to "Radio Drama." Perhaps we have asked the wrong question, not "What are we to make of its reticence regarding Brecht?" but "How might we read Brecht's telecommunicated status, his absent presence in this reticence?" If one consults Gray's *Brecht,* clearly Williams's "guidebook," one might well conclude that this reticence was in fact, due to ignorance. Although in other ways erudite and comprehensive for a slim paperback volume, Gray makes only a passing reference to one of Brecht's early "learning plays" for radio, *The Baden-Baden Learning Play on Acquiescence,* justifying this inattention in aesthetico-political terms: it is dogmatic and therefore failed drama. Indeed, the discussion is so truncated one might not even understand that it was a radio play at all. Moreover, Gray erects an evaluative grid—the familiar organicism of "maturation"—that, for the most part, Williams adopts wholesale and repeats in most of his subsequent statements on the playwright: *Three Penny Opera* immature/failed, *Mother Courage* mature/successful. Of interest here is not the matter of the derivative nature of Williams's perspective—although one can see how ignorance might generate a compromising dependency—but rather the way Gray, unwittingly to be sure, prolongs the indirectness of Williams's encounter with Brecht, a situation that appears to fuel the "haunted" status of the encounter, especially as regards radio.

To engage this "hauntology" (Derrida's neologism) more head on, consider what is to be heard by setting the two early pieces on radio ("Radio Drama" and the review of Llewellyn White's *The American Radio*) side by side. Recall that in the former Williams adduces the mechanical character of the radio institution by establishing that all such institutions necessarily employ devices. At the head of his list stands the newspaper, with its "headlines and other devices of emphasis" ("Radio Drama" 108). In subsequently listing the devices characteristic of the radio, he repeats, among other devices of emphasis, "the headline." I stress this because when we turn to the later review of White we find that when justifying the reader's effort with the volume Williams writes: "At a time when there is still a danger of commercial broadcasting in this country, such an account as Mr. White's ought to be read. The story can be told in his headlines" (Rev. 81). Immediately after the material cited follow five "headlines," at least one extending for a full column inch. On the face of it Williams would appear to be contradicting his earlier position, a fact that one might happily attribute to the imprecision of so-called occasional writing were it not for the rather well-known fact that Williams took such writing, indeed the entire politics of speaking plainly to one another, with utmost seriousness. So let us consider another option: Brecht.

Of the several important differences that distinguish *Drama from Ibsen to Eliot* from *Drama from Ibsen to Brecht*, perhaps the least interesting is the mere addition of Brecht to the table of contents. More interesting, and more immediately relevant, is Williams's retheorization of the concept of convention, a concept that does much heavy lifting in both versions of the study. But this is not the only thing that recommends it to our attention. Recall, for example, that the distinction between "device" and "convention" played a key role in the disagreement with MacNeice, where Williams contrasted them to get at what mechanical institutions, like the radio, *lack*. In the version that stops with Eliot, although there is much familiar discussion of language and what Williams calls there "a mechanical environment" that "has dictated mechanical ways of thought" (*Drama* [1953] 27), convention is rather precipitously depolemicized. Instead, it is spliced into a new analytic configuration, that of convention, method, and technique, where it is used to think through the articulation of dramatic expression and what Williams here calls—as if directly channeling Lukács's *Gemeinschaftsgefühl* from *Theory of the Novel*—"a community of sensibility." What necessitates the depolemicization is Williams's insistence that, in 1953, all contemporary drama is "minority literature," that is, literature deprived in principle of an organic relation to the community of sensibility and thus deprived of the aesthetic circumstance under which the distinction between convention and device made sense.

In the second version, the study that includes Brecht, "community of sensibility" is recast as the now more familiar "structure of feeling," and convention, although still placed within the series "convention, method, technique," is, in effect, repolemicized, not in opposition to "device," but by being put to work in the evaluative schema previously teased out of Gray's study. Starting with the frankly ontological claim that all drama appeals by necessity to conventions, Williams adds the following in coming to terms with Brecht's self-understanding: "When a writer tries to set down the general principles of his work, he is often tempted to define it negatively: by rejecting his predecessors and often collecting them, arbitrarily, into a 'tradition.' Brecht certainly did this: not only because it is an obvious form for an artistic manifesto; but also because the whole cast of his mind was critical—many of his plays, though not indeed the most important ones, are in effect critical replayings of the work of others" (*Drama* [1987] 277). Williams uses this observation to situate Brecht more squarely in the history of drama (to, in effect, justify his inclusion in the study) but also to evaluate Brecht's achievement in terms of the way he either effectively or ineffectively repeated dramatic conventions, a distinction that prompts Williams at one point to distinguish between Brecht the artist and Brecht the pamphleteer. Fundamental to evaluating this repetition with a difference is the recasting of the "community of sensibility" as "structure of feeling," a recasting that allows Williams to begin complicating community—in the singular—with structure, which while written in the singular (at least here) admits of variation; indeed, he appeals in the introductory chapter to one of his signature conceptual innovations, the dominant. What this permits is a determination of efficacy indexed to the conventions that resonate *within* contending structures of feeling. This said, what is nevertheless quite striking about the cited passage is the phrase "critical replayings": that is, the acknowledgment that Brecht, whether in the guise of a convention, a method, or a technique, understood the critical value of repeating something differently. Although it would take us out of range, one might reasonably argue that this articulates the very logic of that practice of "literarization"—among other things, captioning—found by Benjamin to be so powerful in his own struggle to politicize art. Be that as it may, what bears emphasis here is that "critical replaying" might well explain *exactly* what Williams is doing in his review of White. Instead of contradicting himself by resorting to the mere "device" of headlines in his commentary, why not see Williams as critically replaying White's own reliance on the mechanized thought captured in headlines? In effect, Williams is "critically replaying" the device of the headline, but in so doing once again underscoring his conflicted reticence regarding Brecht, though now in a rather different register. Indeed, reticence emerges here as something like very rhythm of replaying.

To replay then a question of my own: So what *is* Williams doing here? What significance can be attached to the present absence of Brecht in his reflection on radio drama? In the end, this is a matter of cultural politics, that is, the articulation between cultural studies (and specifically the Birmingham CCCS) and what Williams called "contemporary Socialism." To clarify how, it is helpful to turn to the closing chapter of *Drama from Ibsen to Eliot*. There, as Williams says in his introduction, "I have tried to show the vital part criticism has played in dramatic reform and development" (38): in other words, it is a chapter that wrestles expressly with the encounter between, if not philosophy, then certainly thought, and art. From the perspective generated here, it is interesting that in his closing formulation regarding this encounter Williams appeals openly to the motif of repetition, aware, it would seem, that repetition functions as an enabling condition *for* the encounter between thought and art. If I stress this, it is in order to highlight Williams's insistence that the repetition is, as it were, lopsided. Criticism encounters drama so as to tease out from it a "continuity of standards" (277), standards that drama articulates but without being able to "think" them. Indeed, he faults Yeats and Eliot for being too willing to learn *from* the theater. What is stressed, and it is an emphasis familiar in the Western context at least since Plato set about legislating poetry and music, is the orthopedic function of criticism. Behind the implied declaration of the unquestionable value of criticism's own standards is the contention—at once aesthetic and political and therefore doubly dubious—that criticism has, as it were, nothing "critical" to learn from drama. Setting aside, for the moment, the question of whether this is true, what seems important to underscore is that it is this very account of the encounter between thought and art that Brecht complicates and, if we are to believe either him or Benjamin, complicates it in the name of politicizing art. I would argue, then, that an active if unthematized dimension of the present absence of Brecht in Williams's reflection on radio is the challenge to criticism, to its epistemological priority, that hangs suspended beneath the telecommunicated "name" Brecht. Because if, in 1953, it is urgent to secure this priority, the capacity of criticism to secure the continuity of standards, then might this not be in reaction to a discovery, in his own critical practice—witness the review of White—of the operation, not simply of Brechtian replaying, but of the "unconscious" (Williams's word) conventions and standards of drama? In effect, what is at issue in the encounter with Brecht is the epistemological integrity of the distinction between criticism and drama, a distinction with far-reaching implications for any sort of intellectual project keen to redress, in Hoggart's words, the fact that "there is not even a moderately precise vocabulary for discussing the cultural questions raised by the study of broadcasting" ("Difficulties" 199).

The dilemma makes itself felt not only in the drifting among terms like *device, technique, method, convention,* and *standards,* but also in the "ugly" phrase "mobile privatization," a phrase thus described so as to register its inadequacy, or, at the very least, the perceived conflict between its sign and its referent. What the encounter between Williams and Brecht suggests is that this dilemma is agitated by the fact that it apparently arises as much because of the constraints of analytical precision, as because of the unsettling, perhaps even delocalizing fact that broadcasting has here fully encroached upon its study. The re: working of radio and drama has "reached" Williams, is active in his critical thinking about radio drama, in ways that both incite and frustrate the drive for a precise critical vocabulary. If this drive is part and parcel with the intellectual and political urgency behind the emergence of cultural studies as an institutionally grounded form of the study of broadcasting (among other things, of course), then one should expect to see this very interplay of incitement and frustration in the establishment of cultural studies. Broadcasting, and I am specifying sound broadcasting, is thus already active within this emergent form of its study, not simply as its object, but as the interrogative instability of its questioning.

Of course, as he himself reminds us, Williams was not actually *at* or *in* Birmingham, but it should now be clear in what sense he was called by the institutional event taking place there beginning in 1963. He was, already in the 1940s, attuned to it. Thus this relation, this affiliation, was itself mediated by radio and its effects. Perhaps more than anyone else, certainly more than Hoggart, Williams recognized that this calling was directed, not to him, but, citing a late work, to "actually existing socialism" ("Beyond") both in Europe and in Britain. Hence the stress in *Tribune* on the chiasmatic circuit connecting Labour and radio.

Radio assumes this urgency because it is where the question of cultural politics is symptomatized in what Thompson referred to as the Marxist tradition. Williams is not avoiding this tradition—although I take Thompson's point—so much as he is attempting to locate within it the zone in which the tradition either has fallen silent or is spoken with garbled precision. That tradition has tended to designate this zone as "art" or "culture" more broadly, and precisely because radio, and mass culture more generally, open a channel—perhaps even a wormhole—between art and everyday life, radio touches on a conflict, a vexed matter, within (but also without) the Marxist tradition. To be sure, Williams has trouble of his own in attempting to sustain the force of this insight. Indeed, one might argue that the name for it in his unconscious is precisely "Brecht." That said, he cannot be faulted for having missed the profound link between radio, education, cultural studies, and the struggle for socialism. He simply had trouble speaking it to others.

CHAPTER 6

"We Are the Word"?

On August 17, 1992, paleoconservative Patrick Buchanan said the following at the Republican National Convention:

> My friends, this election is about much more than who gets what. It is about who we are. It is about what we believe. It is about what we stand for as Americans. There is a religious war going on in our country for the soul of America. It is a cultural war, as critical to the kind of nation we will one day be as was the Cold War itself. And in that struggle for the soul of America, Clinton & Clinton are on the other side, and George Bush is on our side. And so, we have to come home, and stand beside him. (Buchanan 3)

Although these remarks follow the publication of James Davison Hunter's *Culture Wars: The Struggle to Define America,* Dinesh D'Souza's *Illiberal Education,* and Roger Kimball's *Tenured Radicals* by a year or two and are contemporaneous with Gerald Graff's *Beyond the Culture Wars,* because they articulate the distinctly national profile of the "culture wars" they ought to be seen as something like an opening salvo in the war zone known as the public sphere. Even Molly Ivins, whose withering one-sentence rejoinder—"Many people did not care for Pat Buchanan's speech, it probably sounded better in the original German"—missed the point by implying that the German in question was spoken by Hitler instead of Bismarck. After all, it was Bismarck, not even Gramsci, who coined the term *Kulturkampf* as a way to describe the struggle against Roman Catholicism in the domain of German higher education at the end of the nineteenth century. Almost two decades hence it is now easy to overinvest in the emergence of a struggle that is still with us, an overinvestment that loses sight of something decisive, namely, that the "culture wars" refer to what Gramsci did indeed call a "war of position" (as opposed to a "war of maneuver") waged in the broad context of what might be called the neoliberalization of knowledge, that is, the socioeconomic drive to subsume the labor of learning under the logic of market calculation and profitability. In such a context, the university as a publicly funded form of knowledge production and dissemination is at risk. It may indeed be in ruins; for the high-stakes game here is not simply a war over the terms and values of cultural literacy but a war over the enabling conditions of secular knowledge itself.

It is against the noise generated by this background that the following report assumes its significance: "*7. Council Subcommittee.*" The council established an action subcommittee (Gerald Graff, Marianne Hirsch, Michael Holquist, Claire Kramsch, and Naomi Schor) that will meet to discuss various issues, including communication with the general public" (Council, Minutes [May 1993], 594). This appeared in the minutes of the Council of the Modern Language Association published in the May 1993 issue of *PMLA,* and Graff's involvement here is, given *Beyond the Culture Wars,* instructive. The results of the discussions were reported in subsequent issues of the publication, and the textual itinerary is not without interest.

In the October 1993 issue of *PMLA* the following update appeared: "Michael Holquist reported that the subcommittee met on 20 May and that it began its discussion by identifying (1) the goals to be achieved by any effort to use the media in a more proactive and sustained way and (2) the audiences the association might try to reach. The subcommittee focused on the use of radio, identified several topics that could be addressed in radio programs, and recommended to the council that the possibility of using radio be pursued" (Council, Minutes [October 1993], 1202). This was followed, in the same report, by "In response to the subcommittee's report, the council appointed a new subcommittee (Marianne Hirsch, Michael Holquist, chair, Naomi Schor) to continue conceptualizing a series of radio programs, to refine the goals, audiences and topics already developed, and to discuss possible program formats" (Council, Minutes [October 1993] 1202). The newly formed subcommittee was instructed to report back to the council in a year.

Working with apparent urgency, Holquist's committee reported in March of 1994. In the published minutes the subcommittee's task is characterized as that of "conceptualizing a series of radio programs that would present aspects of the study and teaching of languages and literature in ways that would appeal to the general public," and the subcommittee reports having made contact with "an experienced producer of radio programs at the National Humanities Center [NHC]"; as a result subcommittee members now believe that the association could and should "become involved in the production of such programs" (Council, Minutes [March 1994] 312). Subcommittee membership was again expanded to four, with Stephen Greenblatt filling the vacancy left by Graff.

At the May 1994 meeting of the council, the minutes for which refer to Holquist's subcommittee no longer as a reporting subcommittee, but as "National Public Radio Programs," Holquist details the results of his encounter with the NHC, identifying potential radio program topics and noting that as a general rule all topics, where feasible, should have "an international aspect" (Council, Minutes [May 1994] 500). The minutes also report that there was a lively discussion of potential topics and, in its wake a vote taken to develop a "pilot series" of radio programs in concert with the NHC. The council's support was unanimous.

In February of 1996, Holquist appeared before the executive council to both report on the first six radio programs produced in conjunction with the NHC and to request, on behalf of what the minutes refer to as the "radio committee," support for a second series of programs. Suggesting several improvements or changes—better-prepared broadcast participants, collaborators other than the NHC, and so on—Holquist also indicated that a PR firm would be brought in to increase the quality of the second series of programs.

Then things changed. Specifically, a set of activities that had largely achieved visibility through the minutes of the executive council appeared as a piece of association history on the pages of the *MLA Newsletter*. In the Winter 1996 edition, Phyllis Franklin published a two-page piece on what in the interim had become a radio program with a name, *What's the Word?* Her title, "Telling the Field's Story," deserves comment. On the one hand, her piece recounts in considerable detail the history that I have teased out of the published minutes of the executive council's monthly meetings. In this sense, her title refers to her own labor of "telling the story" of how the MLA came to figure out how it was going to approach the problem of telling its ("the field's") story to a suspicious or apathetic public. On the other hand, it is clear that *What's the Word?* is understood by Franklin to be the means by which the MLA has decided to tell its own story. The clap, as it were, between these two hands signals the extent to which the association grasped the continuity between addressing itself and addressing others, especially those not yet turned away by the bad press directed at the MLA by paleoconservatism and its fellow travelers. But this also directs attention to a matter that has achieved thematic status in this book, namely, the problem of how the MLA came to think the relations between education (especially in the postsecondary humanities), cultural politics (the so-called culture wars, but a North American "war of position" more generally), and, of course, radio. Why radio? More to the point, can radio—deployed as the apparatal infrastructure of *What's the Word?*—serve the ends that this configuration of themes appears to set for it?

To respond to the question implicitly broached by Franklin herself—whether a radio program can "reach the public effectively" (4)—it is vital to focus on the word *effectively*. The matter here is not just about the reach of radio and its comparative cost-effectiveness (both issues raised in the minutes) but about the effect of radio *as such* in the context of the culture wars. Although Franklin does not make the link directly, when what was to become the "radio committee" met on May 20, 1993, to identify what goals the association might seek to achieve by using "the media" more proactively, it is clear that at some level the goal that emerged was that of a defensive intervention in the culture wars. This, it would seem, is why in "Telling the Field's Story" Franklin aligns her comments with those of Graff (after all, one of the founding members of the radio committee), citing in full the opening paragraph of his text *Beyond the Culture Wars*. This is the well-known passage in which the humanities are represented through the figure of a neighborhood in decay. It is a risky metaphor because it links deconstruction, feminism, and critical race theory with the effects of poverty on an inner-city neighborhood. In the second paragraph Graff stresses that this metaphor represents the point of view of the cultural warriors opposed to the "new humanities," and it is thus clear that he is giving them more credit than they deserve. Do Kimball, Buchanan, Cheney, et al. actually believe that poverty causes urban blight? I thought they thought it was people of color? This said, in putting this metaphor in play, what Franklin's comments invite is an assessment of the effectiveness of *What's the Word?* indexed to its capacity to challenge and, in the spirit of urban renewal, presumably reverse the decay of the humanities *as construed* by their enemies. This invites two levels of assessment: one, an assessment that considers to what extent a "general public" (listeners of NPR and its affiliates) finds the "urban blight" account of the humanities contradicted by other accounts, and two, an assessment of radio's capacity as an apparatus to support this contradiction.

Though Graff has kind things to say about Franklin (and the MLA) in his book, she does not avail herself of what, under the circumstances of her newsletter report on *What's the Word?*, might have trenchantly crystallized for both her and her readers the urgent question of "effectiveness." I am thinking of one of Graff's several passes over Alan Bloom's *The Closing of the American Mind,* indeed the one that recounts his "debate" with Bloom on *Oprah*. Elaborating on the perennially reliable theme of the North American intellectual as a Cassandra figure, Graff writes: "I am no friend to the Allan Bloom view of education, but once I began to visualize myself debating Bloom before the 'Oprah' audience I was forced to think of him less as an ideological enemy than as a fellow intellectual in a common predicament: how to clarify a debate about relativism, nihilism and other abstractions not commonly presented on daytime network TV" (93). Because Graff's concern in this discussion is to establish the "ambivalence" of the figure of the intellectual, he lets that stand in for the entirety of the question raised about reaching an audience through, in this case, television. Because Holquist's committee took up the question of the audience as job two, we can assume that this sort of consideration led it toward radio and away from television. But there is a more delicate point to be made here. It is the point that surfaced and resurfaced in the earlier chapters of this book, namely, in what way does radio itself become not simply a means but a problem for communication, whether attempted by intellectuals or not? Although he does not say as much, Graff invites us to consider that television itself (and here he aligns himself with the many who have voiced their contempt for the "culture industry") is part of what complicates the relation between North American intellectuals and their publics. Indeed, although this would involve declaring oneself as a partisan, the question of "effectiveness" must at some point crack the nut of the status of the institutions of mass culture, and radio in particular, in the "war of position" called the culture wars. This is in many respects the signature question of the Frankfurt School, and it would not be hard to see that foreclosing the question of the status of radio is part and parcel of the closing of the American mind. Here a different, rather more unsettlingly common ground rises under the feet of Bloom, Graff, and Franklin. Although the politics of mass culture was not immediately on his mind, when Tracy Strong, in his introduction to Carl

Schmitt's *The Concept of the Political,* wondered whether a "Strauss-ianism of the Left" (xx) was possible, he seemed to have forgotten an intellectual position he otherwise was at pains to bring into his discussion: the Frankfurt School. After all, rather little of political substance separates Bloom's critique of rock music from Adorno's formulations in "Jazz: Perennial Fashion," and while this reemphasizes the need to be clear about the Left, it simultaneously raises the problem of whether Strong posed the right question.

To engage the matter of political efficacy more directly, it behooves one to think less obliquely, in general, about the programs aired on *What's the Word?* One in particular calls for attention: "Radio: Imaginary Visions" (or, as it appears in the online index, "Radio: Imaginary Image"). It aired in 1998 (well into the advent of radio studies), was produced, written, and directed by Sally Placksin (who has written about women in jazz), and involved the participation of Everett Frost, Elissa Guralnick, and Thomas Whitaker.[1] The topic: radio drama, about which all three participants had written extensively. What recommends it for special attention in this context is the fact that it is one of the rare engagements with radio as such during the early campaigns of the culture wars. In effect, this is a program in which the MLA might be said to be involved in metacritical self-reflection where the very medium of its public engagement is also the object of scholarly reflection.

The program had its origin in the solicitation for programming ideas that appears routinely in the association newsletter. Responding to it, Elissa Guralnick, in English at the University of Colorado-Boulder, was then contacted by Phyllis Franklin, who urged Guralnick to proceed. Guralnick then involved Frost (in film at New York University) and Whitaker (emeritus from Yale in English). The program follows the design structure developed by Sally Placksin, namely, it opens with something of a teaser—in this instance, short sound bites from each of the academic speakers, recordings of old broadcasts, and a sound effect, followed by the question, "Are these horses' hooves we hear, or only coconut shells? Join us for this edition of *What's the Word?*: 'Radio: Imaginary Visions'"—followed by something that resembles a play of voices. Placksin speaks, then Guralnick speaks. They do not engage each other, but their voices are not utterly unresponsive. This continues for roughly ten minutes, and then there is a break. Guralnick and Placksin give way to Placksin and Frost, who, following another break, give way to Placksin and Whitaker. Guralnick gets the last academic word, followed by Placksin, who brings the program to a close by detailing her role and inviting the audience to tune in next time. The whole thing goes by in less than thirty minutes and it is very professionally done. It is clearly a radio broadcast of the sort imagined by Holquist and his committee.

Although mention is made of the sponsoring association, what could be said—perhaps tendentiously—to establish the MLA's ownership of the program is the fact that sooner or later, with an almost anxious implacability, the "conversation" gets around to Shakespeare. Whitaker concludes his contribution by reading Prospero's oft-cited lines from scene 1, act 4 of *The Tempest*. It is poignantly rendered, as if Prospero's somewhat arch worldliness had been compounded by Whitaker's sense that Placksin's "And it is no accident that Shakespeare's speeches also work well on radio" had raised the stakes unbearably high, virtually requiring the subterfuge of a planned accident. Buried here, even if shallowly, is one of several more philosophical propositions advanced about radio in the program, namely, Whitaker's gingerly proffered suggestion that when Prospero says, "These our actors, / as I foretold you, were all spirits, and / are melted into air" (lines 166–68), he might, "four centuries before Marconi," be talking about radio. In other words, as the program title has insistently adumbrated, radio is fundamentally a locus of "imaginary visions," yet another avatar of the acousmatic character of the medium. If this gesture deserves to be characterized as "anxious," it is because it appears to be where the question of how literature and language connect to radio—and for that matter, the MLA's claim, if you will, on the medium as an object of scholarly attention—are being established.[2] Given that such matters would seem to constitute the very core of the question of political efficacy, it will be important to sort through all the more philosophical propositions advanced about radio there, propositions that by virtue of being "on" the air, sponsored by the MLA, inevitably echo back on the strategic and ultimately political question of turning to radio in order to prosecute the culture wars.

Aware that in bearing down on the content of a brief, quasi-ephemeral radio broadcast I risk making a mountain out of a molehill, I want nevertheless to express my solidarity with Whitaker's insistence, late in the broadcast, upon the important link between education and "sustained attention to thought expressed in words," by paying acute attention to two types of discourse that give the broadcast its deep intellectual structure. On the one hand, there are what I have been calling the philosophical or theoretical propositions. These are characterizations of what radio *is,* often linked to transhistorical practices or psychobiologically grounded assertions about the mind, vision, hearing, and the imaginary. On the other, there are a series of propositions that touch on, sometimes quite directly, the strategic relevance, even importance, of the radio broadcast for the cultural project of the MLA. In one case, the title of the program is itself put in play.

In a certain sense, each academic specialist contributes to the broadcast by developing his or her specific philosophical insight. Guralnick, whose comments bookend the broadcast, opens by sounding a theme then familiar from radio studies, namely, that of the tension between radio and television as opposing, yet complementary solicitations of the human sensorium. Teasing out a central preoccupation of her ambitious 1996 study, *Sight Unseen: Beckett, Pinter, Stoppard and Other Contemporary Dramatists on Radio*, Guralnick says: "There is a sense when you are listening to a radio that, no matter how many millions of listeners have tuned in, that radio is playing for you and only for you. That person is talking to you. There is a very real sense in which only you see what you see, that the scene that you have set is yours and yours alone, which is, of course, not true in a theater or in the movies." As if to underscore the theoretical import of this formulation, Placksin then says: "As we listen to the radio each one of us sees its imaginary visions in his own way. . . . And the image comes instantly to the ready eye of the mind." What emerges here is a version of what Sartre called "serialized" listening, that is, the sense that radio *is* an apparatus endowed with the power to radically individuate a social group. Setting in motion a theme to which she will return, Guralnick stresses not simply that the radio individuates but that it individuates along the troubled continuum between seeing and hearing: the radio's "voice" is singular and addressed intimately to the listener; the scene it evokes is effectively transferred to the listener who "instantly" takes sole possession of it. Invoking her title, Placksin underscores exactly this in saying that "each one of us sees its [the radio's] imaginary visions in his own way." Theoretically then, what this suggests is that radio—in general—is a device that, in the context of mass society, produces individuality as a site of visual, perhaps even imaginary, experience. An interpellation machine?

In a subsequent formulation Guralnick makes it clear that she is indeed situating radio deep within the structure of the human subject. She says:

> Radio depends on your ability to visualize, and playwrights for radio understand that you will see an image instantaneously. When you hear a sound effect, like those coconuts that made the sound of horses' hooves, you will

see a horse. . . . Well, there's that wonderful sense, when you get into a radio play, that you can't be pulled away. You're in a place that you've created and you stay there. . . . But as television grew into its own, it became a more visual medium, and I think we began to lose the verbal characteristics of the old radio play. That sense that we rely on the word rather than on the visual image is what you lose when you move from radio into television and really begin to rely on TV.

"Radio depends on your ability to visualize," but more than that, radio drama (Guralnick's area of academic concentration) depends on the fact that human subjects see images instantaneously, in effect without mediation. We *hear* a simulated horse's trot and immediately we *see* a horse. Here radio is shown to participate intimately in a certain construal of the subject of human perception, indeed, a construal in which a sound effect is allowed to stand in for the aural character of speech—and vice versa. As has been mentioned, in two important papers from the sixties, "Visual and Auditory Signs" and "On the Relation between Visual and Auditory Signs," Roman Jakobson casts some doubt on the model of the subject at work. While the historical point is not without interest (the perceived immediacy of certain sounds actually *came* into being), what Jakobson's remarks foreground is the ambition of Guralnick's claims: she is precisely trying to grasp what I have been calling the apparatal character of the radio.

It is in this context that Guralnick invites us to think about the relation between radio and television. Elaborating on Placksin's observation that "on the radio all the information had been carried on the voice," Guralnick stresses that during the decade of the 1980s a decisive shift took place, "the move from a medium for the voice and for the ear, to a visual medium," implying if not actually suggesting—given the historical claims of Michelle Hilmes, Susan Douglas, and others—that scholarly attention turned again to radio precisely when narrative information became decisively visual, in effect, when the subject of radio listening was displaced by the subject of television watching. Both Placksin and Guralnick seem aware of the troubling character of such remarks—as part, after all, of a *radio* broadcast transmitted in the wake of the shift—and thus Guralnick returns to them in her closing observations, where she makes another pass over the question of radio and subjectivity.

Her remarks are extremely rich and deserve to be cited in full.

As long as children love to be read to, human beings will love to listen to a voice on the radio. It's the same idea in *Heart of Darkness* by Joseph

Conrad. Marlowe's voice comes out of the dark. To hear that book read aloud. Even when you read it to yourself you know that you are listening to Marlowe sitting on that boat in the darkness telling that story. There is a human need for that contact you get with another voice. Radio provides that; film doesn't. Because it is what it is, it's visual, and it *should* exploit the visual image. There is no need to abandon radio just because you also have film. We should have both.

Although here film is the metonymy for visual information instead of television, it is clear that Guralnick wants to soften the blow of what earlier has been characterized as a decisive shift in which something is lost (that sense that we rely on the word) to a more synchronic account of two media standing in complementary relation with one another. Although it certainly seems odd to characterize film as an exclusively visual medium—soundtrack studies have generated a substantial critical literature in both musicology and media studies—what is clear is that Guralnick is freighting the word *sense* ("that sense that we rely on the word") with a lot of conceptual baggage. In other words, the point is not literally that film and television are strictly visual media but that they engage the human sensorium from within a sociohistorical context where information, in its most capacious sense, has become-visual. For this very reason, her account of the voice in the preceding passage likewise assumes great import, and to spell this out it is useful to revisit Freud's evocative account of anxiety in the third of the *Three Essays on the Theory of Sexuality* from 1905.

Freud writes: "Anxiety *[Angst]* in children is originally nothing other than an expression of the fact that that they are feeling the loss of the person they love. It is for this reason that they are frightened of every stranger. They are afraid in the dark because in the dark they cannot see the person they love; and their fear *[Furcht]* is soothed if they take hold of that person's hand in the dark" (224). Explaining the origins of this insight, Freud adds in a footnote: "For this explanation of the origin of infantile anxiety I have to thank a three-year-old boy whom I heard calling from a dark room: 'Auntie, speak to me! I'm frightened because it's so dark.' His aunt answered him: 'What good would that do? You can't see me.' 'That doesn't matter,' replied the child, 'if anyone speaks it gets light'" (224 n.). Freud circles back to this material in "Inhibitions, Symptoms, Anxiety" from 1926 only to further align himself with his infant master. The virtue of these remarks is that they powerfully backlight Guralnick's insistent evocation of "the dark" as the space in which the voice resonates and achieves what Whitaker has called its "auditory power." Moreover, they make clear that her scenario—presumably, the very one instantly appropriated by her listeners—recasts her earlier, more psychobiological account of the human subject, as a distinctly psychoanalytical one, that is, one in which what she calls the "need" for contact with another voice arises as a repetition of an infantile experience of being read to, presumably by one's parents or their surrogates. What Freud contributes here is something like the "cause" of the "need" that Guralnick presents as simply a familiar, and thus familial, fact. Thus might we not say that we "need" contact with the voice of another because we are anxious about losing it, because—to amplify the theoretical resonance of Guralnick's discussion—we are in the dark? And not simply a dark room, but *the* dark, the enigmatic—as Maurice Blanchot might say—"space of literature." In effect, Marlowe's voice, not simply in the dark on that boat, but in the very heart of darkness.

Radio then, for Guralnick, resists the becoming-visual of filmic and televisual information, precisely because it is structured like the voice that addresses us from out of *the* darkness.[3] Here radio—again not *a* radio, but *the* radio, the wireless—is wired deeply into the human subject, assuming the rigorous profile of an apparatus, one that, as Freud suggests, both channels and resists anxiety. It is striking, therefore, that these formulations—precisely to the extent that they shield the broadcast itself from the historical shift between the cultural priorities of listening and seeing, thereby justifying our "attentive listening to serious material"—complicate so provocatively Guralnick's (and for that matter Placksin's) early stress on the visual or imaginary side of radio listening. For it would seem that what gives itself instantly to be seen in the dark is precisely nothing—the void. While it is true that in Conrad the darkness that enshrouds Marlowe's enunciative moment is not total (don't forget the "spectral illumination of moonshine"), Guralnick's evocation of this scene—"Marlowe's voice comes out of the dark"—stresses the fact that the voice isolates itself from the space of visuality, that it sounds *without* producing an image to be possessed by the individuated listener. Indeed, what this voice effects might appear to be the opposite, namely the very withholding, the suspension of individuation. The sound of this voice does not and cannot occasion an act of appropriation where the "imaginary vision" belongs to me, and in this failure it produces the anxiety that the "need for contact" redresses, alas, through exacerbation. It is suggestive, I think, that this anxiety is wedged both within Guralnick's own thinking about radio and in her and Placksin's thinking about the status of *their* broadcast in the period of the eclipse of auditory information. Do their voices come out of the dark? Are their listeners in the dark? About what?

Although here I have clearly clicked forward to those moments in Guralnick's remarks that bear on the strategic value of the broadcast for the MLA, I want to turn first to the philosophical dimensions of the contributions of her colleagues, Frost and Whitaker, before considering her remarks in greater detail.

The Frost segment begins on a directly political note, reminding us that Hitler and Göring believed that the Nazi rise to power would have been impossible without the medium of radio. Frost crystallizes the insight by saying, "The single voice in the mind of all." Although it is clear that he is chiming in on the now familiar modeling of radio sound on the human voice, he also sounds the note that contradicts—in utterly predictable ways—Guralnick's appeal to the essential link between radio and individuation. For Frost, Hitler's voice does not provoke an imaginary vision to be individually appropriated by each listener. On the contrary. Indeed, it is not hard to recognize that the apparent function of his remarks is to conflict—think Graff—with those of Guralnick. For example, when he weighs in on the relation between radio and television he emphasizes: "I don't think of television as a competitor for radio any more than I think of the cinema as a competitor of the book or of the television. These things each have their place, and when they are used properly work synergistically with each other." Although by the time the broadcast concludes Guralnick has come around to a view like this, "We should have both," here Frost sounds as if he is rejecting Guralnick's claim that radio is fatally challenged by the becoming-visual of information. Much hangs, of course, on the adverb *properly,* and Frost himself is compelled to provide it with a "continental" gloss, stressing that in Europe (and Germany in particular) writers move between the various media more freely (properly?), whereas in the United States, "it's all much more segmented," concluding that—and here he rejoins Guralnick—"We've lost something there. We've lost something very real and vital." True, for Frost the matter is much more narrowly professional than for Guralnick ("synergy," after all, deriving from managerial discourse); indeed, his focus is largely on producers, not receivers, but is not for that reason atheoretical. He just stresses that radio is indeed an institutional component of what Adorno and Horkheimer referred to as the "culture industry."

Like Adorno and Horkheimer (with whose work he is doubtless familiar), Frost is concerned about the ontological power of art.

Apparently reacting to his characterization of the public service function of the radio in Germany after World War II, Placksin, in her own invocation of the category of need, says: "There was also a basic need for some form of artistic expression." This is followed by Frost's introduction of Brecht's concept of the *Hörspiel:* "I am forbidding myself here the word 'entertainment' or 'amusement,' but that way the arts have of being in the world, so important and so ephemeral, that makes all the difference in people's lives. They [the Germans] had to find some kind of reflection in themselves of what they had been through that would make it possible to go on. And that was the beginning of radio drama, their word *Hörspiel,* hear-play, play for the ear, not as a substitute but as a different kind of theatrical performance." Like Guralnick, Frost wires the radio deep into the human subject, arguing that the Germans traumatized by the war "had to" (presumably as an expression of Placksin's "basic need") find a reflection of this experience and give it expression. They did so by turning to the radio and capturing there the reflection of the war in the generic innovation of the *Hörspiel.* Again, Frost rewords Guralnick's analysis of seeing and listening by placing a shared "reflection," imaginary vision, of the war at the core of a technical innovation for the ear, suggesting that, however abhorrent Hitler's policies, he was right about the "mind of all." One collective mind, one collective experience, one expressive innovation: radio drama. This conflicts directly with Guralnick's emphasis on the individuality of imaginary visions, perhaps suggesting that while radio drama may *end* as individuated reflections it *begins,* at least generically, as one shared vision—at least for those who produce it. Regardless, there is a different pattern of psychobiological accents falling here, one that invites a different account of radio when conceived in terms of the function of art in the context of an ineluctably politicized cultural history.

Whitaker, whose contributions have been touched on earlier, reverses course, throwing his weight behind Guralnick's stress on radio and subjective individuation. He says: "I think radio does invite listeners to focus more inwardly upon the words than does a stage performance. . . . As a teacher I have come to believe that words and sentences convey much of their meaning through their auditory power. I'm convinced, therefore, that students can't really understand a poem, no matter how brilliant their analyses on paper, unless they can give it a sensitive oral reading. . . . For me, any approach to poetry or drama has to take seriously just those qualities on which we must focus as we listen to radio." The broadcast then turns to a gamut of radio plays

(Thomas, Beckett, and Shakespeare) in which the teacher committed to auditory power submits, albeit implicitly, his reading to the test of "sensitivity," but even more fundamentally the broadcast folds deftly into the object of its attention. When Whitaker is reading, the broadcast *is* a radio drama. In effect, all the other bits and pieces of radio broadcasts woven into this broadcast, for example, the theme music for the Mercury Theater production of *War of the Worlds,* converge here to challenge, if not displace, what has otherwise been commentary "on" the radio. Perhaps it is not then surprising that Whitaker's remarks, as I have noted, touch most directly on the pedagogical scene, where—by virtue of his involvement with the broadcast—he is compelled, as we say, to practice not only what he preaches but *as* he preaches. As important as the inward focus on the auditory power of words might be philosophically—and note that Whitaker stresses words, not, as does Guralnick, visions—what Whitaker effects is a decisive transition between the enumeration of theoretical propositions about radio and the properly strategic dimension of the broadcast, that is, the metacritical fact that he (and the others) are participating in a radio broadcast that, among other things, is seeking to talk about the relation between radio and pedagogy, or, put as bluntly as possible, the relation between *What's the Word?* and, to use Graff's formulation, "American education." Recall that when, during a transitional break, Placksin characterizes the goals of the sponsoring association she describes it, almost as if reading from a fact sheet, as "an organization that encourages the teaching of language and literature."

As intimated earlier, Placksin may well have engineered things so that, the title notwithstanding, Whitaker's stress on the *word*—not as an imaginary vision but as an auditory fact—would arise precisely in a context where the metacritical folding described above takes place. His stress on the link between attention and education, framed as it is by Placksin's observation, "Listening to serious material on the radio does demand a commitment from the listener," obliges the listener, whether inwardly or as part of the mind of all, to consider that *What's the Word?* is not simply a quasi-conspiratorial and obliquely biblical title but, in effect, a restatement of Whitaker's implied pedagogical challenge: Has one paid serious sustained attention to the word? Which word? Certainly those heard during the broadcast, but also the word as a message inscribed with auditory power—in other words, the word as what Derrida would certainly call *logos,* the spoken word that emanates both in and as being, the word approaching us from what Guralnick calls the dark radiating light. As if anticipating this strategic turn, she herself links her historical meditation, her narrative of loss, with the status of the word saying—and I repeat: "That sense that we rely on the word rather than on the visual image is what you lose when you move from radio into television and really begin to rely on TV." Recall that for her this shift of reliance takes places in the "eighties and nineties," that is, presumably, the very period during which the concept of *What's the Word?* arises as a strategy for prosecuting the culture wars. Clearly, Guralnick and Whitaker disagree about the situation of the word on radio, but she, Whitaker, and Placksin nevertheless all manage to produce a sense of urgency about protecting the word in, to invoke Arendt again, "these dark times." Here, "What's the word?" might well be understood as a request for a field report from the frontlines of the culture wars: not "What is the contemporary status of the word?" but "How are the protectors/defenders of the word faring in the current campaign on its behalf?"

Similar points might be made about Frost's awkward, perhaps even Beckettian, observations about art, observations that begin with the avowal that he has violated a prohibition: "I am forbidding myself the word 'entertainment,'" a performative contradiction if there ever was one. Tellingly, this gesture occurs as Frost is explaining Germany's necessary recourse ("they had to") to radio and to radio drama (the *Hörspeil*) in particular. Perhaps this flicker of the word erased as radiophonically uttered is how Frost is preparing us for his subsequent invocation of the "ephemeral" yet absolutely vital being of the arts. Here, and Frost is the only one of the assembled scholars to grind this battleax audibly, the broadcast casts its lot with the traditional defense of humanistic learning in which what is affirmed is the power—it is concerned, after all, with what makes "*all* the difference in people's lives" (my emphasis)—of art, a power that derives from precisely its ephemerality, not in the sense of its transitory character, but in the sense of its deeply attenuated link to what Frost at one point calls the "meat and potatoes, practical ends." It is precisely because the traditional concerns of the humanities, as Whitaker recites Shakespeare, "melt into the air" that they make all the difference. True, there is here no direct evocation of the goals, stated or otherwise, of the MLA. But, in a broadcast conceived as part of a strategic initiative in which a professional association dedicated to the teaching of language and literature (chiefly, but not exclusively, the arts and humanities) is seeking to defend its embattled status, this otherwise "abstract" defense of the arts becomes rather more concrete. As with Whitaker's association of Shakespeare and radio, what gives the broadcast its drama is precisely this encomium to an education in the humanities delivered over a medium more immediately associated with the forbidden but nevertheless uttered word *entertainment*.[4] In this respect, then, "Radio: Imaginary Visions," even if all other broadcasts in the series likewise advocate on behalf of the word, the arts, and the humanities, is utterly singular in bringing the very medium of this advocacy into the field of sustained, auditory attention. As such, it represents the most dramatic wager on the table of the political efficacy of the MLA's investment in radio and asks, willy-nilly, to be reckoned with accordingly.

One will recall that Gerald Graff was initially a member of the MLA committee that formulated the communications strategy that led to *What's the Word?* Moreover, his sense of the moment of intervention shaped Franklin's own as laid out in her piece "Telling the Field's Story." While it is true that Graff soon withdrew from what was fast becoming the Radio Committee chaired by Michael Holquist, it is hard to imagine that his intervention within the culture wars went with him, and this despite the charges of "liberalism" with which his intervention was greeted by people inside and outside the association. So, to pose directly the question intimated throughout this chapter, what opens up when one reflects upon "Radio: Imaginary Visions" as an expression of the politics of "teaching the conflicts"? Moreover, what assessment of the MLA's strategic initiative follows from an answer, however provisional, to such a question?

In sharing with me the design permutations undergone by the program, Franklin made it clear that the idea, popular in Europe and elsewhere, of simply broadcasting a lecture—think J.L. Austin's "Performative Utterances"—was deemed unsuitable by focus groups. She also observed that prospective faculty participants complained about the "interview" format, saying that they often felt unprepared and were reluctant to broadcast their embarrassment, however subtly expressed. Slowly what emerged, and Sally Placksin was crucial here, was a more dialogic model. It was she, apparently, who insisted upon the interrogatory inflection of the title (recall her "Are these horses' hooves we hear, or only coconut shells?"), suggesting, at least to Franklin, that she conceived the programs as modes of questioning, not questions and answers (the interview), but questioning in the form of oral opining and thinking, as it were, on the fly. Here, I would suggest, one can now understand an observation made earlier to the effect that Guralnick, Frost, and Whitaker never *engage* one another (or Placksin for that matter), and this despite the rather obvious way in which—on any number of levels—they are aware of what one another has said or will say. It is as if the program seeks to simulate a seminary space in which participants share views but do not confront one another even when it is perfectly obvious to those assembled that views expressed are at odds with one another. In effect, what dominates are "conflicted views" not "conflicting views." In the foreground are the hesitations or even inconsistencies of the views presented by each speaker, as if what is crucial to the broadcast's message is the simulation of a pedagogy of humility, that is, an enactment of the conviction that the sponsoring association is not dogmatic, or, to invoke a sexist rhetoric, "shrill." To be sure, humility is a vital component of any progressive pedagogy, but its full rigor is compromised when it converts immediately into a form of tolerance sustained by self-doubt. Conflicts among positions, when allowed full articulation, cultivate precisely the form of humility that recognizes as a political principle the fact that no *full* articulation of a position is possible—that even self-reception is bad.

One might argue, then, that "Radio: Imaginary Visions," down to the level of its audio-engineering—the voices passing, as it were, in the dark—refuses to "teach the conflicts." It is as if to do so were deemed too politically risky, as if teaching the conflicts could take the form only of expert bullies screaming one another down (think Lukács and Sartre), and while I agree that nothing is more tedious or professionally counterproductive, teaching conflicts need not succumb to this sort of fraternal disorder. Moreover, if taken seriously, responsibly, teaching the conflicts, even at the rudimentary procedural level, quickly poses the problem of its own limits, its principled inability to secure the definite article *the* in the phrase "teaching the conflicts," in effect, the problem of securing teaching itself from the conflicts it purports to teach—precisely, one should think, the highly charged political matter raised by deploying the radio as a form of "distance learning." This implies, does it not, that even as Graff's view comes to be blinded by its own insight—and let us entertain the idea that this might well have led to its being set aside at the time—the academic discussion of radio avoids with extreme and doubtless symptomatic difficulty the political question of radio's relation to the contemporary fate of humanistic education in the wake of the culture wars. These do not, after all, have to be discussed on air to be happening in the listening space of those following the broadcasts. The very educated, affluent audience imagined to be listening to "Radio: Imaginary Visions" might certainly have been expected to wonder what this broadcast in particular had to say about the MLA's strategic gambit in relation to *these* conflicts.

Oddly, no mention is made of Raymond Williams in this otherwise remarkable set of reflections on radio drama. His name does not appear in the posted bibliography for the program, nor does it appear in the bibliography of Guralnick's obviously generative *Sight Unseen*, a title whose linguistic paradox has clearly influenced if not directly shaped the title of the MLA-sponsored broadcast. Aware that such observations always risk degenerating directly into catty pedantry, let me redeem them by passing over Williams's comments on radio from an angle different from that stressed at the end of the preceding chapter, an angle meant to resound the political questions raised above. Specifically, consider the following remarks from Williams's 1971 statement on the Open University ("Raymond Williams Thinks Well of the Open University"):

> But this [the different challenges of teaching art and science] isn't an educational problem, it's a problem of our expectations in television and radio. And here there is a delicate point. I'd swear that in some cases, producers and staff have been thinking rather conventionally about good television, good radio, in ways that anyone who has done much broadcasting, especially in vision [sic] can recognize. Thinking also about names, about known authorities. There's an observable danger of cliquishness in some of the programs. But if the experiment in combined classes is in the end to work, it will have to be done by long continued collaboration. By people who know each other well enough to have got past the academic side and the production side. Until it's at least as natural as talking anywhere else, and until it's clear that one isn't appearing on television or giving a talk on radio but mainly talking about something, showing something, and that's all that really matters, the present uncertainties of some of the programs will continue.

The tape from which this passage derives is extraordinary in many ways. Thematically, of course, it is rife with metacommentary. This is Williams talking about the use of radio instruction at the Open University while using the BBC (Program 3) to educate the public about the stakes of this experiment in adult and continuing education. Further raising the stakes, this passage in particular talks about talking on radio, thus inevitably attuning listeners to the question raised by Williams himself: Is he talking about "something," or is he, in effect, simply "appearing" on radio? Although I know nothing about the actual reception of this broadcast—the continued if perennially imperiled experiment that is the Open University could be said to say something on the matter—what imposes itself from the recording is Williams's labored breathing. I will come back to this.

While it is obvious that Williams is not here talking about radio drama, he is raising a "delicate point" about radio and education. Although what was to become the culture wars is certainly not yet on his radar, in insisting upon the connection between, in this case, the success of the Open University as a novel project in postsecondary learning and what he calls "thinking" about radio—thinking that he here worries might be "conventional" in a way that would threaten the success of the Open University, that would, in effect compromise the articulation of radio and education—Williams is gesturing ahead to the terrain of the conflict. As we have perhaps come to expect, the question of efficacy is linked almost immediately with Hoggart's formulation "speaking to others," or, to use Williams's word, "talk." The link here is delicate indeed. Specifically, Williams seeks on the one hand to break with a certain conventional thinking about the use of radio, while on the other he calls for a leveling of the distinction between academics and professionals, a leveling that would allow for a form of talk that is strictly speaking anti-Brechtian, in which the medium makes little or no impact on the message. The difficulty lies in the fact that such a formulation seeks to control the significant ambivalence contained in the phrase "on radio." As such, it might be argued that this is precisely the most conventional of conventional thinking about radio, radio as a clear channel for topics, and that Williams is speaking to others at cross-purposes if the point is to challenge conventional thinking about good radio. Put differently, in laying out the terms of his appraisal of the Open University Williams generates the very means by which that appraisal could be said to fall on, to invoke an figure from Nietzsche, large (that is, overly receptive) ears.

In an earlier chapter I stressed the conflicted character of Williams's thinking about Brecht and radio, and his statement "on" the Open University could be said to confirm this point, if from a slightly different angle. But if it makes sense to invoke this issue in the context of a consideration of the efficacy, indeed the political efficacy, of *What's the Word?* this is because in talking about his talking about the conventional thinking about radio, Williams pressures—albeit obliquely—the MLA to wonder aloud about whether *its* thinking about radio isn't too conventional. Consider the terms of his first pass over the matter of conventional thinking: "I'd swear that in some cases, producers and staff have been thinking rather conventionally about good television, good radio, in ways that anyone who has done much broadcasting, especially in vision *[sic],* can recognize. Thinking also about names, about known authorities. There's an observable danger of cliquishness in some of the programs." It would be hard to deny that the MLA, or perhaps even more specifically Sally Placksin (herself a professional broadcaster), has indulged in some conventional thinking about radio. Strictly speaking, of course, this is a churlish point. If the aim is to introduce the listening public to what in effect might be prospective professors of its college-age children, certainly "names and known authorities" are at once essential and frankly obvious. That said, clearly the more provocative if fraught question is that of "talk," of talking about "something" *instead of* appearing to talk about it on radio.

Here we brush back against the issue of "teaching the conflicts," but now—if I may be indulged a slight rewording—as "talking the conflicts." As I have been at pains to establish, "Radio: Imaginary Visions" talks about two "somethings" at great length: radio drama and *the* radio. It also talks, intermittently, about "the voice," indeed more than once it risks reducing all radiophonic sound to the voice, thereby generating the conceptual platform on which radio and radio drama can become the same "something." To this extent, the broadcast meets the standards of unconventional thinking about good radio set forth by Williams, thus complicating its more conventional reliance on "names and known authorities." However, as I have proposed, this is a conflicted standard that at best asks us to fudge the difference between "self-consciousness" (appearing on radio) and, for lack of a better word, estrangement (marking the ambivalent "on" of radio). In meeting this standard, the broadcast reiterates its embrace of what earlier I called "conflicted teaching," as though the question of the relation between radiophonic means and educational ends *should not itself* factor into talk about ("on") those ends. More troubling still is the way "the voice" (as the medium of the mind of all, inwardness, or possessiveness) operates to drown out, to muffle, the question about talk and to foreclose discussion, perhaps even debate, about conflicts that might arise about the educational and political efficacy of radiophonic talk on these topics.

If it is the case that "talk radio" catalyzed, in some sense, the emergence of radio studies, then the questions raised by *What's the Word?* prompt one to consider whether and in what sense these two phenomena belong together. On the face of it, both would appear to have difficulty in hearing in the formulation "talk radio" the "or," that is, talk *or* (in other words) radio. Put differently, what is struggled with—and not necessarily consciously—is the constellation "radio, voice, residualism." For radio studies, "talk radio" functioned as a symptom of the "return of the repressed"; it reminded Northern scholars that a medium thought to have been superseded was, in fact, residual. As I have argued, what renders this version of the residual vestigial is the narrative of technological innovation and progress that powers it. For *What's the Word?* (and perhaps the MLA more generally), "talk (on) radio" is understood to articulate a response to interests, perhaps even forces, bent on reducing instruction in language and literature to a residualism, that is, a superseded practice of education. What brings these endeavors into proximity is the foreclosed question of the residualism of the voice and radio's relation to it. Radio grasped as a medium for or of the voice, or, better, radio conceived of *as* voice (Adorno's "radio voice") urges a vestigial reading of the residual. In "Radio: Imaginary Visions," Guralnick states this plainly when, in explaining the sociohistorical shift from radio to television, she describes radio as a "medium for the voice and ear" and television simply as "a visual medium" (on "mute"?) to which radio yielded. In light of this collaborative foreclosure, one might venture the notion that the becoming-residual of radio, that is, the emergence of radio studies and its object, is the necessary condition for the comeback of the voice as a topic of philosophical reflection. To be sure, as many radio studies partisans have shown, "talk radio" belongs to a geopolitical moment that conditions it in turn. Thus, while on a certain register it seems crucial to acknowledge the white, male rage that fuels much of the talk of "talk radio," this fails to illuminate the more worldly dimension of this rage. Specifically, if the vestigial residualism of radio stands out against a backdrop of its Southern or non-Western ubiquity (not to say dominance), then its decisive relation to the voice might well derive from a broadly perceived and lived Northern need to reclaim the figure and medium of agency in the face of a world less and less responsive to it. As the Voice of America has long demonstrated, the war of the airwaves is an especially difficult war to counter, not because propaganda is compelling, but because propagation as such is more than half the battle. Thus, whether recourse is made to phonocentrism (and the ethnocentrism it hosts) or not, the comeback of the voice that precisely refuses to think its mediation through on and by radio not only fails to think the voice's sonic character but also colludes with a failed strategy for restating the power and value of instruction in languages and literature.

What seems called for under the circumstances is an upgraded version of Williams's labored breathing. This is not to suggest that the focus groups consulted by the MLA were wrong in counseling against lectures. Rather, it is to draw attention to the unwitting effect of reading a written lecture over the radio in which one advocates on behalf of the pedagogical value of talk that is not "on" radio (that is, aware of its appearance on the air), but "about" something, while, during the lecture, the effects of preparation are plainly audible. In other words, precisely because Williams is concerned, even deeply concerned, to address the something that is the Open University, he writes down the precise words he wishes to say. He reads them and he times the reading of them so that what he came to say fits into the time he is given to say them.[5] Because many of his points are delicate, that is, carefully observed, they require one to breathe properly in order to bring the words to life *as if* in ordinary talk. This is difficult to do, and Williams sometimes fails to breathe properly, producing abrupt though faint gasps and words that trail off, asphyxiated. The effect, given the critique of "appearance," is that Williams unwittingly undermines the easy distinction between talk about something and talk "on" radio, prompting listeners to wonder whether, in what sounds like someone contradicting himself, an even more delicate point is being made regarding the difficult and demanding conflict between radio and education. In this albeit subtle textual register his lecture reaches past the question of whether "distance learning" and "wired (or wireless) classrooms" will facilitate postsecondary learning to the matter of whether radio has to be re: worked in order to engage education in an educationally productive, that is, effective way. As we have seen, this is a vital dimension of his thinking about Labour and radio, and for this reason the estrangement effected by Williams's effort, his aspiration to read his lecture "on" the radio, warrants the characterization "labored." In itself it is trivial, but its reception—especially when bad—prompts one to pose a political question about the politics of conventional thinking about radio when bent to the task of educating listeners about the attractions, nay, the importance, of contemporary instruction in languages and literatures.

Here, as intimated earlier, the MLA comes close to, as it were, dropping the signal. In doing so it risks conceding the culture wars before even entering the fray and, in the process, misrepresenting the association. Perhaps these are the same thing, in the sense that to reassure parents about the continuing attraction and relevance of the study of languages and literatures it is apparently necessary to fold radio into drama—the voice—and then suggest, via the principle of the dramatic arc, that Shakespeare himself was speaking to/for/on radio. This risks two unnecessary things. One, under the guise of professional modesty the entwinement of radio drama and *the* radio blankets those members of the association (not to mention un- or differently affiliated researchers) who approach radio as, for example, a sound machine or compositional device. Their signals are, in effect, jammed (and note here that Guralnick herself has written insightfully about Cage's "Roratorio" in her book *Sight Unseen*). Two, as if eager to concede in advance the charge advanced by Richard Bernstein and others of radical silliness, the "radio, drama, Shakespeare" series broadcasts to combatants and noncombatants alike the dubiously reassuring message "No, in fact, we are the same as we ever were. Only different. Now we talk about this sameness on the radio. Now we archive aspects of our radio program on the association's Web site." Of course, these are important advances, but are they not entirely—as Gilles Deleuze might say—reactive? Perhaps even radio-reactive. Indeed, what is called for is an affirmative re: working of radio, one that in refusing to settle for the shiny gadgetry of satellites and the Internet (do these not, in the end, merely aggravate the condition of "mobile privatization"?), not only essays to think the radio as a residual apparatus but discovers there—of all things—the contemporary fate of the posthumanist humanities. After all, this last is or was the true bone of contention in the dogfight of the culture wars. And while it is easy to understand how an association the size of the MLA, in the name of the entirely laudable principle of representative democracy, feels it must refuse this form of tendentiousness, some strategic issues only become more pressing by the day. Witness the broad assault on "academic freedom," "shared governance," and "tenure" that defines our professional moment. While it is true that this assault extends well beyond the precincts of the humanities and the "qualitative" social sciences, it thematizes matters that have long resonated in the humanities in particular, namely, to quote the founding director of the Institute for Advanced Study in Princeton, Alexander Flexner, "the use of useless knowledge," or put less Platonically, the power of thinking that remains unreconciled to the dominant social order. It is false modesty that allows one to separate "languages and literatures" from the humanities, not because languages and literatures might otherwise be thought to stand at the core of the humanities, but because false modesty allows one to avoid the question of what those active in the instruction of languages and literatures might be called to do in this "moment of danger," to cite Benjamin's rhyme for "state of exception/emergency." I fear that the strategy of reassurance is woefully inadequate. It will excite neither members nor the parents of prospective college students, students who obviously incarnate the profession's future. It is not accurate as a strategic assessment of the present, but more damning still it is simply not exciting. What is called for is a real push against onto-political theology (whether negative or not) and an advance toward a mindfully secular humanities, one prepared to broadcast the word. And the word is not love. It is "What?"

Over.

Notes

INTRODUCTION

1. With this formulation I have evoked in a perhaps confusing way Foucault's resonant discussion of "the apparatus" *(le dispositif)* that opens his 1977 interview/discussion with the editorial group of *Ornicar,* a Lacanian journal then published by the fledgling department of psychoanalysis at Vincennes. In English, the piece, titled "The Confession of the Flesh," invokes directly the unpublished fourth volume in *The History of Sexuality, "L'aveu de la chair."* Because at a certain point Foucault is pressed on the matter of the relation between "the apparatus" and "the *episteme,*" and because he responds, after acknowledging the difficulty of the question, by describing the apparatus as "strategies of relations of forces supporting, and supported by, types of knowledge" ("Confession" 196), it would appear that what he means by *apparatus* and what I mean by *object* are one and the same. To clarify: in this study I see the object as precisely addressing the difficulty Foucault acknowledges by articulating the matrix in which force and knowledge are socially and technically organized. Foucault himself earlier gestures in this direction when, in *The Archaeology of Knowledge,* he discusses at length "the formation of objects," clearly putting his own spin on Louis Althusser's concept of the "scientific object." Recently, Giorgio Agamben has reminded us of the importance of Foucault's apparatus (see *What Is an Apparatus?*), but already in 1988 Gilles Deleuze had drawn attention to the conceptual power and rigor of the term (see "What Is a Dispositif?"). Although he does not say as much, it is clear that Deleuze's angle of reading finds inspiration in Félix Guattari's "Machine and Structure," from *Transversalité et psychanalyse,* a book whose preface was written by Deleuze. If the introduction of this bibliographic "clutter" is justified, it is because throughout this study I will have recourse to the vocabulary of objects and apparatuses, and certain "associations" might otherwise pass unremarked.

2. My concentration here on "radio studies" risks creating two false impressions: first, that the only interesting or important writing being done on radio happens under the auspices of "radio studies" (most "radio studies" partisans would *themselves* refuse this notion); and second, that all other writing on radio is somehow symptomatized in "radio studies" and can thus be justifiably ignored. Not only is this false, but it falls, as Michel Foucault might have put it, outside the true, that is, beyond truth and falsity. Indeed, the writing on radio— if one includes here such things as the "spiritual telegraph"—stretching as it does back to the mid–nineteenth century, is voluminous—loud and vast. No one has picked it all up, and I do not pretend to. One is thus obliged, as it were, to scan on a certain frequency, and I have certainly tried to attend diligently to what is out there on radio and philosophy. Of course, diligence reaches only so far, and I hope vital things neglected will be brought to my attention, an attention in no sense turned elsewhere out of disrespect.

3. In "Base and Superstructure," from four years earlier, Williams does appear to apply the alternative/oppositional distinction to both the category of the emergent and that of the residual; indeed, he speaks in passing of an incorporated versus a not incorporated residual. But this distinction does not transform the character of the residual; it merely comprehends its status.

4. The introductory pages to Charles Acland's anthology *Residual Media* (2007) have given an instructive airing of these issues.

5. Important here, at least from the vantage point of enabling micropractices, is the fact that in 1992 the first issue of the *Journal of Radio Studies* (since 2008 the *Journal of Radio and Audio Media*) appeared. The editorial note, "A New Journal for an Old . . . ," by Christopher Sterling, stresses, even elliptically, the theme of novelty. Anticipating a formulation dear to later radio studies partisans, Sterling justifies the establishment of the journal by writing, among other things: "That a journal has finally appeared devoted to serious research on all aspects of *radio* demonstrates academics may finally be broadening their scope of interest from a near obsession with television" (Sterling, n. pag.). Although he continues to adduce several precipitating developments conditioning the establishment of the journal, the language of his formulation—"finally," "obsession"—makes it clear that, at least for him, the becoming new of something old has been a long time coming—that radio studies has overcome something rather like resistance. It may be going too far to say that the radio studies reported on by the *Chronicle* is reactive to this prior development, but surely the preponderance of psychoanalytically charged formulations emitted throughout calls for attention. Also relevant here is acknowledgment of the fact that throughout the 1990s many crucial special issues of journals and anthologies treating radio appeared. The year 1992 alone saw—along with the inauguration of the *Journal of Radio Studies*—the publication of "Radio—Sound," a special issue of *Continuum* edited by Toby Miller; *Radio Rethink*, edited by Daina Augaitis and Dan Lander; and Doug Kahn and Gregory Whitehead's *Wireless Imagination*. These were followed in short order by Neil Strauss's special issue of *Semiotext(e)* entitled "Radiotext(e)," and by a special issue of the *Drama Review*, "Experimental Sound and Radio," edited by Allen Weiss.

6. In the call for papers for *Radio Reader: Essays in the Cultural History of Radio* sent me via e-mail on April 30, 1999, Hilmes and Loviglio make the link I am forging explicit, writing: "In response to recent developments both in the field of media history and in the current state of the media industry, we believe that the time is right to bring together a range of scholarly work focused on the neglected field of radio." Here the psychosocially charged notion of "neglect" emerges to reiterate, even if indirectly, Sperling's emphasis on the contrast between "serious attention" and "obsession."

I. FACING THE RADIO

1. An important exception here is the phenomenological thinker Don Ihde. His *Listening and Voice,* originally published in 1976 and now available in a second, revised edition, is a bold effort to dance around or through the grammatological minefield. Although his direct engagement with Derrida's work is slight, the fact that much of the introduction is given over to the presentation of the virtues of phenomenological method (both Husserl and Heidegger) makes clear that his awareness of the stakes of Derrida's critique is vivid. The fact that his attention turns almost immediately from the voice to sound can be read as something of a concession.

2. In an interview with Ulrich Raulf for the *Süddeutsche Zeitung* of April 6, 2004, Agamben describes *State of Exception* as part of a "tetralogy." As the fourth work in the series, a genealogical study of "forms-of-life" and "life-styles," is as yet unwritten, it seems prudent, if ultimately inaccurate, to describe the texts in question as a trilogy.

3. Although largely focused on television, Lynn Spigel's work on the role of this "box" in the architecture of the postwar suburban home, *Make Room for Television,* is extremely relevant here. What her sociohistorical research establishes is that from the vantage point of room or space the distinction I am drawing between a thing and an object may, to invoke the old saw, be easier held in theory than in practice, at least as concerns television. Before Spigel, Joshua Meyrowitz, in *No Sense of Place,* had recognized the dimension of place in grasping the effects of television, and in Paddy Scannell's *Radio, Television and Modern Life* one finds another rich treatment of these issues that takes up the issue of radio explicitly.

4. In *Psychology of Radio*, Cantril and Allport recount in extraordinary detail the early efforts of broadcasters to craft a "radio voice." Despite their empirical focus—they describe each of the "tests" used to home in on or otherwise identify the proper voice—they do manage to show not simply that the voice was a preoccupation of broadcasters but that this voice was tailored to the medium. Literally, the voice was constructed so as to internalize the constraints of radio as an apparatus. Because their empiricism would prohibit it as a matter of principle, they are not in a position to formulate the critique of phonocentrism their study invites. See in particular their chapters titled "Voice and Personality" (109–26) and "Sex Differences and Radio" (127–38). For a more rigorous philosophical consideration of this issue, see Dyson ("Genealogy" 167–88).

5. Derrida's experiments with stitching together the texts of Heidegger and Francis Ponge urge, under the capacious heading of "Reading Heidegger" (where, in fact, I have placed de Rougement), consideration, however brief, of Ponge's short text from *Pièces,* "La Radio." Written in the winter of 1946 and broadcast over Belgian radio in the following year, the "piece" starts where Adorno starts, with the box: "This varnished box *[boîte]* shows nothing that stands out *[rien qui saille,* a calque of *rien qui vaille,* where the semantic weight of the line falls squarely on the nothing that neither sticks out nor happens], and ends with the can *[la radieuse seconde petite boîte à ordures]."* In transit it hesitates over the ear, noting that the radio improves the ear precisely in order to "pour incessantly into it the worst grossness." Indeed, the text virtually catalogs a scatological flow—"brutal vociferations," "worst grossness," "flood of muck," "manure"—channeling into and through the trash can (748–49). Not only does this flow evoke strongly what Heidegger in his Nietzsche studies would refer to as the "Wasteland," but through the etymological resonances— dear to both Ponge and Heidegger—of *grossièretés* (rendered supra as "grossness" but closer to vulgarities), Ponge presents the radio as caught up in the "bigness," the "giganticism," that sparked Heidegger's fundamental concern. De-severance, the devil and the dump. Perhaps it is this array that prompts Ponge to describe the radio as an apparatus *(un petit appareil).* To extend, by one additional bibliographic click, my "Reading Heidegger" chain of associations, it is interesting in this context to consider Luce Irigaray's powerful little book *The Forgetting of Air in Martin Heidegger* (1983). Although her concern there is to probe the figure of light (and all its attendant associations, the clearing, the shining forth, etc.), her attention to the medium of light, the air, invites us to consider whether its forgetting in Heidegger is linked to his anxious perception of the airwaves. Irigaray herself does not broach the question of radio, or sound transmission more generally, but her analysis might well imply that the Wasteland, the flood of muck, is filler for what is constitutively forgotten.

6. In "Heidegger's Ear: Philopolemology (*Geschlecht IV*)," Derrida elaborates a subtle and trenchant reading of Heidegger's silent call. It ranges well beyond *Being and Time*—including, for example, the still-vexing "Rectorate Discourse"—but sounds several themes that complicate without dismissing Heidegger's silence. Somewhat predictably, Derrida resists the temptation to comment on the radiophonic aspect of this material—his interest in echography comes later—but his appeal to the figure of the friend (who is silent) might be heard to confront Adorno's appeal to the intruder (what Kafka called "the destroyer," *das Verderber*) in an intriguing way.

2. ON THE AIR

1. In April of 1930 Benjamin wrote to Gerhard/Gershom Scholem about his developing friendship with Brecht, a friendship that Scholem misunderstood and of which he disapproved. Specifically, he boasted of his and Brecht's plan, in the context of a reading group they had organized, to "annihilate Heidegger here in the summer" ("To Gerhard Scholem" 365), suggesting rather strongly that Brecht had, if not read, certainly discussed what at the time was *the* Heidegger

text to reckon with, *Being and Time,* where the discourse/chatter distinction appears. Three years later, Scholem writes to Benjamin, in obvious sympathy with what—since it involved Brecht—he might otherwise have regarded an ill-conceived plan, telling him that he intends to declaim Heidegger's Rectoral Address "(in appropriate style)" ("To Walter Benjamin" 85) for dinner guests.

2. "Refunctionalization has emerged as the standard translation of *Umfunktionierung.* While not dissatisfied with this, I propose the perhaps rebarbative alternative "re: working" because it has the advantage of keeping work, working, and workers in focus, while, through the prefix set off by a colon, underscoring both work, working, and workers are under reconstruction and that the term is about itself, its own reworking. Indulge me.

3. To cite some important instances, the hunchback (indeed, a hunchback dwarf) puts in an early and dramatic appearance in the opening aphorism on the late text "On the Concept of History." Here, set opposite the puppet automaton, he assumes allegorical status as the Messianic or theological element in what Scholem called the Janus figure of Benjamin's thought. Slavoj Žižek, in *The Puppet and the Dwarf* (2003), draws on this figure to save Christianity for perversity, although his interests rest primarily on reversing Benjamin's allegorical field, not on reading it. Also, earlier in the decade, in "Berlin Childhood around 1900," in reconstructing, re-membering his childhood, Benjamin invokes a hunchback found on the pages of his edition of the *Deutsches Kinderbuch.* As if establishing a Poe-like and therefore North American subtext for this figure, the hunchback of his childhood is an "imp of the perverse," an urban legend responsible for a sort of superegoic surveillance that triggers incessant parapraxial missteps. In anticipation of the later allegorical treatment (and indeed Žižek's reading of it), the hunchback must be appeased—in prayer.

4. In his brief essay on Benjamin's *Lichtenberg,* Gerhard Schulte details at some length the specificity of the "listening model." Citing Benjamin's program notes, he explains that "the basic tendency of these models is didactic. The subject matter of the instruction deals with typical situations from everyday life. The method of instruction consists of a confrontation of example and counter-example" (33). He lists as Benjamin's first foray a collaboration with Wolf Zucker (organized under the auspices of Ernst Schoen) that deals with how to ask one's employer for a raise. Although Schulte largely ignores the theme of listening—Is it simply the medium of instruction or is it part of what is being instructed?—he clarifies the distinctive status this material had for Benjamin. These issues have also been powerfully amplified by Wolfgang Hagen in his extended treatment of Benjamin's radio work, "On the Minute: Benjamin's Silent Work for German Radio," and by Erik Granly Jensen in his marvelous study of Benjamin's *Much Ado about Punch [Radau um Kasperl],* "Collective Acoustic Space."

5. The figure of "crossed wires" complicates the motif of "encouragement" that has otherwise dominated this construal of the impact of Brecht on Benjamin. A suggestive warrant for the figure is to be found in Benjamin's short article (published in *Die literarische Welt* in the summer of 1927), "Journalism." In it Benjamin with acerbic wit reconstructs the French reception of Lindbergh's achievement, showing how the press, in confusing Lindbergh with the doomed

French airmen François Coli and Charles Nungasser, was attempting to rewrite history. This precedes the friendship between Brecht and Benjamin, but one cannot but be struck by the "coincidence" that the "learning play" with which *The Flight of the Lindberghs* was paired at the Baden Baden Festival was *The Baden Baden Learning Play on Acquiescence,* in which the pilot crashes.

6. It is worth noting that Adorno devotes a section of "Radio Physiognomics" to the phenomenon of "switching off" (172–73). Although there he brings the gesture into instructive relation with Freud's death drive (the "drive for destruction"), in the end he stresses the fruitlessness of this gesture of opposition, listing it among other forms of pseudoactivity that fail to challenge the menace of "ubiquity-standardization." That said, the implicit contrast between solitude and annihilation (two results of "switching off") that arises between Adorno and Sartre invites attention as yet another way to think the encounter between French and German philosophy at midcentury.

3. STATIONS OF EXCEPTION

1. Although in certain respects his text mimics the rowdy material it engages, Gene Fowler's *Border Radio: Quacks, Yodlers, Pitchmen, Psychics and Other Amazing Broadcasters of the American Airwaves* provides indispensable information about precisely the context out of which, and in response to which, the provisions of the Brinkley Act took shape. My remarks here are meant to tease out a more analytical component of this inexhaustible material.

2. See my "Algerian Nation: Fanon's Fetish." A similar version of this point figures centrally in the Pontecorvo/Solanas film *The Battle of Algiers* when the political effectiveness of the general strike is understood to hinge decisively on the extrinsic body of the United Nations, or when Colonel Matthieu responds to a journalist's query about Sartre's position by insisting that he would prefer not to have him as an enemy.

3. See my "Reason, Thus, Unveils Itself," where, in the context of a reading of "Algeria Unveils," I draw out the important textual and political relation between Fanon's discussion of the colonizer's scoptophilic drive and the anaphoric formula *"Nous avons vu."*

4. All citations from Fanon's essay are taken from the available English translation by Haakon Chevalier, the controversial Nuremburg translator and alleged spy on the Manhattan Project. *"Traductori, traditori"* indeed. The discrepancies in wording reflect my own comparisons between this translation and the French version of the essay now available from *La Découverte* that, happily, is reissuing many of the germinal publications from *François Maspero,* the small, largely communist press that ceased operation in 1982.

5. It is crucial here to consider the implications of Adrian Johns's critique of pirate broadcasting in "Piracy as a Business Force." Through a series of theoretically and politically driven readings of specific pirate practices—notably Radio Caroline in the United Kingdom (fetishized as the incitement for the "British Invasion" in rock and roll), Johns draws out the uncomfortable affinities between piracy and rational choice theory in economics and unbridled libertarianism in politics. As we will see, the precise terms of this debate will figure prominently

in the critique of commercial radio in the United Kingdom concurrent with the emergence of the Centre for Contemporary Cultural Studies at Birmingham.

6. In this context it is interesting to consider Alan O'Connor's study of radio in Bolivia, *The Voice of the Mountains: Radio and Anthropology*, as, in some sense, marked by this filter. This slim volume brims over with important ethnographic detail and documents the many stations that, like, El Voz del Minero, appeal immediately to the limitlessly fungible motif of the voice to think about the grounding of popular struggle. In this it calmly transcribes the traumatic scene from Jorge Sanjinés's *El coraje del pueblo* when the Siglo XX radio station is occupied by the army and brutally silenced. The subtitle suggests something more. By establishing an apposite equivalence between the "voice in the mountain" and the radio as conjoined with/grasped by anthropology, it also asks the reader to consider the disciplinary complicity of anthropology in what I have called the filtering of our listening. The point is not that anthropology is in any way remarkable in this respect but rather that some of the forms of interdisciplinary partnering that might be thought to circumvent a strictly disciplinary filtering do not. Here, too, resisting the resistance thought to reside in interdisciplinary research as such becomes urgent.

4. PHONING IN ANALYSIS

1. An important although more constrained pass over this material is to be found in Mark Roberts's "Wired: Schreber as Machine, Technophobe and Virtualist." Neither Roberts nor Hagen pauses to consider Sudre's joint fascination with radio and parapsychology.

2. Fromm's conception of the familiar becomes even more complex when one tries actually to connect his Proppian reconstruction of the plot with any of the cartoon shorts starring Mickey Mouse between 1928 and 1937, the date of the dinner meeting. Strictly speaking cannibals appear, as such, in only two films: *Trader Mickey* and *Mickey's Man Friday*. However, Minnie ("the female") does not appear in either of these films. She does appear in *Pioneer Days*, but there are no cannibals, only offensive "Movie Indians" who have besieged their wagon train but otherwise show no interested in eating either of them. Perhaps the closest film to the plot described by Fromm is *The Gorilla Mystery* from 1930. A virtual prequel to Schoedsack's *King Kong*, this film does not have cannibals, but it does have an enormous gorilla with pronounced gustatory longings (fangs, slobber, etc.) for Minnie, whom he kidnaps and sequesters from Mickey, who must liberate her (in fact, Minnie collaborates with Mickey in her own rescue). In addition, a graphic motif used here dates back to *Plane Crazy* (Disney's 1928 tribute to Lindbergh), in which a character literally swallows the screen by opening wide and engorging the camera. Swallowing is emphasized by Fromm, so the film suggests itself despite the absence of cannibals. In 1938, the year following the meeting with Lazarsfeld et al., Disney released his retelling of the Brothers Grimm's *The Valiant Little Tailor, The Brave Little Tailor*. It likewise lacks cannibals but does have a giant that, in Rabelaisian fashion, swallows Mickey, who is fighting to win the hand of Minnie, daughter of the king. Obviously, this film appears too late to have been thought

of by Fromm, but its existence suggests that Disney was concerned to sound and resound particular themes and motifs, a fact that urges one to consider that Fromm is familiar not so much with a specific film as with the product line of a particular director and studio. Why, then, the demurral on knowing a specific radio program?

3. Having invoked Wolfgang Hagen's work on Schreber, I would be remiss not to indicate that he too has written at some length and with true analytical subtlety on the significance of Charlie McCarthy for the impact of the Mercury Theater broadcast. See in particular the sections titled "Halloween 1938" and "Charlie McCarthy vs. 'War of the Worlds'" in *Das Radio* (229–45). If I assign pride of place to Miller, it is primarily to acknowledge that, if we are to believe publication dates, he got there first. Of course, to insist upon such things as temporal sequence is to deny, preemptively, the claims of telepathy.

4. Relevant, of course, is not simply the term *influence* but Tausk's explicit evocation of radio as an "influencing apparatus" when in listing its main effects he writes: "It produces, as well as removes, thoughts and feelings by means of waves or rays or mysterious forces which the patient's knowledge of physics is inadequate to explain. In such cases the machine is called a 'suggestion apparatus'" (187). Perhaps especially touchy here is Tausk's "anticipation" of Lacan's treatment of broadcasting and analysis through the highly charged Freudianism "suggestion." Remember, Freud struggled continuously with the dismissive claim that psychoanalysis worked only because its results were "suggested" to patients. Surprisingly, given the tenacity of his focus, Hagen does not deal squarely with Tausk in *Das Radio*.

5. The correspondence between Althusser and Lacan assumes a fresh significance in this context. I will draw attention to only two fecund moments, aware that much more than I will say here can be said about both. First, in Lacan's letter to Althusser dated December 1, 1963, one finds the following: "That at the distance at which you are what I address to one close by, often opaque, manages to make itself understood is justification for the faith I *seem* to accord (to the point of disconcerting some) to the pure act of saying" ("To Louis Althusser" 150–51). This is followed eight days later by the following three lines from Althusser: "Your silence has great value for me. I expected it," and "Your silence is priceless" ("To Jacques Lacan" 159). Ostensibly nothing more than the gingerly extended gestures of newfound allies, the details of these remarks in twisting together the Pascalian silence of the analyst and something like a gravitational but clearly Lacanian theory of speaking encourage one to see the link I have drawn between structural causality and the unconscious active and alive in the very event of their friendship. Like politics, theory is in some sense local.

6. Although his interest in Lacan is minimal (it is framed by his interest in Jameson), Jeffrey Sconce's *Haunted Media: Electronic Presence from Telegraphy to Television* contains an astonishing chapter, "The Voice from the Void," that powerfully amplifies the link I am seeking to forge here between radio and void, between utterance and space. His "Alien Ether" chapter, aside from serving as an important (though unacknowledged) opening salvo for Milutis's work, also led me to the *Contact* anecdote through which I began to puzzle over the question where this text came from.

7. In this context one must side with Ricoeur's characterization of Freud, as a practitioner of the hermeneutics of suspicion, over Habermas's contemporaneous assessment, in which he praised Freud for confronting philosophic and scientific knowledge with the principle of self-reflection. For even if, in the end, Ricoeur seeks to rescue philosophy from Freud by establishing that he believed in the possibility of restoring distorted meaning, suspicion unleashes a skeptical contingency that is hard to contain. Gaston Bachelard squares the circle by renarrating the history of science in psychoanalytically charged terms, where the breaks that announce what Kuhn would call paradigm shifts are understood as instances of psychical resistance that give way to the gentle force of rational introspection. Perhaps one way to appreciate the significance of Alain Badiou's effort to bring set theory and psychoanalysis closer together is by noting how much more satisfying his account of such a possibility is than that of either Ricoeur or Habermas. The relevant sources here are Ricoeur's *Freud and Philosophy,* Habermas's *Knowledge and Human Interests,* Bachelard's *New Scientific Spirit,* and Badiou's *Being and Event.*

8. Already in 1901, at least in the French context, Gabriel Tarde, the "sociologist" whom Bruno Latour and others regard as the "father" of ANT (actor network theory), was deploying the precise Newtonian vocabulary of "action at a distance" to talk about publics, specifically crowds. In ANT this notion is developed to account for what in astrophysics is understood as the field, the structure within which elements can interact without contact. As such, it would appear to have a fecund relation to the enigma of "wireless" communication and thus to be "on" the necklace of signifiers Lacan is animating.

9. Genosko, in "Life and Work," has drawn similar attention to the crucial character of "transversality." Although we distribute different accents through this material—Genosko stresses the generative, even foundational, qualities of transversality—we share the sense that something vital is at stake within it.

10. Deleuze has expressed his own ambivalent admiration for Sartre in "Il a été mon maître," from *L'isle déserte* (109–13). This short text, from 1964, is a statement in support of Sartre's refusal of the Nobel Prize for literature awarded him that year. Well before it had become the commonplace with which we are familiar, Deleuze champions Sartre's status as a public intellectual, even as, in the concluding sentence, he concedes that the fresh, even pure, air circulating through Sartre's speech may be impossible to breathe. That he sharply contrasts Sartre to Merleau-Ponty—who sustained a much closer relation to Lacan and his generation—is not entirely unrelated to his attraction for Guattari's project at La Borde.

11. Strictly speaking, what de Beauvoir and Guattari mean by *devenir* are two different things. At issue is a distinction between Hegel and Nietzsche. For de Beauvoir one "becomes a woman" in the sense that one comes to be recognized as such. For Guattari, "becoming woman" (or animal, or plant, or invisible, etc.—and this heterogeneity is part of the point) is a way to designate, not a development, but a proliferation that engages recognition precisely in passing. That said, it is clear that Guattari grasps the subject as a production, an instance of productivity, whose trajectory has little or nothing to do with the determining force of birth. A monograph, provisionally titled "What Became

of Becoming," is waiting to be written on this fragment of French intellectual history.

12. This formulation coupled with the intellectual nationalism of the French—although Deleuze and Guattari are less guilty of this than others—might lead one to think that "free radio" or "pirate radio" (similar if not identical practices) emerged in Italy and France. This is false. Scholarly consensus appears to be that Radio Mercur in Denmark, which began broadcasting in 1958, was the first of such radiophonic practices. In fact, if one thinks about the postwar deployment of the Voice of America (founded in 1944 and located outside Cincinnati) in Eastern Europe, where it was used to broadcast illegally into the USSR from sites outside its recognized national borders, it might be possible to complicate the notion of pirate radio in any number of politically crucial ways. It has nothing essential to do with either Europe or the 1970s.

13. This takes silence well beyond the Sartrean republic and links both it and radio to Lacan's more metapsychological, not to say astrophysical, concerns without thereby sacrificing the critical edge of the *Critique*. The line, "The silence, the uncanny, the 'unstated,' that which remains to be said . . . frightens," bears an unmistakable, perhaps even uncanny, resemblance to Pascal's aphorism from Section Three of *Pensées:* "The eternal silence of these infinite spaces frightens me" (61). This might well reflect Radio Alice's sense that the Judeo-Christian beliefs of the "radio for the participants" are what trigger the charge of obscenity, but what Pascal seems to find obscene is the all-too-obvious fact that god has absconded. The Bible is far from straightforward, and there are no obvious answers to rather basic questions like, to paraphrase the *Pensées,* "Why are we on this planet as opposed to another?" or "How many realms out there will never be known to us?" Why so clearly evoke such post-Galilean sentiments if Pascal's silence—the withdrawal or absence of a transcendental instance, god's voice—is not meant to illuminate "the unstated," not by getting at its cause (religious anxiety), but by getting at its effect, the way it marks radio and free radio in particular with a structuring absence? For Lacan, this structuring absence grips radio at the level of the nothing over which radiophonic transmission is projected, the ethereal nothing that connects everything. For Radio Alice and Guattari the matter is rather different. For them, the question is that of the everywhere—the everywhere that is the new nothing.

14. It is worth noting here that Foucault, in the interview with the members of *Ornicar* cited earlier, attempts to get under the skins of his interlocutors by drawing out an analogous link to Grégoire. See "Confessions" (219). As if on cue, Miller turns in his very next query to the question of the homosexual rights movement in France.

5. BIRMINGHAM CALLING

1. In the many historical reconstructions of the Birmingham School, tracing the waning of Hoggart's influence—at once administrative and intellectual—has become essentially generic. It is important to note, however, that Hoggart initiates a feature of much contemporary cultural studies scholarship, namely, its deep attraction to and reliance upon self-ethnography. We now tend to

confuse this with "identity politics," but it is clear that Hoggart's identification with the British working class (as he writes in *Uses of Literacy:* "I am from the working classes and feel even now both close to them and apart from them" [18]) matters more than the methodological precaution he presents it as. Precisely because of the motif of "feeling" and the way this authorizes his analysis, Hoggart is building into the structure of literature and contemporary cultural studies the epistemological and political value of writing—and expressly in an academic setting—about one's people or one's self. Asserting or otherwise feigning objectivity is, of course, no alternative. But what this difficulty invites is more sustained reflection on the status of identity—From where does concern about it arise, and what forms of recognition does it require?—within contemporary incarnations of cultural studies. It should be noted in passing that the oft-heard assertion that class is not an identity may be true, but from within an argument, at once historical and theoretical, that has not yet been convincingly made. Here, I should think, Hoggart is a headache.

2. In Stuart Hall's introduction to *Culture, Media Language* (part of the CCCS series at Routledge), he draws attention to the fact that, although Sartre's *Search for a Method* (the methodological introduction to the *Critique*) was familiar to cultural studies partisans and the editors (including Williams) of *New Left Review*, the *Critique* itself was not, or at least was not available to non-Francophone readers ("Cultural Studies"). In this context, what substituted for one's encounter with the *Critique* was R.D. Laing and David Cooper's *Reason and Violence*, where, although Sartre's discussion of the radio broadcast is summarized, very little attention overall is devoted to what mattered to Williams, namely, a cultural materialist account of communications. It remains a bit surprising that when Williams circles back to "private mobilization" in "Problems of the Coming Period" from 1983 and the Falkland Islands reoccupation, he makes no gesture to what he would ordinarily have valued deeply, the word forging of another committed socialist.

3. Given that Powell's repudiation of commercial broadcasting is unsparing, it may strike the reader as odd that she aligns it directly and immediately with pirate radio, a form of cultural politics more typically associated with the Left, if not socialism more specifically. To appreciate the urgency of doing so it suffices to recall here the discussion of piracy in Adrian Johns's "Piracy as a Business Force" in the closing paragraphs of chapter 3. On the matter of Radio Caroline (named, let us recall, after the daughter of JFK) and the "British Invasion," see Chapman.

4. The allusion above to Bakhtin's "dialogism" was a knowing one. It is interesting, with regard to the articulation of sociology and linguistics in and around the emerging CCCS, to reread Williams's chapter in *Marxism and Literature* titled "Language." While it can certainly be parsed as an explication of the work of Bakhtin, Volosinov, and Vygotsky, it is also a probing meditation on the concept of the social in the wake of the "linguistic turn," a dimension of the piece perhaps inadvertently emphasized in *The Raymond Williams Reader*, where its editor, John Higgins, retitles the piece, "Language as Sociality."

5. Although in the summer issue of *Politics and Letters* Williams, under the name *(de plume)* Michael Pope, reviews Llewellyn White's *The American*

Radio, whose "journalistic breeze" he finds compromising, Williams seems to show no familiarity here with Rudolph Arnheim's certainly less "breezy" study of what he called "an art of sound," though *Radio* had been translated (by Herbert Read) and published by Faber and Faber in 1936. I will pass briefly back over this review in what follows.

6. "WE ARE THE WORD"?

1. The citations from the "Radio: Imaginary Visions" broadcast that follow are all taken from the tape of this program provided to Elissa Guralnick by Sally Placksin and the MLA. The tape is identified as "WHAT'S THE WORD? Radio. Modern Language Association. (212) 614–6301" and is dated April 1998. I am grateful to all for access to and permission to use this material.

2. Contributing to what I am calling the anxious tone of this moment is the fact that Whitaker, who has, prior to this, been throwing his weight behind Roger Shattuck's contentious claim that the true understanding of literature arises not in analysis but in reading aloud, here actually ventures what certainly appears to be an analytical interpretation of Shakespeare. This, I would suggest, and not the more common, though no less problematical, assertion of the bard's prophetic powers is what requires the obvious linguistic delicacy (the "might almost," the "perhaps") of the passage. For reasons that will soon become apparent, this "teaching the conflicted" needs to be measured against Graff's call for "teaching the conflicts" as the way to save American education.

3. Confirming its importance, this point is made in *Sight Unseen* as follows: "If radio drama has survived in spite of movies, not to mention the television and video industries, there is just one explanation: radio plays are well served by the dark from which they issue. How that darkness contributes to their meaning and effect is at issue in what follows, analyses of plays that do radio proud" (Guralnick xvi). In fact, while the motif of loss remains important—Guralnick circles back to it in her "Afterword"—the darkness is dissipated. While it thus invites what might be called a symptomatic reading, more important is the implicit invitation here to think about the sound of the dark. In an earlier chapter I linked this to the motif of the void, but might one not also think here of Hegel's Jena lecture titled "Man, That Night *[Nacht],*" where among other things he writes: "Man is that night, that empty nothing, which contains everything in its simplicity: a wealth of infinitely many representations, images, none of which occurs to it directly, and none of which not present. . . . We see this Night when we look a human being in the eye, looking into a Night that turns terrifying; it is the Night of the World that rises up before us" (87). For that matter, it might be useful in this context to consider what Hannah Arendt meant by titling her 1959 Lessing Prize lecture "On Humanity in Dark Times." What relation is there between "these times" and the loss Guralnick is anxious to recover? Indeed, if there is such a relation, does this not invite one to consider how radio—not *a* radio—belongs to the "ethereal" Hegelian night, "the empty nothing that contains everything in its simplicity"? One might argue, although I'll not do it here, that this is precisely the animating conceit of Michael Curtiz's 1947 film *The Unsuspected,* where a radio dramatist, Victor Grandison, uses

the tele-technology of radio to fill the dark with the unsuspected, in this case, a murderous, because economically impotent, maternal uncle (what Lévi-Strauss understood as the linchpin of "the avunculate").

4. When I spoke to Phyllis Franklin about the program, she made it clear that while the initiative began as one designed to "get the word out" about the MLA in the context of its negative press, this developed, in concert with the program concept itself, in the direction of a more general outreach to the parents of prospective postsecondary students. The goal, as Franklin put it, was to convince these parents that the study of language and literature was not an ill-advised investment—in effect, to convince these parents not only that study in these fields would not be "useless" but that humanities majors are not destined to become the butt of the sorts of jokes lavished upon the profession by Richard Bernstein and others. Today, of course, the harder sell is the implacable entry into debt to which all students and parents seemed doomed by the economics of higher learning, regardless of major.

5. Benjamin, as Detlev Holz, sketches a painful yet hilarious account of the problem of timing a reading in "On the Minute" (407–9). Hagen's pass over this material is rife with insight (see Hagen, "On the Minute"), but in the context of the present chapter the more pressing questions might be pedagogical. Consider, for example, in light of what is said about the lecture (its preemptive condensation, its premature conclusion, its reactive resumption, its silent pause, etc.), whether it would have been heard to have been about "something." In being, perhaps inevitably, about the something that *is* the radio talk, it may well constitute the upgrade of Williams's breathing.

Works Cited

Acland, Charles. *Residual Media*. Minneapolis: U of Minnesota P, 2007.

Adorno, Theodor Wiesengrund. *Current of Music: Elements of a Radio Theory*. Ed. Robert Hullot-Kentor. Frankfurt: Suhrkamp, 2006.

———. *The Jargon of Authenticity*. Trans. Kurt Tarnowski and Frederic Will. Evanston: Northwestern UP, 1973.

———. "Radio Physiognomics." Adorno, *Current*.

———. "The Radio Symphony." *Essays on Music*. Ed. R. Leppert. Berkeley: U of California P, 2002. 251–70.

———. "The Radio Voice." Adorno, *Current*.

———. "To Walter Benjamin." 5 Apr. 1934. Adorno and Benjamin, *Complete Correspondence* 36–39.

———. "To Walter Benjamin." 7 Mar. 1938. Adorno and Benjamin, *Complete Correspondence* 240–41.

Adorno, Theodor Wiesengrund, and Walter Benjamin. *Complete Correspondence, 1928–1940*. Ed. Henri Lonitz. Cambridge, UK: Polity, 1999.

Adorno, Theodor Wiesengrund, and Max Horkheimer. *Dialectic of Enlightenment*. Trans. Edmund Jephcott. Stanford: Stanford UP, 2002.

Agamben, Giorgio. *Homo Sacer: Sovereign Power and Bare Life*. Trans. Daniel Hiller-Roazen. Stanford: Stanford UP, 1998.

———. Interview by Ulrich Raulf. *Süddeutsche Zeitung* 6 Apr. 2004.

———. *The Open: Man and Animal*. Trans. Kevin Attell. Stanford: Stanford UP, 2004.

———. *State of Exception*. Trans. Kevin Attell. Stanford: Stanford UP, 2005.

———. *What Is an Apparatus? and Other Essays*. Trans. David Kishick and Stefan Pedatella. Stanford: Stanford UP, 2009.

Althusser, Louis. "To Jacques Lacan." 9 Dec. 1963. *Writings* 159.

————. *Writings on Psychoanalysis: Freud and Lacan*. Ed. Olivier Carpet and François Matheron. Trans. Jeffrey Mehlman. New York: Columbia UP, 1996.

Arendt, Hannah. "On Humanity in Dark Times: Thoughts about Lessing." *Men in Dark Times*. New York: Harcourt Brace, 1968. 3–32.

Aristotle. *The Politics. The Basic Works of Aristotle*. Ed. Richard McKeon. New York: Random House, 1941.

Arnheim, Rudolph. *Radio: An Art of Sound*. Trans. Margaret Ludwig and Herbert Read. New York: Da Capo, 1972.

Augaitis, Daina, and Dan Lander, eds. *Radio Rethink: Art, Sound, and Transmission*. Banff, Canada: Walter Phillips Gallery, 1994.

Bachelard, Gaston. *The New Scientific Spirit*. Trans. Arthur Goldhammer. Boston: Beacon, 1984.

Badiou, Alain. *Being and Event*. Trans. Oliver Feltham. London: Continuum, 2005.

Barnouw, Erik. *A Tower in Babel: A History of Broadcasting in the United States to 1933*. New York: Oxford UP, 1966.

Barthes, Roland. "From Work to Text." *Textual Strategies: Perspectives in Poststructuralist Criticism*. Ed. Josue V. Harari. Ithaca: Cornell UP, 1979. 73–81.

Benjamin, Walter. "The Author as Producer." *Selected Writings* 2: 768–82.

————. "Berlin Childhood around 1900." *Selected Writings* 3: 344–413.

————. "Bert Brecht." *Selected Writings* 2: 365–77.

————. "Conversation with Ernst Schoen." *Work of Art* 397–402.

————. "Curriculum Vitae (VI)." *Selected Writings* 4: 381.

————. "Journalism." *Selected Writings* 2: 50.

————. *Lichtenberg: Ein Querschnitt. Drei Hörmodelle*. Frankfurt: Suhrkamp, 1971.

————. "Mickey Mouse." *Selected Writings* 2: 545–46.

————. "On the Concept of History." *Selected Writings* 4: 389–400.

————. "On the Minute." *Work of Art* 407–10.

————. "On the Trail of Old Letters." *Selected Writings* 2: 555–58.

————. "Reflections on Radio." *Selected Writings* 2: 543–44.

————. *Selected Writings*. 4 vols. Ed. Michael Jennings. Cambridge, MA: Harvard UP, 1996–2003.

————. "Theater and Radio." *Selected Writings* 2: 583–86.

————. "To Gerhard Scholem." 25 Apr. 1930. *The Correspondence of Walter Benjamin, 1910–1940*. Ed. Gershom Scholem and Theodor Adorno. Trans. Manfred and Evelyn Jacobson. Chicago: U of Chicago P, 1994. 365.

————. "What Is the Epic Theater?" *Selected Writings* 4: 302–10.

————. "The Work of Art in the Age of Its Technical Reproducibility." *Work of Art* 19–55.

————. *The Work of Art in the Age of Its Technological Reproducibility and Other Writings on Media*. Ed. Michael Jennings, Brigid Doherty, and Thomas Levin. Cambridge, MA: Harvard UP, 2008.

Bennett, Tony. "Texts in History: The Determinations of Readings and Their Texts." *Journal of the Midwest Modern Language Association* 18:1 (1985): 1–16.

Berardi, Franco ["Bifo"], and Ermanno Guarneri ["Gomma"]. *Alice è il diavolo: Storia di una radio sovversiva*. Milan: ShaKe, 2002.

Brecht, Bertolt. "Aufbau einer Rolle: Laughtons Galilei." *Gesammelte Werke* 17: 1117–26.

———. *Brecht on Film and Radio*. Ed. and trans. Marc Silberman. London: Methuen, 2000.

———. "Brecht on Radio." Trans. Stuart Hood. *Screen* 20 (Winter 1979–80): 16–23.

———. *Brecht on Theatre: The Development of an Aesthetic*. Ed. and trans. John Willet. New York: Hill and Wang, 1964.

———. "Building up a Part: Laughton's Galileo." *Brecht on Theatre* 163–68.

———. *Der Flug der Lindberghs*. *Versuche* 3.

———. "Der Rundfunk als Kommunikationsapparat: Rede über die Funktion des Rundfunks." *Gesammelte Werke* 8.2: 127–134.

———. "Explanations [about 'The Flight of the Lindberghs']." *Brecht on Film* 38–40.

———. *Gesammelte Werke*. Ed. Elizabeth Hauptmann. Frankfurt: Suhrkamp, 1967.

———. "Radio: An Antediluvian Invention?" *Brecht on Film* 36–37.

———. "The Radio as a Communications Apparatus" [1932]. *Brecht on Film* 41–48.

———. "Radio: Eine vorsintflutliche Erfindung?" *Gesammelte Werke* 8.2: 119–121.

———. "A Radio Speech." *Brecht on Theatre* 18–19.

———. "Suggestions for the Director of Radio Broadcasting." *Brecht on Film* 35.

———. *Versuche 1–3*. Berlin: Kiepenhauer, 1930.

Buchanan, Patrick. "1992 Republican National Convention Speech." http://buchanan.org/blog/1992-republican-national-convention-speech/. Accessed 6 Feb. 2009.

Cage, John. "Experimental Music." *Silence*. Middletown, CT: Wesleyan UP, 1973.

Cantril, Hadley. *The Invasion from Mars: A Study in the Psychology of Panic*. New York: Harper and Row, 1966.

———. "To John Marshall." 11 May 1937. "Selected Correspondence." Hadley Cantril Papers at the Mudd Library, Princeton U, Princeton, NJ.

Cantril, Hadley, and Gordon Allport. *The Psychology of Radio*. New York: Harper and Brothers, 1935.

Césaire, Aimé. Contribution to "Hommages à Frantz Fanon." *Présence Africaine* 12 (1962): 120–22.

Chapman, Robert. *Selling the Sixties: The Pirates and Pop Music Radio*. London: Routledge, 1992.

Clemens, Justin, and Russell Grigg, eds. *Jacques Lacan and the Other Side of Psychoanalysis*. Durham: Duke UP, 2006.

Collective A/Traverso. "Radio Alice—Free Radio." Lotringer and Marazzi 130–35.

Council of the Modern Language Association. Minutes. *PMLA* 108 (May 1993): 594.

———. Minutes. *PMLA* 108 (Oct. 1993): 1212.

———. Minutes. *PMLA* 109 (Mar. 1994): 312.

———. Minutes. *PMLA* 109 (May 1994): 500.

Currid, Brian. *A National Acoustics: Music and Mass Publicity in Weimar and Nazi Germany*. Minneapolis: U of Minnesota P, 2006.

Deleuze, Gilles. "Il a été mon maître." *L'isle déserte et autres textes: Textes et entretiens, 1953–74*. Paris: Minuit, 2002. 109–13.

———. "What Is a *Dispositif?*" *Michel Foucault Philosopher*. Trans. Timothy Armstrong. New York: Routledge, 1992.

Derrida, Jacques. "Heidegger's Ear: Philopolemology (*Geschlecht IV*)." *Reading Heidegger: Commemorations*. Ed. John Sallis. Bloomington: Indiana UP, 1993. 163–218.

———. *Of Grammatology*. Trans. Gayatri Chakravorty Spivak. Baltimore: Johns Hopkins UP, 1974.

———. *Of Spirit: Heidegger and the Question*. Trans. Geoffrey Bennington and Rachel Bowlby. Chicago: U of Chicago P, 1989.

———. "'To Do Justice to Freud': The History of Madness in the Age of Psychoanalysis." *Resistances of Psychoanalysis*. Trans. Peggy Kamuf, Anne Brault, and Michael Naas. Stanford: Stanford UP, 1998. 70–118.

Doherty, Thomas. "Return with Us Now to Those Thrilling Days of Yesteryear: Radio Studies Rise Again." *Chronicle of Higher Education* 21 May 2004: B12–13.

Dolar, Mladen. *A Voice and Nothing More*. Cambridge, MA: MIT P, 2006.

Douglas, Susan. *Listening In: Radio and the American Imagination*. New York: Times Books, 1999.

Dyson, Frances. "The Genealogy of the Radio Voice." Augaitis and Lander.

Enzensberger, Hans Magnus. "Constituents of a Theory of Media." *Critical Essays*. Ed. Reinhold Grimm and Bruce Armstrong. New York: Continuum, 1982. 46–76.

Fanon, Frantz. "Here Is the Voice of Algeria." *A Dying Colonialism*. Trans. Haakon Chevalier. New York: Grove P, 1967. Originally published as "Ici, la voix d'Algérie." *L'an cinq de la révolution algérienne*. Paris: Maspero/ Découverte, 1959.

Fink, Bruce. *Lacan to the Letter: Reading Écrits Closely*. Minneapolis: U of Minnesota P, 2004.

Foucault, Michel. *The Archaeology of Knowledge*. 1972. New York: Routledge, 2002.

———. "The Confession of the Flesh." *Power/Knowledge: Selected Interviews and Other Writings, 1972–1977*. Ed. Colin Gordon. New York: Pantheon, 1980.

———. *The History of Sexuality.* Vol. 1. *An Introduction.* Trans. R. Hurley. Harmondsworth, UK: Penguin, 1981.

———. *Psychiatric Power: Lectures at the Collège de France, 1973–1974.* Ed. Jacques Lagrange. Trans. Graham Burchell. New York: Picador, 2006.

Fowler, Gene. *Border Radio: Quacks, Yodlers, Pitchmen, Psychics and Other Amazing Broadcasters of American Airwaves.* Austin: U of Texas P, 2002.

Franklin, Phyllis. "Telling the Field's Story." *MLA Newsletter* Winter 1996: 4–5.

Freud, Sigmund. "Three Essays on the Theory of Sexuality." *The Standard Edition of the Psychological Works of Sigmund Freud.* Vol. 7. Ed. James Strachey. London: Vintage, 2001.

Fromm, Erich. "Radio." Erich Fromm Papers, 1929–1980. Manuscript and Archives Division, New York Public Library. New York City, NY.

Genosko, Gary. "The Life and Work of Félix Guattari: From Transversality to Ecosophy." Afterword. *The Three Ecologies.* By Félix Guattari. Trans. Ian Pindar and Paul Sutton. London: Athlone, 2000.

Graff, Gerald. *Beyond the Culture Wars: How Teaching the Conflicts Can Revitalize American Education.* New York: Norton, 1992.

Grégoire, Menie. "'L' homosexualité, ce douloureux problème.' Transcript of a March 10, 1971, radio program." *La revue h,* no. 1 (Summer 1996): 52–59. www.france.qrd.org/media/revue-h/001/probleme.html. Accessed 28 Mar. 2011.

Guattari, Félix. *The Anti-Oedipus Papers.* Ed. Stéphane Nadaud. Trans. Kélina Gotman. New York: Semiotext(e), 2006.

———. "Anti-Psychiatry and Anti-Psychoanalysis." *Molecular Revolution* 45–50.

———. *Chaosmosis: An Ethico-Aesthetic Paradigm.* Trans. Paul Bains and Julian Pefanis. Bloomington: Indiana UP, 1995.

———. *Chaosophy.* Ed. Sylvère Lotringer. New York: Semiotext(e), 1995. 187–208.

———. "Des millions et des millions d'Alices en puissance." Introduction. *Radio Alice, radio libre.* By Collective A/Traverso. Paris: Delarge, 1977.

———. "Everywhere at Once." *Chaosophy* 27–35.

———. "The Group and the Person." *Molecular Revolution* 24–44.

———. "Interview à propos de l'*Anti-Oedipe* par Arno Munster." *Frankfurter Rundschau* 17 Jan. 1973.

———. "La Borde: A Clinic Unlike Any Other." *Chaosophy* 187–208.

———. *Molecular Revolution: Psychiatry and Politics.* Trans. Rosemary Sheed. London: Penguin, 1984.

———. "Popular Free Radio." *Soft Subversions.* Ed. Sylvère Lotringer. Trans. David Sweet and Chet Wiener. New York: Semiotext(e), 1996. 73–78.

———. "Pragmatic/Machinic: Discussion with Félix Guattari (19 March 1985)." Interview by Charles Stivale. *Pre/Text* 14:3–4 (1993): 215–50. rpr/ Works, 3 June 1997, http://webpages.ursinus.edu/rrichter/stivale.html. Accessed 26 Mar. 2011.

———. "Three Group Problems." *Semiotext(e)* 2:3 (1977): 99–109.

———. *Transversalité et psychanalyse: Essais d'analyse institutionnelle.* Paris: Maspero, 1972.

———. "Why Italy?" Trans. John Johnston. Lotringer and Marazzi 234–37.

Guralnick, Elissa. *Sight Unseen: Beckett, Pinter, Stoppard and Other Contemporary Dramatists on Radio.* Athens: Ohio UP, 1996.

Habermas, Jurgen. *Knowledge and Human Interests.* Trans. Jeremy J. Shapiro. Boston: Beacon, 1971.

Hagen, Wolfgang. *Das Radio: Zur Geschichte und Theorie des Hörfunks—Deutschland/USA.* Munich: Fink, 2005.

———. "'On the Minute': Benjamin's Silent Work for the German Radio." Lecture, U of California, Santa Barbara. 2006. www.whagen.de/vortraege/2006/20061201Benjamin/OnTheMinute.pdf. Accessed 27 Mar. 2011.

———. "On the Place of Radio." Opening lecture for the conference "Recycling the Future," ORF-Kunstradio. 4 Dec. 1997. www.kunstradio.at/FUTURE/RTF/SYMPOSIUM/LECTURES/HAGEN/hagen-txt-e.html. Accessed 27 Mar. 2011.

———. *Radio Schreber: Der "moderne Spiritismus" und die Sprache der Medien.* Vienna: VDG, 2001.

Hall, Stuart. "Cultural Studies and the Centre: Some Problematics and Problems." Hall et al. 3–33.

Hall, Stuart, Dorothy Hobson, Andrew Lowe, and Paul Willis, eds. *Culture, Media, Language* . London: Routledge, 1992.

Hardt, Michael, and Antonio Negri. *Empire.* Cambridge, MA: Harvard UP, 2000.

Hegel, Georg Friedrich. "Man, That Night." *Hegel and the Human Spirit: A Translation of the Jena Lectures on the Philosophy of Spirit.* Trans. Leo Rauch. Detroit: Wayne State UP, 1983.

Heidegger, Martin. "Age of the World Picture." *The Question Concerning Technology and Other Essays.* Trans. William Lovitt. New York: Harper and Row, 1977. 115–54.

———. *Being and Time.* Trans. John Macquarrie and Edward Robinson. New York: Harper and Row, 1962.

———. *Early Greek Thinking.* Trans. David Farrell Krell and Frank Capuzzi. San Francisco: Harper and Row, 1984.

———. *The Fundamental Concepts of Metaphysics: World, Finitude, Solitude.* Trans. William McNeill and Nicholas Walker. Bloomington: Indiana UP, 1995.

Hilmes, Michelle, and Jason Loviglio. *Radio Reader: Essays in the Cultural History of Radio.* New York: Routledge, 2002.

Hobson, Dorothy. "Housewives and the Mass Media." Hall et al. 85–95.

———. "A Study of Working Class Women at Home: Femininity, Domesticity and Maternity." MA thesis. U of Birmingham, 1978.

Hoggart, Richard. "Difficulties of Democratic Debate." *Speaking* 1: 182–96.

———. "Schools of English and Contemporary Society." *Speaking* 2: 246–58.

———. *Speaking to Each Other.* 2 vols. New York: Oxford UP, 1970.

———. *The Uses of Literacy: Changing Patterns in English Mass Culture.* Boston: Beacon, 1961.

Ihde, Don. *Listening and Voice: Phenomenologies of Sound*. Albany: State U of New York P, 2007.

Irigaray, Luce. *Martin Heidegger and the Forgetting of Air*. Trans. Mary Beth Mader. 1983. Austin: U of Texas P, 1999.

Jakobson, Roman. "On the Relation between Visual and Auditory Signs." *Selected Writings* 2: 338–44.

———. *Selected Writings*. Vol. 2. *Word and Language*. The Hague: Mouton, 1971.

———. "Visual and Auditory Signs." *Selected Writings* 2: 334–37.

Jameson, Frederic. *Brecht and Method*. London: Verso, 1998.

Jensen, Erik Granly. "Collective Acoustic Space: LIGNA and Radio in the Weimar Republic." *Radio Territories*. Ed. Erik Granly Jensen and Brandon LaBelle. Los Angeles: Errant Bodies, 2007.

Johns, Adrian. "Piracy as a Business Force." *Culture Machine* 10 (2009): 44–63.

Kahn, Douglas, and Gregory Whitehead. *Wireless Imagination: Sound, Radio, and the Avant-Garde*. Cambridge, MA: MIT P, 1994.

Karr, Rick. "Prometheus Unbound." *Nation* 23 May 2005: 22–27.

Kittler, Friedrich. *Gramophone, Film, Typewriter*. Trans. Geoffrey Winthrop-Young and Michael Wurtz. Stanford: Stanford UP, 1999.

———. "Observations on Public Reception." Augaitis and Dan Lander 75–85.

Koyré, Alexandre. *Newtonian Studies*. Chicago: U of Chicago P, 1965.

Lacan, Jacques. *Autres écrits*. Paris: Seuil, 2001.

———. "Discours de Rome." *Autres écrits* 133–64.

———. *Écrits*. Trans. Bruce Fink. New York: Norton, 2006.

———. "Impromptu at Vicennes." *Television* 117–28.

———. "The Instance of the Letter in the Unconscious, or Reason since Freud." *Écrits* 138–68.

———. "Overture to This Collection." *Écrits* 3–5.

———. "Petit discours a l'ORTF." ORTF, France. 2 Dec. 1966. www.ubu.com/sound/lacan.html. Transcript, *Autres écrits* 221–26.

———. "Radiophonie." RTB, Belgium, and ORTF, France. 5 June 1970. www.ubu.com/sound/lacan.html. Transcript, *Autres écrits* 403–47.

———. "Sign, Symbol, Imaginary." *On Signs*. Ed. Marshall Blonsky. Baltimore: Johns Hopkins UP, 1985. 203–9.

———. "Télévision." ORTF, France. 1973. www.ubu.com/sound/lacan.html. *Autres écrits* 509–46.

———. "Television." *Television* 3–48.

———. *Television/A Challenge to the Psychoanalytic Establishment*. Ed. Joan Copjec. Trans. Denis Hollier, Rosalind Krause, Jeffrey Mehlman, and Annette Michelson. New York: Norton, 1990.

———. "To Louis Althusser." 1 Dec. 1963. Althusser, *Writings* 150–51.

Lang, Berel. *Heidegger's Silence*. Ithaca: Cornell UP, 1996.

Lazarsfeld, Paul. "Notes," 16 Dec. 1939, meeting. "Correspondence" file. Paul Lazarsfeld Papers [ca. 1930]–1976. Boxes 25–28. Rare Book and Manuscript Library, Columbia U. New York City, NY.

Lotringer, Sylvère, and Christian Marazzi, eds. *Italy: Autonomia*. New York: Semiotext(e), 1980.

Loviglio, Jason. *Radio's Intimate Public: Network Broadcasting and Mass-Mediated Democracy*. Minneapolis: U of Minnesota P, 2005.

Lukács, Georg. *The Destruction of Reason*. Trans. Peter Palmer. Atlantic Highlands, NJ: Humanities, 1981.

———. "Existentialism." *Marxism and Human Liberation: Essays in History, Culture and Revolution*. Ed. Epifanio San Juan Jr. New York: Delta, 1973.

Marx, Karl. *Das Kapital*. Vol. 1. Berlin: Dietz, 1973.

Mehlman, Jeffrey. *Walter Benjamin for Children: An Essay on His Radio Years*. Chicago: U of Chicago P, 1993.

Meyrowitz, Joshua. *No Sense of Place: Impact of Electronic Media on Social Behavior*. New York: Oxford UP, 1985.

Miller, Edward. *Emergency Broadcasting and 1930s American Radio*. Philadelphia: Temple UP, 2003.

Miller, Toby, ed. *Radio—Sound*. Spec. iss. of *Continuum* 6:1 (1992).

Milutis, Joe. *Ether: The Nothing That Connects Everything*. Minneapolis: U of Minnesota P, 2006.

Monaghan, Peter. "Exploring Radio's Sociocultural Legacy." *Chronicle of Higher Education* 19 Feb. 1999: A17–19.

Mowitt, John. "Algerian Nation: Fanon's Fetish." *Cultural Critique* 22 (1992): 165–86.

———. "Reason, Thus, Unveils Itself." *Mosaic* 40 (June 2007): 179–88.

———. *Text: The Genealogy of an Antidisciplinary Object*. Durham: Duke UP, 1992.

O'Connor, Alan. *The Voice of the Mountain: Radio and Anthropology*. Lanham, MD: UP of America, 2006.

Pascal, Blaise. *Pensées*. Trans. W. F. Trotter. New York: Dutton, 1958.

Pierce, Brian. "Oscar Romero, the Preacher." *Witness Magazine* 10 Mar. 2005. www.thewitness.org/article.php?=812.

Ponge, Francis. "La Radio." *Oeuvres completes*. Vol. 1. Ed. Bernard Beugot. Paris: NRF/ Gallimard, 1999.

Powell, Rachel. *Possibilities for Local Radio*. Finsbury Park, UK: Goodwin, 1965.

"Radio: Imaginary Visions." *What's the Word?* NPR, Apr. 1998. Dir./writ./prod. Sally Placksin. Participants, Elissa Guralnick, Sally Placksin, Everett Frost, and Ted Whitaker. Tape of radio broadcast, privately owned.

Rancière, Jacques. *The Philosopher and His Poor*. Ed. Andrew Parker. Trans. John Drury, Corinne Oster, and Andrew Parker. Durham: Duke UP, 2003.

Ricoeur, Paul. *Freud and Philosophy: An Essay on Interpretation*. Trans. Denis Sauvage. New Haven: Yale UP, 1970.

Roberts, Mark. "Wired: Schreber as Machine, Technophobe and Virtualist." *Drama Review* 40:3 (1996): 31–46.

Rougement, Denis de. *The Devil's Share: An Essay on the Diabolical in Modern Society*. Trans. Haakon Chevalier. New York: Meridian, 1956.

Sartre, Jean-Paul. "Aminadab or the Fantastic Considered as a Language." *Literary and Philosophical Essays*. Trans Annette Michelson. New York: Collier Books, 1962. 60–77.

———. *Critique of Dialectical Reason.* Vol. 1. *A Theory of Practical Ensembles.* Trans. Alan Sheridan-Smith. London: Verso, 1982. Originally published as *Critique de la raison dialectique.* Paris: Gallimard, 1960.

———. "La république du silence." *Situations III.* Paris: Gallimard, 1947.

———. *Search for a Method.* Trans. Hazel Barnes. New York: Vintage, 1968.

Scannell, Paddy. *Radio, Television and Modern Life.* Cambridge, MA: Blackwell, 1996.

Schaeffer, Pierre. *Traité des objets musicaux.* Paris: Le Seuil, 1966.

Scholem, Gershom. "To Walter Benjamin." 24 Oct. 1933. *The Correspondence of Walter Benjamin and Gershom Scholem, 1932–1940.* Ed. Gershom Scholem. Trans. Gary Smith and Andre Lefevere. Cambridge, MA: Harvard UP, 1992. 83–85.

Schulte, Gerhard. "Walter Benjamin's Lichtenberg." *Performing Arts Journal* 14:3 (1992): 33–36.

Sconce, Jeffrey. *Haunted Media: Electronic Presence from Telegraphy to Television.* Durham: Duke UP, 2000.

Scriven, Michael. *Sartre and the Media.* London: Saint Martin's, 1993.

Shakespeare, William. *The Tempest.* New Haven: Yale UP, 1955.

Spigel, Lynn. *Make Room for Television: Television and the Family Ideal in Postwar America.* Chicago: U of Chicago P, 1992.

Sterling, Christopher. "A New Journal for an Old . . ." *Journal of Radio Studies* 1 (1992): n. pag.

Strauss, Neil, ed. *Radiotext(e).* Spec. iss. of *Semiotext(e).* 16 (June 1992).

Strong, Tracy. "Foreword: Dimensions of the New Debate around Carl Schmitt." *The Concept of the Political.* By Carl Schmitt. Chicago: U of Chicago P, 1996. ix–xxviii.

Subcomandante Marcos. "On Independent Media: A Message from Subcomandante Marcos to 'Free the Media' Teach-In, NYC. January 31, 1997." *Our Word Is Our Weapon: Selected Writings.* New York: Seven Stories, 2001. 180–82.

Sudre, René. *Le huitième art: Mission de la radio.* Paris: Julliard, 1945.

Tarde, Gabriel. *Monadologie et sociologie.* Paris: Le Seuil, 2003.

Tausk, Victor. *Sexuality, War and Schizophrenia: Collected Psychoanalytic Papers.* Ed. Paul Roazen. Trans. Eric Mosbacher. New Brunswick, NJ: Transaction, 1991.

Thompson, E.P. "The Long Revolution." Part 1, *New Left Review* 9; part 2, *New Left Review* 10.

Vigil, José Ignacio López. *Rebel Radio: The Story of El Salvador's Radio Venceremos.* Willimantic, CT: Curbstone, 1994.

Weiss, Allen, ed. *Experimental Sound and Radio.* Spec. iss. of *Drama Review* 40:3 (1996). Rpt. as *Experimental Sound and Radio.* Cambridge, MA: MIT P, 2001.

Williams, Raymond. "The Achievement of Brecht." *Critical Quarterly* 3 (1961): 153–62.

———. "Base and Superstructure in Marxist Cultural Theory." *Problems in Materialism and Culture.* London: Verso, 1980. 31–49.

———. "Beyond Actually Existing Socialism." *Problems in Materialism and Culture*. London: Verso, 1980. 252–73.

———. "Communication and Community." *Resources of Hope*. London: Verso, 1989.

———. "Creators and Consumers." Rev. of *Brecht,* by Ronald Gray. *Guardian* 24 Mar. 1961: 15.

———. *Drama from Ibsen to Brecht*. London: Hogarth, 1987.

———. *Drama from Ibsen to Eliot*. New York: Oxford UP, 1953.

———. "Just What Is Labour's Policy for Radio?" *Tribune* 18 Feb. 1966: 8.

———. *Marxism and Literature*. London: Oxford UP, 1977.

———. "Practical Critic." *Guardian* 26 Feb. 1970: 18.

———. "Problems of the Coming Period." *New Left Review* 1 (July–Aug. 1983): 1–18.

———. "Radio Drama." *Politics and Letters* 1:2–3 (1947): 106–9.

———. "Raymond Williams Thinks Well of the Open University." Tape of BBC radio broadcast. British Library, BBC Sound Archive, M4024R (1971).

———. *Resources of Hope*. London: Verso, 1989.

——— [Michael Pope]. Rev. of *The American Radio,* by Llewellyn White. *Politics and Letters* 1:4 (1948): 86.

———. *Television: Technology and Cultural Form*. New York: Schocken, 1975.

Williamson, John. "What Washington Means by Policy Reform." *Latin American Readjustment: How Much Has Happened*. Ed. John Williamson. Washington, DC: Institute for International Economics, 1989. 5–20.

Winchester, Simon. *The Meaning of Everything: The Story of the Oxford English Dictionary*. New York: Oxford UP, 2003.

Žižek, Slavoj. *The Puppet and the Dwarf: The Perverse Core of Christianity*. Cambridge, MA: MIT P, 2003.

———. "Series Foreword." *A Voice and Nothing More*. By Mladen Dolar. Cambridge, MA: MIT P, 2006. vii–viii.

Index

TEXT:
10/13 Sabon Open Type

DISPLAY:
Sabon Open Type

COMPOSITOR:
BookComp, Inc.

INDEXER:
Paige Sweet

PRINTER AND BINDER:
IBT Global